WHO IS THIS GOD?

A HANDBOOK FOR LIFE WITH HIM

PAUL BRYAN

LUCIDBOOKS

Who Is This God?
A Handbook for Life with Him

Copyright © 2023 by Paul Bryan

Published by Lucid Books in Houston, TX
www.LucidBooks.com

All rights reserved. No part of this publication may be reproduced, stored in a retrieval system, or transmitted in any form by any means, electronic, mechanical, photocopy, recording, or otherwise, without the prior permission of the publisher, except as provided for by USA copyright law.

Scripture quotations marked (ESV) are taken from the ESV® Bible (The Holy Bible, English Standard Version®), copyright © 2001 by Crossway, a publishing ministry of Good News Publishers. Used by permission. All rights reserved.

Scripture quotations marked (NIV) are taken from the Holy Bible, New International Version®, NIV®. Copyright ©1973, 1978, 1984, 2011 by Biblica, Inc.™ Used by permission of Zondervan. All rights reserved worldwide. www.zondervan.com The "NIV" and "New International Version" are trademarks registered in the United States Patent and Trademark Office by Biblica, Inc.™

Scripture quotations marked (NASB) are taken from the (NASB®) New American Standard Bible®, Copyright © 1960, 1971, 1977, 1995, 2020 by The Lockman Foundation. Used by permission. All rights reserved. www.lockman.org

Scripture quotations marked (NLT) are taken from the Holy Bible, New Living Translation, copyright ©1996, 2004, 2015 by Tyndale House Foundation. Used by permission of Tyndale House Publishers, Carol Stream, Illinois 60188. All rights reserved.

Scripture quotations marked (NET) are taken from the New English Translation Bible®, Copyright ©1996, 2019 by Biblical Studies Press, L.L.C. http://netbible.com. All rights reserved.

ISBN: 978-1-63296-608-7
eISBN: 978-1-63296-609-4

Special Sales: Most Lucid Books titles are available in special quantity discounts. Custom imprinting or excerpting can also be done to fit special needs. Contact Lucid Books at Info@LucidBooks.com

DEDICATION

This book is dedicated to you, our readers. It was created to help you personally know the God of the Bible. May you discover that God loves and cherishes you and that He wants you to spend eternity with Him. May you learn to experience Him in your daily life as the three persons of God: the Heavenly Father, Jesus Christ, Savior and Lord, and the Holy Spirit, Helper, Teacher, and Guide.

SPECIAL THANKS

I can't express in words my appreciation for those who worked alongside me during the writing of this book. They have spent many hours reviewing, editing, and providing invaluable feedback to help make this book what it is. Their personal relationship with God and knowledge of the Bible were essential to this end. My wife, Linda, and two close friends were stalwarts in this assistance as they reviewed every chapter multiple times. I am also indebted to my Men's Group and the ten "Beta Readers" who spent many hours reviewing and providing input that made this book better in every way.

TABLE OF CONTENTS

PART A
THE GOD OF THE BIBLE: DO YOU KNOW HIM?

PART B
CHANGE IS NEEDED IN YOUR LIFE

PART C
DEVELOP NEW HABITS TO KNOW GOD

PART D
GOD IS SUPERNATURAL AND STILL DOES MIRACLES

INTRODUCTION

This book begins and ends with a foundational message: everyone believes in someone or something. But who or what do you believe in? Concepts, your own ideas, or the God of the Bible? *Who Is This God?* is a Christian nonfiction book that unravels the confusion so you can discover God's true nature and character. It demonstrates how to develop a personal relationship with God and grow spiritually to enjoy eternal life with Him.

Everyone Believes in Someone or Something

People put their faith in what they believe to be true. The perception of truth is the basis on which beliefs are built.

The following describes what some people believe to be true about God and religion:

- Atheists don't believe in the existence of God or any supreme being.

- Agnostics have neither belief nor disbelief in the existence of a supreme being. Instead, they look at the material world and believe there is nothing else.

- Anti-theists oppose belief in any god. They believe all religions are detrimental to society and the world.

- Extremists and cultists have a distorted view of God and often use it to control people.

Other people believe in the scientific theory of evolution by natural selection; their own abilities; in another person; in their church and its teachings; in another religion of the world; or in a universal god ("All roads lead to god").

You Can Find God in This Book

This book is intended to demonstrate that the God of the Bible exists, cares about you, loves you, is available to you, and that He wants an eternal relationship with you. Look for God and His involvement in people's lives as I recount His story throughout this book. You can see Him everywhere if you choose to find Him. How exciting it is to know that the supernatural God who created the universe loves you and wants you to spend eternity with Him!

The Great Commission

My earnest desire is that you will find God in this book and, therefore, be participants in the "Great Commission" of Jesus Christ, as stated in the following scripture:

> Then Jesus came up and said to them, "All authority in heaven and on earth has been given to me. Therefore go and make disciples of all nations, baptizing them in the name of the Father and the Son and the Holy Spirit, teaching them to obey everything I have commanded you. And remember, I am with you always, to the end of the age." (Matthew 28:18-20 NET)

In the above verses, Jesus tells His followers to go into the world and make disciples for Him. To *make disciples* starts with helping people know and accept Jesus Christ as their Savior and Lord. Then it's about these new disciples maturing as followers of His. Every follower of Jesus Christ has something they are called and equipped by God to do in helping to fulfill The Great Commission.

NOTE: For those of you not familiar with the Bible, I use a standard format for denoting a scripture reference: For example, Matthew 28:18-20 is the New Testament book of Matthew, the 28th chapter, and verses 18-20 in that chapter. The Bible version is included with the scripture, such as "NET" (New English Translation).

Use of this book. This book can be read or studied by individuals or groups as well as used for discipleship. As you will see in the next section, it was constructed to benefit a diverse audience and provide a variety of learning methods.

Construction of this Book

All the chapters in *Who Is This God?* include narratives, Bible verses, and questions. Most also include true stories. These provide factual information to help you know God based on truth and reality.

The major themes about God and life with Him include:

- There is one God in three persons, the Father, the Son—Jesus Christ, and the Holy Spirit.

- God created you to experience His love and know Him personally.

- Everyone needs to be rescued and born-again to enter the Kingdom of God.

- God has a purpose and plan for you (your life is not meaningless).

- The Holy Spirit was sent to dwell within, guide, help, and teach the followers of Jesus.

- Believers must mature spiritually to live an authentic Christian life.

- God is supernatural, and you live in the natural and supernatural realms of this world where miracles and other supernatural interventions by God still occur.

Questions and additional information. There are two types of questions throughout the book. The first is intended to stimulate thinking about the related topic. These are prefaced with **"What Do You Think?"** Some of these include answers to help with learning. The **"What Do You Think? (Advanced)"** questions are for those who want to delve deeper into understanding the topic or scripture. The second type of question applies to the reader personally and is prefaced with **"Personal Application."** There are also **"Practice It"** actions similar to Personal Application questions. They are personal and provide an opportunity to practice the topic to learn from doing.

Information related to the text is indented and has an initial word in all capital letters, such as NOTE, IMPORTANT, INFORMATION, or CAUTION. They provide explanations, definitions, and other information to assist in understanding the text.

IMPORTANT: Know what you believe and why you believe it. This book is a teaching resource for everyone who wants to know the God of the Bible. That's why this book includes the following:

- Scripture quotations – 660
- What Do You Think? questions – 151
- What Do You Think? (Advanced) questions – 33
- Personal Application questions – 99
- Practice It – 21
- True stories – 70

The many true stories illustrate the reality of God and the Christian life. They confirm that the God of the Bible is real and actively engaged in people's lives. The experiences I describe, including the supernatural, are true and without embellishments. Some stories describe unusual experiences that are not common to many followers of Christ. This is true of the Father God speaking audibly to me. He chose to do this as part of His plan to save me and bring me into His eternal Kingdom. Either the hand of the Father God from Heaven, the Holy Spirit, or an angel pushed Linda's car off a railroad track just seconds before an oncoming train would have killed her and her friends when here car stalled on the tracks. You will see that several of us heard a choir of angels sing praises to God along with us as we worshiped Him. Also, you will learn about the haunted house I rented, how God protected me from a life-altering back injury while sumo wrestling in Japan, and how God healed me miraculously on two occasions.

NOTE: Pseudonyms are used for people in the book, except for my wife, Linda, and me (Paul).

Each story is included because it points to the God of the Bible and the realities of the Christian life. When you read each story in the book, ask yourself the following questions:

- What is God doing in the story?
- How is He impacting people's lives?
- How is He changing their hearts?

- Why did He do what He did – what was His purpose?
- And finally, how can God use the story to impact your own life?

God works differently in each of our lives. The experiences I have had may not occur in your life. His plan is different for each person. As you earnestly seek His presence and will, you will discover a new life you could never have imagined.

PERSONAL APPLICATION

When you read something in this book you have not heard before, why should you ask the Holy Spirit to help you understand its truth and application to you?

As you seek to know God, you may find He will reveal Himself to you in ways you have never experienced. He may astound you as He teaches you about Himself and His enduring love for you.

PART A

THE GOD OF THE BIBLE: DO YOU KNOW HIM?

1

God Doesn't Try to Prove His Existence

Does the God of the Bible really exist? Apparently, not to ninety-four percent of adult Americans. George Barna's 2020 *American Worldview Inventory* concludes that ninety-four percent of adult Americans have created their own idea of who they want God to be. That means only six percent believe in and live for God as He describes Himself in the Bible. The survey results were discussed in an *American Pastor's Network* interview with Mr. Barna in 2021 entitled "America's New 94% Religion: The Results and Implications of an unbiblical Worldview." Many studies indicate unbelief in the God of the Bible exists worldwide.

Who Is This God? A Handbook for Life with Him is a resource for anyone seeking to know the God of the Bible as He truly exists.

"OUR book will change people's lives!" I started writing this book in early October 2020. Several weeks later, on the morning of October 23, 2020, I was dressing and thinking about people in America and our crises of unbelief. Then, I heard the voice of the Holy Spirit in my mind say, "OUR book will change people's lives!"

WOW! But who does the "OUR" refer to?

Well, of course, myself. It also refers to the dozen people who reviewed and edited the book.

Most importantly, it includes the Holy Spirit! This audible voice in my head was the Holy Spirit speaking what Jesus Christ wanted me to know for this book.

> When the Spirit of truth comes, He will guide you into all truth. He will not speak on His own but will tell you what He has heard. He will tell you about the future. He will bring Me glory by telling you whatever He receives from Me. All that belongs to the Father is Mine; this is why I said, "The Spirit will tell you whatever He receives from Me." (John 16:13-15 NLT)

But how will this book "change people's lives?" My written words will not do that. So this book about God was written under the inspiration of the Holy Spirit. That's what's so important about the meaning of "Our book will change people's lives." He is the one who will use His words in this book to transform your thinking so you can know Him. So ask Him to do this.

> Don't copy the behavior and customs of this world, but let God transform you into a new person by changing the way you think. Then you will learn to know God's will for you, which is good and pleasing and perfect. (Romans 12:2 NLT)

NOTE: Since you are reading this book, I believe you were on His mind when He told me to write it.

Philosophy of religion. In undergraduate school in college, I took a class on philosophy that focused on world religions. We studied the major philosophers and their views on religion. We studied Christianity along with other world religions. At the end of the class, I remember the professor asking us what religion did we want to believe in: Christianity which says you are a sinful person, or another religion that says you are a good person? The professor didn't teach us that the God of the Bible is the only God who loves you and wants to have an eternal relationship with you.

After reading this book, you will know what the professor didn't understand—that the Christian God loves you so much that He sent His only Son to die on the cross to pay the penalty for all your sins (John 3:16). When you accept Jesus as your Savior, His resurrection from the dead provides what no other religion can: eternal life with God and a changed life with a new nature like Jesus. (You will learn more about this later.)

PERSONAL APPLICATION
In which god do you want to believe? Your god? Someone else's god? Or the God of the Bible?

There is only one God. In the Introduction, I stated that, "everyone believes in someone or something." In this chapter, I provide a few ways to know that the God of the Bible exists. I have included Bible verses so you can see that these are based on what God says about Himself. In the following verses, God says He alone is God. No other god in any form exists. He says that many people have created their own ideas of who He is, but they don't know Him as He truly is, the God of the Bible.

God Doesn't Try to Prove His Existence   11

"What fools they are who carry around their wooden idols and pray to gods that cannot save! Consult together, argue your case. Get together and decide what to say. Who made these things known so long ago? What idol ever told you they would happen? Was it not I, the LORD? For there is no other God but Me, a righteous God and Savior. There is none but Me. Let all the world look to Me for salvation! For I am God; there is no other. I have sworn by My own name; I have spoken the truth, and I will never go back on My word: Every knee will bend to Me, and every tongue will confess allegiance to Me." The people will declare, "The LORD is the source of all my righteousness and strength." And all who were angry with Him will come to Him and be ashamed. (Isaiah 45:20-24 NLT)

The Bible doesn't try to prove God's reality. The Bible simply states He exists. This is evident in the first verse of the Bible.

> In the beginning God created the heavens and the earth. (Genesis 1:1 NET)

Faith in God's Reality Is Needed to Experience Him

I know it's obvious, but you must believe that God is real to have a personal relationship with Him and experience His life.

> And it is impossible to please God without faith. *Anyone who wants to come to Him must believe that God exists* and that He rewards those who sincerely seek Him. (Hebrews 11:6 NLT, author's emphasis)

WHAT DO YOU THINK?
Why is faith in God's reality essential to knowing and experiencing Him?

God's Reality Is Evident in His Creation

The Bible states simply and clearly that God created everything.

> This is the account of the heavens and the earth when they were created – when the LORD God made the earth and heavens. (Genesis 2:4 NET)

The following verses say the evidence that God created everything can be seen in creation itself:

> By faith we understand that the entire universe was formed at God's command, that what we now see did not come from anything that can be seen. (Hebrews 11:3 NLT)

> For ever since the world was created, people have seen the earth and sky. Through everything God made, they can clearly see His invisible qualities—His eternal power and divine nature. So they have no excuse for not knowing God. (Romans 1:20 NLT)

I knew God was real, but I didn't know who He was. I remember, as a teenager, sitting under the fig trees on my grandparent's farm on hot summer days and looking up into the sky and talking to God. I just knew from His creation that He existed.

> The heavens proclaim the glory of God. The skies display His craftsmanship. Day after day they continue to speak; night after night they make Him known. They speak without a sound or word; their voice is never heard. Yet their message has gone throughout the earth, and their words to all the world. (Psalm 19:1-4 NLT)

I believed in God long before I knew who He was. As a committed Christian now, I study the Bible, meet with other believers, and experience God in many genuine ways. I live by faith in Him and enjoy experiencing His presence in my life. My faith in God rests on what He says about Himself. Real-life experiences with Him bolster this faith.

You also can discover God and experience His reality when you seek to know Him with all your heart. If you want to know God, ask Him to reveal Himself to you.

> You will seek Me and find Me when you search for Me with all your heart. (Jeremiah 29:13 NASB)

WHAT DO YOU THINK? (ADVANCED)

Why do you think God wanted to create the universe, planet earth, all living creatures, and people?

God's Reality Is Evident through Science

Some people think science and Christianity are polar opposites. That you can't believe in both but must choose one over the other. Central to this conflict is the theory of evolution by natural selection and the opposing Christian belief that there is an intelligent design and, therefore, a Designer behind creation. Some people fail to understand evolution is still just a theory that can't be proven by science and the scientific method.

NOTE: Scientists seeking truth use the scientific method to prove that a theory is true and only then confirm it as science. Despite many attempts, the theory of evolution has never been proven to be valid and reliable as a scientific fact.

The young atheist. I remember shortly after committing my life to Jesus Christ, discussing evolution and creation with a person at a party. He was a biology major and an atheist who was convinced the theory of evolution was the answer to the age-old question, "How did we get here?" I was staunchly advocating God as the Creator. We came to an impasse, neither of us willing to budge in our firmly held beliefs.

The young Christian. Many years later, I had a discussion about science and Christianity with a young Christian lady in an adult Sunday School class I was teaching. She mistakenly thought evolution was science. Due to her strong belief in creation, she considered all science to be opposed to the Bible and Christianity. I told her evolution is a theory and not a proven science. I said that true science and the Bible are not only compatible but inseparable because unbiased science is a study of God's creation. I explained the Bible was replete with verses related to the sciences, such as biology, physics, astronomy, geography, and so on. The chapter "The Natural World" further describes this compatibility.

WHAT DO YOU THINK?

After all, if God created everything, why isn't science, without bias, a study of the natural world He created?

God's Reality Is Evident in Changed Lives

When people accept Jesus Christ as their Savior and ask Him to be the Lord of their life, He sends the Holy Spirit to live within them. Because of this, they become a Christian. In biblical terms, they are a new creation on the inside. As they strive to live for Christ, their outward behavior begins to change to reflect the transformations occurring in their hearts and minds.

She was a vulgar and immoral woman. I didn't like being around this friend of my mother's. (She was very different from my mother, so I wondered why they were friends.) However, she was also my good friend's mother, so there was no avoiding her. Then one day, my friend told me his mother had committed her life to Jesus Christ. He said she was radically different because Jesus Christ had changed her. She no longer used vulgar language. She stopped going to bars and stopped drinking alcohol. She was radically different on the outside and the inside. I was not a Christian and didn't believe this could happen to such a disreputable woman. I would have to see her to believe it. Well, I did see her, and she was indeed different! She was sweet and kind but constantly talked about Jesus Christ. I was not sure what to make of her.

Later, my friend told me his mother had gone home to be with Jesus. I didn't know what he meant, so he told me she had died and gone to Heaven. She was divorced and had been battling serious cancer for many years. After she committed her life to Jesus, she asked Him to take her home to be with Him when her alimony payments stopped. She was too ill to return to work and would be destitute without financial income. The Father God honored her faith and prayer, so she died a few days after she received her last alimony check. Her son committed his life to Jesus because he saw God's life-changing power in his mother.

WHAT DO YOU THINK?
How is this woman's changed life evidence of God's existence?

More information about the existence of God. Richard E. Simmons III wrote a book published in 2019 titled *Reflections on the Existence of God*. It's a compilation of fifty-five short essays presented in ten groupings based on their similarity. Within the ten groupings, he provides a variety of perspectives to help you understand the reality of God's existence. Examples of the essays include God has a personal name, existence of evil, human morality, belief in God, meaning of life, evolution and God, and more.

PERSONAL APPLICATION
Why do you want to know more about the realities of God's existence?

Did Jesus Really Exist, or Was He a Myth?

How can you know that Jesus Christ was actually a person who lived on earth some two thousand years ago? Is there actual evidence that He existed? Unfortunately, many people treat His existence as a myth, simply the imagination of some zealous religious followers of His. Titus Kennedy answers these questions in his book, *Excavating the Evidence for Jesus: The Archaeology and History of Christ and the Gospels.* He uses extensive archeological discoveries in Israel to trace the birth, life, ministry, death, and resurrection of Jesus Christ to prove His existence. He follows Jesus through the New Testament Gospels, identifying scientific findings and historical literature to confirm the story of Jesus Christ.

PERSONAL APPLICATION
How has this chapter helped you confirm that the God of the Bible exists?

The next chapter provides a glimpse of how mighty and awesome God truly is. You will also learn that He is the Triune God, that is, ONE God in three persons.

2

The Greatness of God

God Is Spirit and Has a Supernatural Existence

God doesn't have a physical existence like human beings. Instead, He is a supernatural being existing beyond the natural realm. The Bible says *God is spirit* (John 4:24 NASB).

> God is spirit, and the people who worship him must worship in spirit and truth. (John 4:24 NET)

Yet, for people to relate to Him, He describes Himself as having a form throughout the Bible. For example, the *hand of God* (Isaiah 62:3 NLT). He does this because He wants people to relate to Him as an actual being who knows and cares about them.

God's Nature and Greatness

God is sovereign. This means He reigns and is supreme over everything. Nothing is outside His absolute authority. He is perfect in every respect. He is holy and separate from His creation. He is eternal and can't die. He can't be harmed or injured. He is the Creator of everything. He is majestic. He is just and righteous in all His ways. He is loving and compassionate toward people.

People are like a grain of sand compared to God. Each person on earth is like a grain of sand on the bottom of the Pacific Ocean, and God is the ocean. If you were a grain of sand and you could think and see, would it be possible to comprehend the magnitude and vastness of the entire 64,196,000 square miles of the Pacific ocean? No, it would not be possible. You might see a few feet around you, but not the 64 million square miles. Even this analogy is limited by our lack of human ability to comprehend the minutest aspects of Almighty God's nature, His majesty, and powerful existence.

Even when God reveals Himself, our human nature and brain limit our comprehension, as the following scriptures reveal:

> Can you discover the essence of God? Can you find out the perfection of the Almighty? (Job 11:7 NET)

> "My thoughts are nothing like your thoughts," says the LORD. "And My ways are far beyond anything you could imagine." (Isaiah 55:8 NLT)

Here are a few descriptions of the nature and greatness of God:

> O LORD, our Lord, Your majestic name fills the earth! Your glory is higher than the heavens. (Psalms 8:1 NLT)

> Yours, O LORD, is the greatness, the power, the glory, the victory, and the majesty. Everything in the heavens and on earth is Yours, O LORD, and this is Your kingdom. We adore You as the One who is over all things. (1 Chronicles 29:11 NLT)

> The LORD is great and certainly worthy of praise! No one can fathom his greatness! (Psalms 145:3 NET)

WHAT DO YOU THINK?
How would you describe the greatness of God to someone who has never heard of Him?

God Exists as the Trinity (ONE God in Three Persons)

His greatness can be seen in the triune nature of His existence. The following verse states that the God of the Bible is ONE God.

> Jesus answered, "The foremost is, 'Hear, o Israel! The LORD our God is one LORD'" (Mark 12:29 NASB).

However, He is also the Triune God, that is, ONE God in three persons. This is referred to as the "Trinity." This word doesn't appear in the Bible. Biblical scholars created it to help people understand the unity, yet reality of one God existing in three persons: Jehovah (God the Father), His Son, Jesus Christ, and the Holy Spirit. They are each equally God in every aspect of their being and nature.

Jesus told His disciples, "Therefore, go and make disciples of all the nations, baptizing them in the name of the Father and the Son and the Holy Spirit." (Matthew 28:19 NLT)

WHAT DO YOU THINK?

Why did Bible scholars create the word "Trinity?"

Trinity in the Old Testament

The writers of the Old Testament often refer to God in such a way that the casual reader may think they are referring to Him as an individual person. But a careful study reveals that even though they do speak of Him as ONE God, they also identify Him as existing in the three persons of God.

Following is the most apparent identification of the three persons of the Trinity in the Old Testament:

> "Listen to Me, O family of Jacob, Israel My chosen one! I alone am God, the First and the Last. It was My hand *[Jesus]* that laid the foundations of the earth, My right hand that spread out the heavens above. When I call out the stars, they all appear in order. . . . And now the Sovereign LORD *[Jehovah]* and His Spirit have sent me with this message." Isaiah 48:12-16 NLT, author's emphasis)

An inference to the Triune God appears in the Old Testament book of Genesis when God said *Let **Us** make human beings in **Our** image, to be like **Us**.*

> Then God said, "Let Us make human beings in Our image, to be like Us." (Genesis 1:26 NLT)

WHAT DO YOU THINK?

What other possibility besides the Trinity could explain the use of the plural in this verse?

Answer: Some think this refers to Jehovah God and His angels. I wonder about this since Jehovah is Almighty God who created everything, including angels. So how can the Creator and His creation say, *Let **Us** make human beings in **Our** image, to be like **Us?*** Angels are not equal to God, so they are not the same. So I believe this verse refers to the Trinity of God.

Jesus is God in the Old Testament. There are hundreds of verses in the Old Testament about Jesus that solidify He is God and part of the Trinity. Many of these are prophecies about His first and second coming. Following are several examples.

> "Look! I am sending My messenger *[John the Baptist]*, and he will prepare the way before Me *[Jesus]*. Then the Lord *[Jesus]* you are seeking will suddenly come to His Temple. The messenger of the covenant, whom you look for so eagerly, is surely coming," says the LORD of Heaven's Armies *[Jesus]*. (Malachi 3:1 NLT, author's emphasis)

> As my vision continued that night, I saw someone like a son of man *[Jesus]* coming with the clouds of heaven. He approached the Ancient One *[Jehovah]* and was led into His presence. He *[Jesus]* was given authority, honor, and sovereignty over all the nations of the world, so that people of every race and nation and language would obey Him. His rule is eternal—it will never end. His kingdom will never be destroyed. (Daniel 7:13-14 NLT, author's emphasis)

The Holy Spirit is God in the Old Testament. There are also many verses in the Old Testament about the Holy Spirit that validate He is God and part of the Trinity. Following are a few examples.

> Then the LORD said, "My Spirit will not put up with humans for such a long time, for they are only mortal flesh. In the future, their normal lifespan will be no more than 120 years." (Genesis 6:3 NLT)

> The Spirit of the LORD speaks through me; His words are upon my tongue. (2 Samuel 23:2 NLT)

WHAT DO YOU THINK?

When you consider these Old Testament verses about Jesus and the Holy Spirit, why are they evidence that both are God and part of the Trinity?

Trinity in the New Testament

The Old and New Testaments of the Bible are consistent in their teachings, which include who God is. Following are New Testament scriptures that teach about the existence of the Trinity as the Father, Jesus Christ, and the Holy Spirit.

> God the Father knew you and chose you long ago, and His Spirit has made you holy. As a result, you have obeyed Him and have been

cleansed by the blood of Jesus Christ. May God give you more and more grace and peace. (1 Peter 1:2 NLT)

The grace of the Lord Jesus Christ and the love of God and the fellowship of the Holy Spirit be with you all. (2 Corinthians 13:14 ESV)

WHAT DO YOU THINK? (ADVANCED)

Along with the Father, Jesus and the Holy Spirit are mentioned many times in the New Testament as equal to Jehovah. Why is this continuity between the Testaments important in understanding who the God of the Bible is?

The chapter "Prayer to Know God" describes how you can enter into an eternal relationship with the Almighty God, who created everything when nothing existed. If you already have a personal relationship with God, this book can help enhance that relationship. It can help you learn to experience each person of God more fully in your life.

PERSONAL APPLICATION

Why does the unfathomable greatness of God give you faith that the God of the Bible is true?

The next five chapters describe each person of the Trinity. It's essential to have a basic understanding of who each person of God is before you read further in the book.

3

Jehovah (Father God)

As we have seen, the Trinity is ONE God existing as three separate persons. As such, they each have their own names and titles. The following New Testament verse identifies each person of the Trinity.

> According to the foreknowledge of God the Father by being set apart by the Spirit for obedience and for sprinkling with Jesus Christ's blood. (1 Peter 1:2 NET)

The Triune nature of God is a mystery, yet, as you will see in this book, God has revealed aspects of each person.

PRACTICE IT
Why don't you ask each person of God to help you know Him better as you continue to study this book?

Roles and Responsibilities of God

I remember telling an adult Sunday School class that each person of the Trinity had certain roles in relation to each other and people. And that each role had its designated responsibilities. Some of them looked at me with bewilderment, so I used examples such as the following:

Jehovah: Chose the role of **Father** for everyone He would declare to be His children. Jesus even referred to Him as Father (*Abba*).

Jesus Christ: Chose the roles of **Savior** and **Lord** for everyone who accepted His death and resurrection for their salvation.

Holy Spirit: Chose the role of **Helper** and **Teacher** for all followers of Jesus.

You will discover additional roles as you read the chapters describing Jehovah (the Father), Jesus Christ, and the Holy Spirit. However, each person of God is exceedingly more complex than their roles reflect.

WHAT DO YOU THINK?

Why can understanding their roles help people know each of them personally? How could we distinguish between them if we didn't know their roles?

God (Jehovah, Father God)

Christians identify Jehovah, the Father God as the first person of the Trinity. When we see the word *God* in the Old and New Testaments of the Bible, it's typically referring to Him. Sometimes, it also refers to the Trinity, emphasizing their oneness. In the Hebrew language of the Old Testament, **God gives Himself one personal name, Yahweh** (Exodus 3:13-14). Because the people of Israel thought of this as His sacred name, they referred to it as "YHWH," leaving out the vowels. In English Bibles, this is **sometimes written as *I AM WHO I AM*, lord (with small capital letters), *Adonai*, or *Jehovah*.** When I use *Jehovah* in this book (instead of *Yahweh*, YHWH), it is to honor this Jewish tradition.

The following verses in the New Living Translation Bible (NLT) include God's personal name and other words for Him:

> Then the LORD told Moses, "Now you will see what I will do to Pharaoh. When he feels the force of My strong hand, he will let the people go. In fact, he will force them to leave his land!" And God said to Moses, "I am Yahweh—'the LORD.' I appeared to Abraham, to Isaac, and to Jacob as El-Shaddai—'God Almighty'—but I did not reveal My name, Yahweh, to them." (Exodus 6:1-3 NLT)

Following are explanations of these words for God:

- *LORD* (*Yahweh* in Hebrew) – *Yahweh* is God's personal name. His name means God is self-existent. *Jehovah* is a translation in English Bibles for *Yahweh*.

- *God* (*Elohim* in Hebrew) – This means God is the strong one with great authority. Some people think of *Elohim* as the Creator God.
- *El Shaddai* (*God Almighty* in Hebrew) – This means God is the all-sufficient God, powerful to meet all His children's needs.

WHAT DO YOU THINK? (ADVANCED)

Why are these three names important in helping people understand God's nature, that is, who He is?

Names and titles for Jehovah God reveal aspects of His divine nature and represent who He is. Two names seem to contrast but are important to understand Him: *Abba* (Father God) and *El Shaddai* (God Almighty).

Father God

Father God in the Old Testament. Jehovah has always been the Father to His children. However, this personal relationship is not emphasized throughout the Old Testament. The following Old Testament verses demonstrate that the people of Israel were His beloved children.

> Surely You are still our Father! Even if Abraham and Jacob would disown us, LORD, You would still be our Father. You are our Redeemer from ages past. (Isaiah 63:16 NLT)

> "My wayward children," says the LORD, "come back to Me, and I will heal your wayward hearts." "Yes, we're coming," the people reply, "for You are the LORD our God." (Jeremiah 3:22 NLT)

Father God in the New Testament. The Aramaic word *Abba* in the New Testament depicts Jehovah in an intimate sense as daddy or papa. However, this name also implies obedience to Him. His eternal children are to love, obey, and respect Him as their God and spiritual Father. The following verses say that the Holy Spirit within believers confirms they are *Abba's* children.

> For all who are led by the Spirit of God are children of God. So you have not received a spirit that makes you fearful slaves. Instead, you received God's Spirit when He adopted you as His own children. *Now we call Him, "Abba, Father."* For *His Spirit joins with our spirit to affirm*

that we are God's children. And since we are His children, we are His heirs. (Romans 8:14-17 NLT, author's emphasis)

In the New Testament, Jesus continually referred to Jehovah as His *Abba*, Father. In doing so, He introduced the intimacy of a personal relationship with Jehovah not usually depicted in the Old Testament. His disciples later understood this and began to call Jehovah their *Abba*, Father (1 John 3:1). On one occasion, Jesus taught this personal relationship by telling His disciples to pray to their Father in Heaven (Matthew 6:9). In addition to Jehovah, I refer to Him as the Father God, Heavenly Father, the Father, or God the Father often in this book.

PERSONAL APPLICATION
Is Jehovah God *Abba* to you? If not, why?

God Almighty

The Hebrew word *El Shaddai* is often translated as Almighty God or God Almighty. It means God is all-sufficient and all-powerful to meet all His children's needs. Quite simply, He is enough. He can sustain His people in every situation. Another aspect is that He is all-powerful in doing whatever He wants. This includes altering the natural world He created through what we perceive as miracles.

> For nothing will be impossible with God. (Luke 1:37 ESV)

> Great is our Lord, and abundant in power; his understanding is beyond measure. (Psalms 147:5 ESV)

> Ah, Lord God! It is you who have made the heavens and the earth by your great power and by your outstretched arm! Nothing is too hard for you. (Jeremiah 32:17 ESV)

When I think of the Father as God Almighty, I remember how omnipotent (all-powerful) He is in everything.

How almighty is Jehovah God? Following are some verses that describe Jehovah in His majesty, power, and sovereign greatness.

> Ascribe to the LORD the glory due his name; bring an offering and come before him! Worship the LORD in the splendor of holiness; tremble before him, all the earth; yes, the world is established; it shall never be moved. Let the heavens be glad, and let the earth rejoice, and

let them say among the nations, "The LORD reigns!" Let the sea roar, and all that fills it; let the field exult, and everything in it! Then shall the trees of the forest sing for joy before the LORD, for he comes to judge the earth. (1 Chronicles 16:29-33 ESV)

Yours, O LORD, is the greatness and the power and the glory and the victory and the majesty, for all that is in the heavens and in the earth is yours. Yours is the kingdom, O LORD, and you are exalted as head above all. Both riches and honor come from you, and you rule over all. In your hand are power and might, and in your hand it is to make great and to give strength to all. (1 Chronicles 29:11-12 ESV)

WHAT DO YOU THINK?

Knowing how great someone is can change our attitude toward him. How can Jehovah's almighty greatness impact how people view Him as God?

Almighty God sits on His throne of majesty and power. Jehovah (God Almighty, the Father) sits on His throne in Heaven and is surrounded by His mighty angels who constantly worship and praise Him for His majesty, greatness, and might.

I saw the Lord sitting upon a throne, high and lifted up; and the train of his robe filled the temple. Above him stood the seraphim. Each had six wings: with two he covered his face, and with two he covered his feet, and with two he flew. And one called to another and said: "Holy, holy, holy is the LORD of hosts; the whole earth is full of his glory!" And the foundations of the thresholds shook at the voice of him who called, and the house was filled with smoke. (Isaiah 6:1-4 ESV)

Jehovah in the Old Testament

When you read the names *God, Adonai, Elohim, El Shaddai,* or *Jehovah* in the Old Testament, they almost always refer to the first person of the Trinity, Jehovah (Father God).

Following are some Old Testament names that can provide additional insight into who this person of God is. These all start with God's personal name, *Jehovah (Yahweh* in Hebrew). So, we know these are names, not titles, since they start with His personal name, *Jehovah.*

God is our righteousness (*Jehovah-Tsidekenu*). Jehovah does what people cannot do by making them right with Himself through the death and resurrection of Jesus Christ. Since people cannot be good enough to earn the right to live with God eternally, He provided the only way for them to receive His perfect righteousness.

> "Behold, the days are coming, declares the LORD, when I will raise up for David a righteous Branch, and he *[Jesus Christ]* shall reign as king and deal wisely, and shall execute justice and righteousness in the land. In his days Judah will be saved, and Israel will dwell securely. And this is the name by which he will be called: 'The LORD is our righteousness.'" (Jeremiah 23:5-6 ESV, author's emphasis)

God is our peace (*Jehovah-Shalom*). Jehovah gives perfect peace of body, soul, and spirit. This carries a sense of completeness and wholeness since nothing needs to be added for this peace to occur.

> May the LORD *[Jehovah-Shalom]* give strength to his people! May the LORD bless his people with peace! (Psalms 29:11 ESV, author's emphasis)

PERSONAL APPLICATION

Is there anything hindering you from having God's Shalom peace in your life? If so, ask Jehovah to forgive you and help you receive His peace.

God provides (*Jehovah-Jireh*). Jehovah sees our needs and can make provision for them. This includes our eternal need for salvation as well as the daily needs of life. However, this does not mean He grants all our wishes. He knows what's best and provides according to His plan, will, and timing.

> So Abraham called the name of that place, "The LORD will provide"; as it is said to this day, "On the mount of the LORD it shall be provided." (Genesis 22:14 ESV)

God who heals (*Jehovah-Rophe, also Rapha*). Jehovah brings healing to the body, soul, and spirit of His people. It's a healing that can occur at all levels of the person's being. This includes healing the sin-sick soul with salvation when a person accepts Jesus as Savior and Lord.

> For I, the LORD, am your healer. (Exodus 15:26 NET)

God is our banner (*Jehovah-Nissi*). This means His people do not fight their battles alone against the flesh (old nature), the devil, and the world. Instead, *Jehovah-Nissi* helps them live in victory over all their enemies.

> The LORD said to Moses, "Write this as a memorial in the book, and rehearse it in Joshua's hearing; for I will surely wipe out the remembrance of Amalek from under heaven." Moses built an altar, and he called it "The LORD is my Banner." (Exodus 17:14-15 NET)

God is our Shepherd (*Jehovah-Roi*). This indicates the personal, caring relationship of the Father for His children. It's translated as the *LORD is my shepherd* in Psalms 23. *Jehovah-Roi* cares for and guides His children for their safety and well-being.

> The LORD is my shepherd; I shall not want. He makes me lie down in green pastures. He leads me beside still waters. He restores my soul. He leads me in paths of righteousness for his name's sake. (Psalms 23:1-3 ESV)

PERSONAL APPLICATION

Is there an Old Testament name for Jehovah that you are currently experiencing as a blessing? Is there one you want to experience more to help you know Him better?

Jehovah in the New Testament

We know the Father God's personal name is *Yahweh*, sometimes translated as *Jehovah* in the Old Testament. However, the Hebrew names for God don't appear in most New Testament English translations of the Bible. Instead, the New Testament Greek word *theos* is translated as *God* and *kurios* as *Lord*.

NOTE: It's important to know that the Triune God of the Old Testament is the same Triune God of the New Testament, even though different names are used in these two partitions of the Bible.

We see the use of *theos* and *kurios* used for God (*Jehovah*) in the following verses:

> Now one of the experts in the law came and heard them debating. When he saw that Jesus answered them well, he asked him, "Which

commandment is the most important of all?" Jesus answered, "The most important is: 'Listen, Israel, the Lord *[kurios]* our God *[theos]*, the Lord is one. Love the Lord your God with all your heart, with all your soul, with all your mind, and with all your strength.'" (Mark 12:28-30 NET, author's emphasis)

Theos. The Greek word *theos* refers to a deity, particularly the supreme divinity. This Greek word is used the most in the New Testament for Jehovah God.

Kurios. The Greek word *kurios* has several different meanings in the New Testament. One of those is *Lord*, the one who is supreme in authority. It's used to refer to both Jehovah and Jesus.

WHAT DO YOU THINK? (ADVANCED)

Why do you think the New Testament writers used more general names for *Jehovah*, such as *theos* and *kurios,* instead of descriptive names, such as *Jehovah, El Shaddai,* and *Elohim*?

Answer. In this chapter, you have seen a shift in focus from Jehovah in the Old Testament to the Father God in the New Testament. This shift emphasizes the personal relationship of Jesus and His followers with Jehovah as their spiritual Father. Also, the heart of the New Testament is to demonstrate that everyone needs a personal relationship with Jesus as their Savior and Lord. It's about salvation and eternal life with God. Therefore, the Old Testament descriptive names for Jehovah are not necessary to accomplish this purpose in the New Testament books.

PERSONAL APPLICATION

Why is this shift from the Old Testament descriptive names for Jehovah to frequent references to Him as the Father in the New Testament important to you?

Consider that ALMIGHTY God loves you so much He wants to be your *Abba,* Father God. This incredible news can change your life if you accept its truth and choose to live in a personal relationship with Him.

4

Jesus Christ: Old Testament

Christians identify Jesus Christ as the second person of the Trinity. He is entirely God and fully divine in His nature. He is found throughout the Old and New Testaments of the Bible and has many names and titles to help us understand who He is and what He does.

NOTE: *Jesus* is the personal name of *Jesus Christ*. It was given at His first coming to earth when He was born to the Virgin Mary (Matthew 1:21). Therefore, it's not used in Old Testament verses about Him. *Christ* is one of His New Testament titles, as *Messiah* is an Old Testament title.

Jesus Is God in the Old Testament

As you read earlier, many Bible scholars think the words *Us* and *Our* in the following verse refers to the Trinity. That being the case, this is the first indication that Jesus is God in the Bible.

> Then God said, "Let Us make human beings in Our image, to be like Us." (Genesis 1:26 NLT)

The next reference to Jesus in the Old Testament is in Genesis 3:15. Jehovah, the Father, tells Satan (devil) that a descendent of Eve, *her Offspring* [Jesus], *will strike your head*. This event occurred when Jesus died and rose again, and the devil's power over believers was broken (Hebrews 2:14). Only God could die, rise from the dead, and destroy the devil's power over the followers of Jesus.

> And I will cause hostility between you and the woman, and between your offspring and her Offspring *[Jesus]*. He will strike your head, and you will strike His heel. (Genesis 3:15 NLT, author's emphasis)

There are many Old Testament verses that indicate that Jesus is God. For example, in the following verse, Jesus is referred to as ***the** angel of God*:

> Then the angel of God said to me in the dream . . . "I am the God of Bethel, where you anointed a pillar and made a vow to me. Now arise, go out from this land and return to the land of your kindred." (Genesis 31:11-13 ESV)

NOTE: "**The** angel of God" is Jesus. Whereas "**An** angel of God" is an angel.

WHAT DO YOU THINK?
Why is it essential to the Christian religion to know that Jesus is identified as God in the Old Testament of the Bible?

Hundreds of Old Testament Prophecies

Hundreds of verses in the Old Testament are prophecies about the first and second coming of Jesus Christ to earth. Some estimate there are over three hundred Old Testament prophecies about His first coming alone, all of which were fulfilled.

First coming of Jesus (Savior). This is about Jesus coming to earth to be the Savior of all people.

When He comes, He will:
Come from the tribe of Judah.

> The scepter will not depart from Judah, nor the ruler's staff from between his feet, until he comes to whom it belongs; the nations will obey him. (Genesis 49:10 NET)

Be declared the Son of God.

> The king says, "I will announce the LORD's decree. He said to me: 'You are my son! This very day I have become your father!'" (Psalm 2:7 NET).

Start His ministry in the region of Galilee.

> The gloom will be dispelled for those who were anxious. In earlier times he humiliated the land of Zebulun, and the land of Naphtali; but now he brings honor to the way of the sea, the region beyond the Jordan, and Galilee of the nations. The people walking in darkness see a bright light; light shines on those who live in a land of deep darkness. (Isaiah 9:1-2 NET)

Come as the Savior to redeem people from their sins.

> This is what the LORD says—Israel's King and Redeemer, the LORD of Heaven's Armies: "I am the First and the Last; there is no other God." (Isaiah 44:6 NLT)

Proclaim Jehovah's messages (by the Holy Spirit).

> The Spirit of the Sovereign LORD is upon me, because the LORD has chosen me. He has commissioned me to encourage the poor, to help the brokenhearted, to decree the release of captives, and the freeing of prisoners. (Isaiah 61:1 NET)

Rise from the dead.

> O LORD, you have brought up my soul from Sheol; you restored me to life from among those who go down to the pit. (Psalms 30:3 ESV)

PERSONAL APPLICATION

Jesus fulfilled all the above verses at His first coming. So why do these help you believe in Him as your Savior?

Second coming of Jesus (Judge). This is about Jesus' second coming to render judgment on everyone who rejected Him as Savior.

When He returns, He will:
Land on the Mount of Olives.

> Behold, a day is coming for the LORD *[Jesus]*, when the spoil taken from you will be divided in your midst . . . . Then the LORD will go out and fight against those nations as when he fights on a day of

> battle. On that day his feet shall stand on the Mount of Olives that lies
> before Jerusalem on the east, and the Mount of Olives shall be split
> in two from east to west by a very wide valley, so that one half of the
> Mount shall move northward, and the other half southward. . . . Then
> the LORD my God [Jesus] will come, and all the holy ones with him.
> (Zechariah 14:1-5 ESV, author's emphasis)

Eliminate sin in the world.

> A period of seventy sets of seven has been decreed for your people and
> your holy city to finish their rebellion, to put an end to their sin, to
> atone for their guilt, to bring in everlasting righteousness, to confirm
> the prophetic vision, and to anoint the Most Holy Place. (Daniel 9:24
> NLT)

Return in a fury to judge those who rejected Him as Savior.

> For behold, the LORD will come in fire, and his chariots like the
> whirlwind, to render his anger in fury, and his rebuke with flames of
> fire. For by fire will the LORD enter into judgment, and by his sword,
> with all flesh; and those slain by the LORD shall be many. (Isaiah
> 66:15-16 ESV)

Find the nations (unbelievers all over the world) gathered to make war with Him.

> Why are the nations so angry? Why do they waste their time with futile
> plans? The kings of the earth prepare for battle; the rulers plot together
> against the LORD and against His anointed one. (Psalms 2:1-2 NLT)

WHAT DO YOU THINK?
Why does Jesus want to return to earth?

Mathematical Probability Jesus Is the Messiah

The probability of one person fulfilling just eight first-coming prophecies is astronomical. In his book *Evidence that Demands a Verdict*, Josh McDowell refers to the book *Science Speaks* by author Professor Peter W. Stoner. He states the mathematical probability that one person could fulfill just eight of the more than 300 prophecies of Jesus' first coming. **His purpose is to demonstrate that the science of mathematics rules out mere coincidence that one person could fulfill just eight of these prophecies.**

The eight prophecies included in this probability about His first coming follow:

1. His birth. (Micah 5:2)

2. Preceded by a messenger. (Malachi 3:1)

3. Entered Jerusalem on a donkey. (Zechariah 9:9)

4. Betrayed by a friend and wounded in His hands. (Zechariah 13:6)

5. Betrayed for 30 pieces of silver. (Zechariah 11:12)

6. Judas threw 30 pieces of silver to the potter into the temple. (Zechariah 11:13)

7. Silent before His accusers. (Isaiah 53:7)

8. Pierced His hands and feet. (Psalms 22:16)

This probability is 1 in 10^{17} (1 in 100,000,000,000,000,000).

To put this in perspective, you could lay 1017 silver dollars on the entire state of Texas two feet deep. Then mark one of these, mix it in, and try to find it. The probability you could locate it is 1017. I doubt you would ever discover it in your lifetime.

Jesus fulfilled not only these eight prophecies, but all the prophecies of His first coming—over three hundred. The probability of one person fulfilling all of these is astronomical! Yet we see in the New Testament scripture that He fulfilled all of them. Only the God of the Bible could give these specific prophecies to multiple Old Testament prophets and have Jesus Christ fulfill them several thousand years later.

WHAT DO YOU THINK?
Why do you think Jesus is God if He fulfilled all (not just the eight) Old Testament prophecies about His first coming?

Old Testament Appearances of Jesus in Human Form

Jehovah (Father God) says no human being on earth can see Him and live (Exodus 33:20). We also read in the following verses that Jehovah is a spirit and is invisible to people on earth:

> God is spirit, and those who worship him must worship in spirit and truth. (John 4:24 ESV)

> Christ is the visible image of the invisible God. (Colossians 1:15 NLT)

Where is Jehovah God located? Jehovah resides and reigns from His throne in Heaven.

> God reigns over the nations, God sits on His holy throne. (Psalms 47:8 ESV)

Jesus pre-incarnate and incarnate. All Old Testament Bible references to people seeing God as a man on earth are Jesus Christ. These appearances are called a "Christophany" and are referred to as Jesus Christ "pre-incarnate." This means Jesus appeared in human form prior to His birth to the Virgin Mary (Matthew 1:18). His physical birth to Mary as a man is Jesus "incarnate." Incarnate is a Latin word that means "in the flesh."

Jesus appears in human form. Following are some Old Testament verses about the pre-incarnate Jesus appearing in the form of a man. Notice that Jesus is called by the same Hebrew names used for the Father God: *Jehovah*, *El Shaddai*, and *Adonai*. Jesus is part of the Trinity of God and is, therefore, equally God in all respects. Even though they are separate persons of God, they share the nature of each name for God.

> When Abram was ninety-nine years old, the LORD *[Jehovah]* appeared to him and said, "I am El-Shaddai—'God Almighty.' Serve Me faithfully and live a blameless life." (Genesis 17:1 NLT, author's emphasis)

> Then the angel of the LORD *[Jehovah]* put out the end of the staff that was in his hand and touched the meat and the unleavened bread; and fire sprang up from the rock and consumed the meat and the unleavened bread. Then the angel of the LORD vanished from his sight. When Gideon saw that he was the angel of the LORD, he said, "Alas, O Lord *[Adonai]* GOD *[Jehovah]*! For now I have seen the angel of the LORD face to face." The LORD said to him, "Peace to you, do not fear; you shall not die." (Judges 6:21-23 NASB, author's emphasis)

WHAT DO YOU THINK?

Why is it appropriate to call Jesus by the same biblical names as His Father, Jehovah?

Jehovah God's physical manifestations. When God manifests Himself in a physical form in the Bible, it's referred to as a "Theophany." There are several views about these physical manifestations of God on earth when He is not in the form of a man. Some believe these are always Jesus Christ, while others believe some or all are Jehovah God.

The following New Testament scripture is about Jehovah manifesting His presence as a cloud while speaking from Heaven in Jesus' presence. This does not mean that all physical manifestations of God in the Old Testament are Jehovah. But it's an example that indicates at least some are likely Jehovah, while others may be Jesus (when not in the form of a man).

> And after six days Jesus took with him Peter and James and John, and led them up a high mountain by themselves. And he was transfigured before them . . . And a cloud overshadowed them, and a voice came out of the cloud, "This is my beloved Son; listen to him." (Mark 9:2-7 ESV)

Not exhaustive. The above is not intended to be an exhaustive study of Theophanies and Christophanies in the Bible. Instead, I have included this glimpse to demonstrate that this is another way Jesus Christ can be seen as God in the Old Testament.

Old Testament Messiah of Israel

Jehovah God promises in the Old Testament that He would send the Messiah to save Israel. The Hebrew word *Mashiah* is translated *Messiah* or *Anointed One* in the Bible. It means the anointed one of Jehovah God.

> So you are to know and discern that from the issuing of a decree to restore and rebuild Jerusalem until Messiah the Prince there will be seven weeks and sixty-two weeks; it will be built again, with plaza and moat, even in times of distress. (Daniel 9:25 NASB)

Other Old Testament verses don't use the Hebrew word *Mashiah* but instead use other titles that represent who the Messiah is and what He will do when He comes to earth. The following verse is an example of this:

> But you, O Bethlehem Ephrathah, are only a small village among all the people of Judah. Yet a ruler of Israel will come from you, One whose origins are from the distant past. (Micah 5:2 NLT)

Jesus is the New Testament name for this promised Messiah.

> Jacob was the father of Joseph, the husband of Mary. Mary gave birth to Jesus, who is called the Messiah. (Matthew 1:16 NLT)

Incorrect expectations. The Jewish people were expecting the Messiah to be a military and political leader who would free them from the tyranny of the Roman government. But this was not the Father's purpose in sending Jesus as the Messiah. Instead, He came to save both Jewish and non-Jewish people from the eternal consequences of their sins.

WHAT DO YOU THINK?
Why do you think most Jewish people rejected Jesus as their Messiah?

The next chapter pictures Jesus Christ as God in the New Testament of the Bible. In contrast to the Old Testament and its focus on God, nearly all New Testament is about Jesus.

5

Jesus Christ: New Testament

No Christianity If Jesus Christ Is Not God

If Jesus Christ is not God, there is no New Testament Christianity. The entire Christian religion is based on this one simple fact – Jesus is God.

Following are a few scriptures where Jesus is proclaimed to be God:

> "My Lord and my God!" Thomas exclaimed. (John 20:28 NLT)

> "But to the Son *[Jesus]* He *[Father God]* says, 'Your throne, O God, endures forever and ever. You rule with a scepter of justice.'" (Hebrews 1:8 NLT, author's emphasis)

Jesus said He and the Father (Jehovah) were one, saying He was God.

> "The Father and I are one." Once again the people picked up stones to kill Him. Jesus said, "At My Father's direction I have done many good works. For which one are you going to stone Me?" They replied, "We're stoning you not for any good work, but for blasphemy! You, a mere man, claim to be God." (John 10:30-33 NLT)

Josh McDowell wrote *More than a Carpenter* in 1977 to help people develop a biblical understanding that Jesus Christ is God. Initially, he was a skeptical non-believer who wanted to prove to fellow college students that Christianity and Jesus were fake. But, in his determined effort to prove them wrong, he discovered they were right! Trying to prove that the resurrection of Jesus never happened was a key to his change of heart, mind, and eternal destiny. Josh wrote this book after he committed his life to Christ to help people realize that Jesus is who He said He was: the resurrected Son of God. So Jesus was *More than a Carpenter*, and more than a great man and great prophet, as some say.

WHAT DO YOU THINK?

To say Jesus was a great man and a great prophet ignores what He said about Himself. How can He be just a prophet and good man if He claimed to be God?

Son of God and Son of Man

Jesus Christ is called the Son of God and Son of Man in the New Testament. Each title represents a picture of who He is.

> Then Nathanael exclaimed, "Rabbi, You are the Son of God—the King of Israel!" . . . Then He *[Jesus]* said, "I tell you the truth, you will all see heaven open and the angels of God going up and down on the Son of Man, the One who is the stairway between heaven and earth." (John 1:49-51 NLT, author's emphasis)

Son of God - No biological father. Jesus did not have a biological father. Instead, He had a spiritual father, the Holy Spirit. It was through Him that Jesus received His spiritual nature as the Son of God at conception.

> The angel replied, "The Holy Spirit will come upon you, and the power of the Most High will overshadow you. So the baby to be born will be holy, and He will be called the Son of God". (Luke 1:35 NLT)

As the Son of God, He was born fully divine, fully God, and equal to His Father, Jehovah.

> And we know that the Son of God has come, and He has given us understanding so that we can know the true God. And now we live in fellowship with the true God because we live in fellowship with His Son, Jesus Christ. He is the only true God, and He is eternal life. (1 John 5:20 NLT)

Son of Man - Biological mother. Jesus' biological mother was a young virgin woman, Mary. It was through her that He received His human nature as the Son of Man. Because she became pregnant by the Holy Spirit, people refer to this as the "virgin birth" of Jesus.

> This is how Jesus the Messiah was born. His mother, Mary, was engaged to be married to Joseph. But before the marriage took place, while she was still a virgin, she became pregnant through the power of the Holy Spirit. (Matthew 1:18 NLT)

WHAT DO YOU THINK?

If Mary was pregnant by Joseph instead of the Holy Spirit, why would there not be a Christian religion?

As the Son of Man, He was born fully human. He had a human body that became tired, hungry, and thirsty.

> Jacob's well was there; and Jesus, tired from the long walk, sat wearily beside the well about noontime. (John 4:6 NLT)

Jesus suffered and experienced temptations in His human form but did no wrong.

> This High Priest of ours understands our weaknesses, for He faced the same tests that we do, yet He did not sin. (Hebrews 4:15 NLT)

Only in His human form as the Son of Man could Jesus' body suffer and die physically. His spirit/soul could never die because He is the eternal God.

> And he began to teach them that the Son of Man must suffer many things and be rejected by the elders and the chief priests and the scribes and be killed, and after three days rise again. (Mark 8:31 ESV)

The Son of Man *gave up His divine privileges.* He didn't use His divine, supernatural abilities and majesty as God when He lived as fully God and fully human in this world. Instead, he chose to forego these and rely on the Holy Spirit.

> You must have the same attitude that Christ Jesus had. Though He was God, He did not think of equality with God as something to cling to. Instead, He gave up His divine privileges; He took the humble position of a slave and was born as a human being. When He appeared in human form, He humbled Himself in obedience to God and died a criminal's death on a cross. (Philippians 2:5-8 NLT)

Every supernatural miracle He did was by the Holy Spirit (Matthew 12:28). This enabled Him to demonstrate that His followers must also rely on the presence and power of the indwelling Holy Spirit.

WHAT DO YOU THINK?
What can a believer do in their Christian life and serving the Father without the work of the Holy Spirit?

Savior and Lord

Jesus Is Savior. To save people from the eternal consequences of sin, He became the sacrifice for their sins. Because He sacrificed His physical human life, He became the *Savior* for all people.

> But now he has appeared once for all at the consummation of the ages to put away sin by his sacrifice. (Hebrews 9:26 NET)

> While we look forward with hope to that wonderful day when the glory of our great God and Savior, Jesus Christ, will be revealed. He gave His life to free us from every kind of sin, to cleanse us, and to make us His very own people, totally committed to doing good deeds. (Titus 2:13-14 NLT)

No one else can save people from the eternal consequences of their self-centered life.

> And there is salvation in no one else, for there is no other name under heaven given among men by which we must be saved. (Acts 4:12 ESV)

Jesus Is Lord.

For Him to be Lord means people have given Him control of their life. He is in charge, not them. They have relinquished their will to that of Jesus. Therefore, maturing believers continually seek to know and do His will in all things.

In the following verses, Jesus is referred to as *Lord.*

> If you confess with your mouth that Jesus is Lord and believe in your heart that God raised him from the dead, you will be saved. (Romans 10:9 ESV)

Therefore God has highly exalted him and bestowed on him the name that is above every name, so that at the name of Jesus every knee should bow, in heaven and on earth and under the earth, and every tongue confess that Jesus Christ is Lord, to the glory of God the Father. (Philippians 2:9-11 ESV)

There is no salvation for people if He is not the Lord of their life.

WHAT DO YOU THINK?
Why aren't people saved if they have not asked Jesus to be in charge of their life?

Additional New Testament titles for Jesus Christ. These help us better understand who He is and what He came to do. For example, we know His personal name is Jesus and that Christ is the title that identifies Him as the Savior.

Following are some additional titles for Jesus Christ:

Emmanuel.

> "Look! The virgin will conceive and give birth to a son, and they will name him Emmanuel," which means "God with us." (Matthew 1:23 NET)

The Great Shepherd.

> And when the chief Shepherd appears, you will receive the unfading crown of glory. (1 Peter 5:4 ESV)

High Priest.

> Therefore he had to be made like his brothers and sisters in every respect, so that he could become a merciful and faithful high priest in things relating to God, to make atonement for the sins of the people. (Hebrews 2:17 NET)

King of kings and Lord of lords.

> He has a name written on his clothing and on his thigh: "King of kings and Lord of lords." (Revelation 19:16 NET)

WHAT DO YOU THINK? (ADVANCED)
What's the benefit of many titles for Jesus Christ in the New Testament?

The Supremacy of Christ

Supremacy refers to His sovereignty and superiority over all creation, including people, angels, and the devil and his demons. Seven things can be learned about the supremacy of Jesus Christ from the following verses in Colossians 1:15-19 (NLT).

1. Exact image of His Father God.

When you see the nature and character of Jesus Christ described in the Bible, you also see the Father God. Jesus is the exact image of the Father (Philippians 2:6). Jesus doesn't just look like God. He is God.

Christ is the visible image of the invisible God. (Colossians 1:15 NLT)

2. Jesus existed before creation and is supreme over everything.

Before the beginning of time and creation, He was God and was with God. (John 17:5; Revelation 22:13). Because Jesus is God, He is supreme over everything that exists.

He existed before anything was created and is supreme over all creation. (Colossians 1:15 NLT)

3. Jehovah created everything through Jesus.

Jesus spoke everything into existence (Genesis 1:1-31). This includes physical things that can be seen and invisible things that can't be seen (John 1:1-3; Hebrews 1:10).

For through Him God created everything in the heavenly realms and on earth. He made the things we can see and the things we can't see—such as thrones, kingdoms, rulers, and authorities in the unseen world. Everything was created through Him and for Him. (Colossians 1:16 NLT)

4. Jesus existed before anything and holds everything together.

Jesus existed before He created anything. And because He created everything, He sustains it, upholds it, and maintains it to continue as long as He desires (Hebrews 1:3).

He existed before anything else, and He holds all creation together. (Colossians 1:17 NLT)

WHAT DO YOU THINK?
What do these verses tell you about the superiority of Jesus Christ over every human being, even the most extraordinary people throughout world history?

5. Jesus is the head of His church.

Christ's church consists of every born-again follower of Jesus throughout the world and in Heaven (Colossians 2:19; Ephesians 1:20-23). So, His church is not a building, institution, or organization.

> Christ is also the head of the church, which is His body. (Colossians 1:18 NLT)

6. He is first in everything, including rising from the dead.

Jesus Christ's human physical body was put to death on the cross. He was buried and rose from the dead (Luke 23:44-56, 24:1-6). As a result, His followers will also have their dead physical bodies resurrected at His second coming (1 Corinthians 15:23-24).

> He is the beginning, supreme over all who rise from the dead. So He is first in everything. (Colossians 1:18 NLT)

7. Jehovah God in all His fullness lives in Jesus.

Jehovah lives in Jesus because Jesus is God (John 14:9; Colossians 2:9). The mystery of the Trinity, one God in three persons, is incomprehensible to the limited human mind.

> For God in all His fullness was pleased to live in Christ. (Colossians 1:19 NLT)

Jesus Sits on His Throne

The following verses say Jesus is seated on His throne at the Father's right hand in Heaven. This occurred when He ascended into Heaven after His resurrection from the dead.

> So then the Lord Jesus, after he had spoken to them, was taken up into heaven and sat down at the right hand of God. (Mark 16:19 ESV)

> But of the Son He *[Jehovah, Father]* says, "Your throne, O God, is forever and ever, and a righteous scepter is the scepter of your kingdom." (Hebrews 1:8 NET, author's emphasis)

From His Heavenly throne, He rules over the Kingdom of God and His followers. He presides with His majesty, glory, might, and full divinity as God. As the King of kings and Lord of lords, no one is like Him.

PERSONAL APPLICATION
If you were standing before the throne of Jesus in Heaven, how do you think you would feel?

Mediator of the New Covenant

Jesus Christ is the only one who died and rose again to bring salvation and eternal life to people. This Good News is the New Covenant that Jesus instituted at the "Last Supper" (Luke 22:14-20). Therefore, He is the only Mediator for this Covenant (agreement or contract) between His followers and Jehovah.

NOTE: The term *mediator* applied to Jesus does not mean He is settling disputes between the Father and people. Instead, it refers to Him as the only one who reconciled sinful people to the Father by His death and resurrection, which is the New Covenant.

For there is only one God and one Mediator who can reconcile God and humanity—the man Christ Jesus. (1 Timothy 2:5 NLT)

And so he is the mediator of a new covenant, so that those who are called may receive the eternal inheritance he has promised since he died to set them free from the violations committed under the first covenant. (Hebrews 9:15 NET)

The Old and New Covenants. The Old Covenant was based on the Law of Moses described in the Old Testament of the Bible. It required complete obedience to every law of God. Its purpose was to show that people could not perfectly obey all the Laws to earn eternal life with God (Galatians 3:23-26). Instead, the Old Covenant pointed toward the need for the New Covenant that is based on grace and faith and not the efforts of people. The purpose of the New Covenant is to offer salvation as the free gift of God's grace (unmerited favor).

For by grace you have been saved through faith. And this is not your own doing; it is the gift of God, a result of works, so that no one may boast. (Ephesians 2:8-9 ESV)

WHAT DO YOU THINK?

Why was there a need to replace the Old Covenant with the New Covenant? What is the benefit of the New Covenant to the followers of Jesus Christ?

Jesus intercedes for His followers. The following verses indicate that Jesus is interceding to the Father on behalf of His brothers and sisters:

> Therefore He is able, once and forever, to save those who come to God through Him. He lives forever to intercede with God on their behalf. (Hebrews 7:25 NLT)

> Who then will condemn us? No one—for Christ Jesus died for us and was raised to life for us, and He is sitting in the place of honor at God's right hand, pleading for us. (Romans 8:34 NLT)

PRACTICE IT

What would you like Jesus to say to the Father God on your behalf? Why don't you ask Him to do this now?

Jesus Is The Judge

The Father God gave His Son, Jesus Christ, the authority to judge every human being. He did this because Jesus lived on earth in human form as the Son of Man and Son of God. As such, He experienced all the temptations that people experience but did not sin. Therefore, He is qualified to judge people for how they lived their lives on earth (Ecclesiastes 12:14).

> And he commanded us to preach to the people and to testify that he is the one appointed by God to be judge of the living and the dead. (Acts 10:42 ESV)

> And he has given him authority to execute judgment, because he is the Son of Man. (John 5:27 ESV)

In the following verses, you see Jesus sitting on His *great white throne* to judge all people on Judgment Day:

> Then I saw a great white throne and him who was seated on it. From his presence earth and sky fled away, and no place was found for them. And I saw the dead, great and small, standing before the throne, and books were opened. Then another book was opened, which is the book of life. And the dead were judged by what was written in the books, according to what they had done. (Revelation 20:11-12 ESV)

WHAT DO YOU THINK?
Why did the Father God give Jesus the right to judge all people to determine their eternal destiny?

He Is the Alpha and Omega

Jesus Christ is the beginning and the end of everything.

> I am the Alpha and the Omega, the first and the last, the beginning and the end. (Revelation 22:13 ESV)

He was God before creation and will be God for eternity in the new heavens and new earth.

> Then the angel showed me the river of the water of life – water as clear as crystal – pouring out from the throne of God and of the Lamb, flowing down the middle of the city's main street . . . . And there will no longer be any curse, and the throne of God and the Lamb will be in the city. His servants will worship him, and they will see his face, and his name will be on their foreheads. (Revelation 22:1-4 NET)

In the following verses, you see He has always existed and will always exist as God:

> In the beginning was the Word, and the Word was with God, and the Word was God. He was in the beginning with God. (John 1:1-2 ESV)

This means that He is the whole of everything, including what exists between the beginning and end.

> Christ, who fills all things everywhere with Himself. (Ephesians 1:23 NLT)

PERSONAL APPLICATION

Is there anyone else you want to put faith in for eternal life? Why not ask the Holy Spirit to reveal the real, biblical Jesus Christ to your heart and mind?

The next two chapters are about the Holy Spirit. They will help you see Him as God in the Old and New Testaments of the Bible. You will learn why the Holy Spirit is vital to the believer's ability to know God and live an authentic Christian life that pleases the Father.

6

Holy Spirit: Old Testament

The Holy Spirit is identified as the third person of the Trinity. As you will see in this chapter, He is not some cosmic, impersonal force. Instead, He is a real person of God in the form of a spirit who loves and cares (Romans 15:30). Following is an Old Testament verse that indicates He's part of the Trinity:

> Look at My Servant *[Jesus]*, whom I strengthen. He is My Chosen One, who pleases Me *[Jehovah]*. I have put My Spirit upon Him. He will bring justice to the nations. (Isaiah 42:1 NLT, author's emphasis)

He is also identified as part of the Trinity in the New Testament.

> Therefore go and make disciples of all nations, baptizing them in the name of the Father and the Son and the Holy Spirit. (Matthew 28:19 NET)

He Is God in the Old Testament

In the following verse, the Holy Spirit is declared to be the *Spirit of the Sovereign LORD* (Jehovah). Therefore, He's entirely God, as Jehovah and Jesus are.

> The Spirit of the Sovereign LORD *[Jehovah]* is upon Me *[Jesus]*, for the LORD has anointed Me to bring good news to the poor. (Isaiah 61:1 NLT, author's emphasis)

WHAT DO YOU THINK?
Why is it important that both Old and New Testament verses agree that the Holy Spirit is God?

Spirit's Divine Attributes of God

Since He is God, He has all the divine attributes of Jehovah God and His Son, Jesus Christ. Following are three key attributes that only God can have. They demonstrate how superior the Triune God (Holy Spirit in this case) is to everything in creation, including people.

He is omniscient. (All-knowing)

The Holy Spirit knows everything because the Triune God lives in eternity, that is, in the past, present, and future, all at once. There is no boundary of space and time with Him. Therefore, since they created everything, there is nothing He doesn't know.

> The Spirit of the LORD will rest on Him, The spirit of wisdom and understanding, The spirit of counsel and strength, The spirit of knowledge and the fear of the LORD. (Isaiah 11:2 NASB)

He is omnipresent. (All-present)

The Spirit was everywhere before creation and is everywhere now. The following verse confirms His universal presence:

> I can never escape from Your Spirit! I can never get away from Your presence! (Psalms 139:7 NLT)

He is omnipotent. (All-powerful)

The Triune God is sovereign in power, so the Holy Spirit can do whatever He wants. Nothing or no one can prevent His will from being done. There are no limitations on His abilities; nothing physical or supernatural. His power is infinite and limitless.

> You send forth Your Spirit, they are created. (Psalms 104:30 NASB)

WHAT DO YOU THINK?

Why is it essential for the Holy Spirit to have God's three key divine attributes? If He did not have them, could He still be part of the Triune God?

Spirit of Life in Creation

Each person of the Trinity was involved in creation. In the following verses, I believe *hovering* means that the Holy Spirit is preparing to be involved in creation:

> In the beginning, God created the heavens and the earth. The earth was without form and void, and darkness was over the face of the deep. And the Spirit of God was hovering over the face of the waters. (Genesis 1:1-2 ESV)

The next verse indicates the Spirit breathed the life force of Almighty God into people:

> The Spirit of God has made me, and the breath of the Almighty gives me life. (Job 33:4 ESV)

Author of the Bible

The Holy Spirit gave both Old and New Testament men of God inspired words to write the sixty-six books of the Bible.

> All Scripture is breathed out by God and profitable for teaching, for reproof, for correction, and for training in righteousness, that the man of God may be complete, equipped for every good work. (2 Timothy 3:16-17 ESV)

We see in the next verse that He gave prophetic words to the Old Testament prophets:

> In Your love, You were patient with them for many years. You sent Your Spirit, who warned them through the prophets. (Nehemiah 9:30 NLT)

We see this in the New Testament as well.

> For no prophecy was ever produced by the will of man, but men spoke from God as they were carried along by the Holy Spirit. (2 Peter 1:21 ESV)

PERSONAL APPLICATION
When have you experienced the Holy Spirit giving you a prophecy or teaching in some way?

Activities of the Spirit in the Old Testament

Many verses in the Old Testament refer to the Holy Spirit. These help us know more about His divine nature and what He does in this world. He is often referred to as "the Spirit" or "the Spirit of God."

Following are some examples that reflect who He is as a person of the Triune God.

The Holy Spirit:

Was active on earth.

> The earth was without form and void, and darkness was over the face of the deep. And the Spirit of God was hovering over the face of the waters. (Genesis 1:2 ESV)

Was sent by the Father to be present with His people.

> Where is the One who sent His Holy Spirit to be among His people? (Isaiah 63:11 NLT)

Gave God's people rest.

> As with cattle going down into a peaceful valley, the Spirit of the LORD gave them rest. (Isaiah 63:14 NLT)

Came upon people for a purpose.

> At that time the Spirit of the LORD came upon Jephthah, and he went throughout the land of Gilead and Manasseh, including Mizpah in Gilead, and from there he led an army against the Ammonites. (Judges 11:29 NLT)

Put instructions into people's minds.

> He gave him the plans of all that the Spirit had put in his mind for the courts of the temple of the LORD and all the surrounding rooms, for the treasuries of the temple of God and for the treasuries for the dedicated things. (1 Chronicles 28:12 NIV)

Gave people skills to serve God.

> He has filled him with the Spirit of God – with skill, with understanding, with knowledge, and in all kinds of work. (Exodus 35:31 NET)

Gave prophecies to people.

> So Saul went to Naioth in Ramah. The Spirit of God came upon him as well, and he walked along prophesying until he came to Naioth in Ramah. (1 Samuel 19:23 NET)

Gave people visions from God.

> Then a wind lifted me up and carried me to the exiles in Babylonia, in the vision given to me by the Spirit of God. (Ezekiel 11:24 NET)

WHAT DO YOU THINK?

How should these activities help people see clearly that the Holy Spirit is God in the Old Testament?

Did the Spirit Indwell Old Testament Believers?

Many Christians wonder if the Holy Spirit dwelled within ALL Old Testament believers as He does all New Testament believers today. There are two common views about this.

VIEW #1: Holy Spirit did NOT indwell ALL Old Testament believers.

While the Holy Spirit was clearly active in the lives of many Old Testament believers, there is no biblical evidence that He permanently lived within every believer. There is no Old Testament promise by the Father that He would do this, as there is for New Testament believers (Acts 1:4-5).

New Testament validates the lack of Old Testament evidence. Jesus stated that the Holy Spirit was WITH the New Testament believers prior to Pentecost and would later be IN them. (This Pentecost event occurred just after the ascension of Jesus Christ.)

> He is the Holy Spirit, who leads into all truth. The world cannot receive Him, because it isn't looking for Him and doesn't recognize Him. But you know Him, because He lives with you now and later will be in you. (John 14:17 NLT)

> When He said "living water," He was speaking of the Spirit, who would be given to everyone believing in Him. But the Spirit had not yet been given, because Jesus had not yet entered into His glory. (John 7:39 NLT)

We see in the Old Testament that the Spirit would temporarily *come upon* certain people for a specific purpose.

> Then the Spirit of the LORD will come upon you mightily, and you shall prophesy with them. (1 Samuel 10:6 NASB)

And again that He would empower individuals for a specific purpose.

> When the Israelites cried out for help to the LORD, he raised up a deliverer for the Israelites who rescued them. His name was Othniel son of Kenaz, Caleb's younger brother. The LORD's Spirit empowered him and he led Israel. (Judges 3:9-10 NET)

A few scriptures, such as the following, indicate the Spirit indwelled selected individuals:

> The LORD replied to Moses, "Take Joshua son of Nun, a man in whom is the Spirit, and lay your hand on him." (Numbers 27:18 NET)

It's also thought that if He permanently lived within all Old Testament believers, He would not leave them, as He did King Saul (1 Samuel 16:14). King David asked Jehovah not to take the Spirit away from him (Psalms 51:11).

VIEW #2: Holy Spirit did indwell ALL Old Testament believers.
I could not find any verses clearly stating that the Holy Spirit dwelled within ALL Old Testament believers. However, those who believe this say it's impossible for Old Testament believers to love and serve God without the Spirit's presence and power. They say that when scripture indicates the Spirit came upon someone, it was a special anointing that didn't preclude Him from living within them. Another argument for this view is that when the Spirit left someone (as He did King Saul), it was His anointing that left, not His presence.

WHAT DO YOU THINK?
Which view do you think is Biblically correct? Why do you believe this to be true?

My conclusion. I believe the Holy Spirit didn't permanently indwell ALL Old Testament believers. This universal indwelling did not occur until after the life, death, resurrection, and ascension of Jesus in the New Testament. Then, it occurred for the first time at Pentecost. As we have seen, however, He likely indwelled some Old Testament believers and anointed or came upon others for specific purposes.

The next chapter describes the indwelling life, presence, and power of the Holy Spirit in New Testament believers.

7

Holy Spirit: New Testament

There are many verses in the New Testament about the Holy Spirit. **He is so essential to the life and service of Christians that Jesus said it was better for Him to leave so that the Holy Spirit would come.** This was the Father's plan so that the Holy Spirit could indwell and be present with all geographically dispersed believers, while Jesus could only be present in one place with a limited number of them.

> Nevertheless, I tell you the truth: it is to your advantage that I go away, for if I do not go away, the Helper will not come to you. But if I go, I will send him to you. (John 16:7 ESV)

This chapter provides a picture of who the Holy Spirit is and what He is doing during the New Testament period in which we live.

He Is God in the New Testament

Following is a verse that says the Holy Spirit is God.

> But Peter said, "Ananias, why has Satan filled your heart to lie to the Holy Spirit...You have not lied to people but to God!" (Acts 5:3-4 NET)

Many names and titles. The Holy Spirit has many names and titles in the Bible that indicate He is divine, fully God in nature, and part of the Trinity. For example, the following verse indicates He is equal to the Father and Jesus since He is the *Spirit of God* and the *Spirit of Christ.*

> But you are not controlled by your sinful nature. You are controlled by
> the Spirit if you have the Spirit of God living in you. (And remember
> that those who do not have the Spirit of Christ living in them do not
> belong to Him at all.) (Romans 8:9 NLT)

The Forgotten God

There is little preaching or teaching about the Holy Spirit today. Author and speaker
Francis Chan wrote a book titled *The Forgotten God* because many people don't know
Him. Unfortunately, I have witnessed this in many churches across multiple Christian
denominations.

WHAT DO YOU THINK?

When have you experienced consistent, solid biblical preaching and teaching
about the Holy Spirit? How did this impact the congregation's belief in
Him?

Some people reject the existence of the Holy Spirit. Leonardo Blair wrote an
article for The Christian Post entitled *Most adult US Christians don't believe Holy Spirit
is real: study.* His source was George Barna's 2021 *America's Dominant Worldview*
survey. He says that more than half of adult Americans do not believe in the existence
of the Holy Spirit.

WHAT DO YOU THINK?

Why do you think many adult Americans don't believe in the existence of the
Holy Spirit? What can be done to remedy this?

Why He's Important

The Holy Spirit was Jesus' supernatural power on earth. Everything Jesus did while
on earth requiring divine power was done by the Holy Spirit working in and through
Him.

> But if I am casting out demons by the power of God, then the Kingdom
> of God has arrived among you. (Luke 11:20 NLT)

The following verses indicate that the Holy Spirit is the Father's power at work within believers to enable them to accomplish His will and purposes:

> Now all glory to God, who is able, through His mighty power at work within us, to accomplish infinitely more than we might ask or think. (Ephesians 3:20 NLT)

> For the Kingdom of God is not just a lot of talk; it is living by God's power. (1 Corinthians 4:20 NLT)

This same Holy Spirit and His power are within every born-again follower of Jesus. But if they don't understand this or choose to ignore Him, their life as a Christian will have little value to God, and their eternity with Him will certainly be diminished (1 Corinthians 311-15).

The One Called Alongside

He is the person of God who enables the followers of Jesus Christ to know God and live for Him. Jesus used the Greek word *Paraclete* to indicate the importance of the Holy Spirit to believers. This word is translated as *Helper* (NASB, ESV), *Comforter* (KJV), and *Advocate* (NET, NLT, NIV) in various Bible versions. It means **one called alongside to help**. It depicts how essentially close the Holy Spirit is to believers as He works within and through them. In fact, it could be said that **the Holy Spirit should be the believer's closest companion and co-worker in God's Kingdom.**

PERSONAL APPLICATION
If you are a follower of Jesus, what must you change to live in this close relationship with the Holy Spirit?

Because of this closeness, Jesus said that the Holy Spirit would never leave His followers.

> And I will ask the Father, and he will give you another Helper, to be with you forever. (John 14:16 ESV)

The *paraclete's* help. The following scriptures identify why Jesus's followers cannot live and serve effectively without knowing and living by the *Paraclete*:

But the Helper, the Holy Spirit, whom the Father will send in my
name, he will teach you all things and bring to your remembrance all
that I have said to you. (John 14:26 ESV)

But when the Helper comes, whom I will send to you from the Father,
the Spirit of truth, who proceeds from the Father, he will bear witness
about me. (John 15:26 ESV)

When the Spirit of truth comes, He will guide you into all truth. He
will not speak on His own but will tell you what He has heard. He will
tell you about the future. (John 16:13 NLT)

Those who are controlled by the Holy Spirit think about things that
please the Spirit . . . letting the Spirit control your mind leads to life
and peace. (Romans 8:5-6 NLT)

The above verses indicate that the Holy Spirit does the following for believers:

- Helps them
- Teaches them
- Guides them
- Reminds them about the life, death, and resurrection of Jesus,
  which brings salvation and eternal life with God
- Communicates to them for the Father and Jesus, as well as Himself
- Controls their thinking and minds (which gives spiritual life and
  peace)

PERSONAL APPLICATION

Which of the above do you need to experience more from the Holy Spirit to live
your life with Him more fully? Why is this the case?

There is no situation where the Holy Spirit can't help. He lives in believers to
assist and enable them in every situation of life. The following story demonstrates this
when He supernaturally intervened in Linda's and my life as our *Helper* to save us from
a potentially fatal car accident.

Holy Spirit stops our car from hitting a concrete pole. A miracle of the Holy
Spirit's intervention in our lives occurred in 2007 in Orlando, Florida. Linda and I
were driving down a busy thoroughfare. The traffic was moving fast with a 55-mile-an-

hour speed limit. We were in the slow lane of the three-lane road when a large SUV lost control and suddenly struck our car. I didn't even see it coming. The right front of the SUV rammed my driver's door, and then the entire SUV slammed into the full side of our car. The impact was so violent that it catapulted our car (traveling at 55 miles an hour) off the road and onto the grass and sidewalk. This sudden violence caused me to black out momentarily. However, when I shortly began to come to, I realized my foot was on the brake, and our car was slowly decreasing in speed as we traveled toward a giant concrete pillar. (Streetlights hang on these across major roads.) Linda said all she could do was watch as our car traveled toward the concrete pillar. She said our car somehow began to slow down as we gently came to a stop a few feet from the pillar.

WHAT DO YOU THINK?

When I momentarily blacked out, I wasn't aware and, therefore, was not able to move my foot from the accelerator to the brake pedal, so who did this? Who applied the steady pressure on the brake to slow our car down as it approached the concrete pillar? An angel or the Holy Spirit?

Answer. We believe the indwelling presence and power of the Holy Spirit did this. I was unconscious, so it wasn't me. Death was not the Father's plan for us at that time.

When Does He Indwell Believers?

As you saw in the previous chapter, I believe that in the days of the Old Testament, the Holy Spirit did not live within all believers.

In the New Testament book of John, Jesus said that the Holy Spirit was *with* His followers but later would live *in* them.

> He is the Holy Spirit, who leads into all truth. The world cannot receive Him, because it isn't looking for Him and doesn't recognize Him. But you know Him, because He lives with you now and later will be in you. (John 14:17 NLT)

Promise fulfilled at Pentecost. When Jesus' promise was fulfilled on Pentecost, everything changed for God's people. In the following verses, Jesus told His disciples this would happen on Pentecost just before He ascended into Heaven:

> Once when He was eating with them, He commanded them, "Do not leave Jerusalem until the Father sends you the gift He promised, as I

told you before. John baptized with water, but in just a few days you will be baptized with the Holy Spirit." . . . But you will receive power when the Holy Spirit comes upon you. And you will be My witnesses, telling people about Me everywhere—in Jerusalem, throughout Judea, in Samaria, and to the ends of the earth." After saying this, He was taken up into a cloud while they were watching, and they could no longer see Him. (Acts 1:4-9 NLT)

One hundred and twenty believers were baptized with the Holy Spirit as He came to live within them at Pentecost about 33 AD. These were the first followers of Jesus Christ to be indwelled by the Holy Spirit.

They were all filled with the Spirit as He spoke through them, thus proving the reality of His presence *with* and *in* them.

On the day of Pentecost all the believers were meeting together in one place. Suddenly, there was a sound from heaven like the roaring of a mighty windstorm, and it filled the house where they were sitting. Then, what looked like flames or tongues of fire appeared and settled on each of them. And everyone present was filled with the Holy Spirit and began speaking in other languages, as the Holy Spirit gave them this ability. (Acts 2:1-4 NLT)

Holy Spirit indwells all believers since Pentecost. When people profess faith in Jesus Christ as their Savior and Lord, the Holy Spirit comes to live within them. They are given a spiritual birth. Only then are they born-again and become a Christian.

Jesus said, "I tell you the truth, unless you are born-again, you cannot see the Kingdom of God." . . . "Humans can reproduce only human life, but the Holy Spirit gives birth to spiritual life. So don't be surprised when I say, 'You must be born-again.'" (John 3:3-7 NLT)

WHAT DO YOU THINK? (ADVANCED)
The Holy Spirit is a spirit, so how does His living within believers give them *spiritual life*?

You will learn more about born-again in the chapter "'Born-again' Is Misunderstood."

Indwelling, Baptism, Anointing, and Filling

You have seen that when the Holy Spirit comes to live within a believer, they are born-again. But what about baptism, anointing, and filling with Him? When do these occur?

Baptism with the Holy Spirit. Baptism in the Bible is the idea of being completely immersed in something. For example, think about putting a cup completely under water to wash it. So, baptism with the Holy Spirit means being completely immersed in the Spirit's presence, power, and life. There are differences of opinion about when this occurs. I believe it happens when a person is born-again. They are baptized with the Holy Spirit at this moment of spiritual birth. Spiritual life is derived from spiritual birth. And I believe this spiritual life results from believers being completely immersed in the Holy Spirit.

I think the following verses indicate that baptism with the Holy Spirit occurs at the moment of spiritual birth (when they are born-again):

> Some of us are Jews, some are Gentiles, some are slaves, and some are free. But we have all been baptized into one body by one Spirit, and we all share the same Spirit. (1 Corinthians 12: 13 NLT)

> And all who have been united with Christ in baptism have put on Christ, like putting on new clothes. There is no longer Jew or Gentile, slave or free, male and female. For you are all one in Christ Jesus. (Galatians 3:27-28 NLT)

The baptism with the Holy Spirit results in unity among the followers of Jesus Christ, as identified in the following verses:

> There is one body and one Spirit, just as you too were called to the one hope of your calling, one Lord, one faith, one baptism, one God and Father of all, who is over all and through all and in all. (Ephesians 4:4-6 NET)

"Second blessing of the Spirit." Some Christians think they were baptized with the Holy Spirit later after spiritual birth. While others baptized with the Holy Spirit at spiritual birth believe they later received what they refer to as a "second blessing of the Spirit." By this, they mean there was an incident later when the Holy Spirit came upon them in a powerful way that changed their life by giving them more spiritual insight and power than they previously had experienced.

WHAT DO YOU THINK?

> **WHAT DO YOU THINK?**
>
> Why should this issue of when believers are baptized with the Holy Spirit not divide Christians? What should their attitude be toward one another instead of divisiveness?

Anointing with the Holy Spirit.

In the New Testament, believers receive an anointing of the Holy Spirit as part of being born-again and baptized with Him. The following verses indicate this:

> Nevertheless you have an anointing from the Holy One. (1 John 2:20 NET)
>
> Now as for you, the anointing that you received from him resides in you. (1 John 2:27 NET)

In the Old Testament, certain religious positions (such as priest and king) required an anointing of oil on the head to install them into the role. In the New Testament, the Holy Spirit's anointing (instead of oil) initiates the ministry or service. The start of Jesus' ministry on earth is an example of this in the following verse:

> You know of Jesus of Nazareth, how God anointed Him with the Holy Spirit and with power, and how He went about doing good and healing all who were oppressed by the devil, for God was with Him. (Acts 10:38 NASB)

Occasionally, the Spirit's anointing causes believers to experience His presence and power more significantly for a particular purpose. For example, I have experienced many short-term anointings of the Spirit while teaching adult Sunday School classes. When this occurs, I sense His enhanced presence and teach with greater knowledge and authority than otherwise. Therefore, I always ask the Holy Spirit for His anointing in all spiritual matters. I have been doing this as I write and edit this book.

> **WHAT DO YOU THINK?**
>
> When have you witnessed an anointing of the Holy Spirit on yourself or other believers? In what ways were His presence and power more discernible than otherwise?

Filling with the Holy Spirit.

Like the anointing of the Holy Spirit, the filling occurs at the time of spiritual birth. The following verse says that when this happens, the Spirit will flow like *rivers of living water* from the believer's heart:

> Whoever believes in me, as the Scripture has said, "Out of his heart will flow rivers of living water." Now this he said about the Spirit, whom those who believed in him were to receive, for as yet the Spirit had not been given, because Jesus was not yet glorified. (John 7:38-38 ESV)

The New Testament Greek word translated *filled* (for example, Acts 4:31; Ephesians 5:18) means to be full, filled to the top with no more room. The goal is for believers to be so full of the Holy Spirit's presence, influences, and power that there is no room in their hearts and minds for their old self-centered nature to prevail. The following verse says that believers should be filled continually with the Spirt:

> And the disciples were continually filled with joy and with the Holy Spirit. (Acts 13:52 NASB)

However, they will not always experience this continual filling since their old nature strives against their new nature for control. When it wins, they are not being filled with the Spirit's presence and power. This is one reason believers must seek to be transformed by the Spirit to be filled continually with Him. (More on the two natures and this transformation later.)

The following verses equate the experience of being drunk (filled) with alcohol to being filled with the Holy Spirit. In both cases, the individual acts or behaves under the influence of something other than themselves. However, this does not imply that being filled with the Holy Spirit results in thoughtless and reckless actions that alcohol can cause. On the contrary, the believer's actions are intentional choices to follow the Spirit's leading.

> Don't be drunk with wine, because that will ruin your life. Instead, be filled with the Holy Spirit, singing psalms and hymns and spiritual songs among yourselves, and making music to the Lord in your hearts. And give thanks for everything to God the Father in the name of our Lord Jesus Christ. And further, submit to one another out of reverence for Christ. (Ephesians 5:18-21 ESV)

These verses also say that when believers live by the filling of the Spirit, they will thank the Father for Jesus and willingly help one another because of their love for Christ.

PERSONAL APPLICATION
When have you experienced a filling of the Holy Spirit's life and power? When did it flow within and out from you like *rivers of living water*?

God's Seal and Guarantee

The seal is the Holy Spirit's presence within every born-again believer. It's the Father's guarantee of their eternal inheritance with Christ. It identifies them as belonging to the Father as His children.

> In him you also, when you heard the word of truth, the gospel of your salvation, and believed in him, were sealed with the promised Holy Spirit, who is the guarantee of our inheritance until we acquire possession of it, to the praise of his glory. (Ephesians 1:13-14 ESV)

WHAT DO YOU THINK?
Why does the Father want His children to know they are sealed with the Holy Spirit and guaranteed an eternal inheritance with Him?

The Holy Spirit and Non-Believers

The Holy Spirit opens people's hearts and minds to understand the Gospel that Jesus died for their sins and was resurrected to provide eternal life with God. He gives them the faith needed to believe and accept this salvation (Ephesians 2:8-9). The Father doesn't want anyone to perish but all to have this eternal life with Him (John 3:16; 2 Peter 3:9).

PERSONAL APPLICATION
If you are a Christian, describe how the Holy Spirit opened your heart and mind to believe in Jesus and accept Him as Savior and Lord.

As He opens people's hearts and minds, He also convicts (proves to) non-believers that they live a life contrary to the will of God and His righteousness.

> And when he comes, he will prove the world wrong concerning sin and righteousness and judgment – concerning sin, because they do not believe in me; concerning righteousness, because I am going to the Father and you will see me no longer; and concerning judgment, because the ruler of this world has been condemned. (John 16:8-11 NET)

NOTE: The word *world* in this context doesn't mean the physical planet earth. Instead, it refers to people who live without God and without His morals, standards, and values. These are people who don't know God.

Books to learn about the Holy Spirit. Some excellent books have been written to help you know the Holy Spirit. Authors such as Billy Graham, Jim Cymbala, and Francis Chan are examples. I have learned much about the Holy Spirit from the book *Disciple's Guide to the Holy Spirit* by Dr. Ralph F. Wilson, published by JesusWalk Publications. This excellent book and Bible study provides scripture to develop your knowledge of the Holy Spirit and expand your relationship with Him.

Your greatest need. You have no greater need than to give your heart and life to Jesus Christ and be born-again by the Holy Spirit. When you do this, everything changes for you. For the first time, through the Holy Spirit, you begin to live, think, and behave as an eternal child of the Father. The chapter "Prayer to Know God" can help you know how to have this eternal relationship with God through His Son, Jesus Christ.

8

Imagine Never Talking to Someone You Love

Think about your relationship with a special person in your life. Someone you care about. How would you describe the relationship? What aspects of it do you think could relate to a relationship with God?

Knowing about and Knowing Personally

There is a significant difference between knowing facts about people and knowing them personally. For example, you can look someone up on the Internet and learn facts, such as place of birth, schools, spouse, and career. You can do all that without ever having personal contact. However, you can never know people personally without spending time with them. When you talk with them, you learn about their lives in ways you can't know otherwise. You learn things only they can tell you, such as their desires, hurts, frustrations, joys, and hopes for the future. Likewise, you must spend time with God to develop a personal relationship with Him.

The following verses talk about knowing God personally, not just knowing things about Him:

> I will be faithful to you and make you Mine, and you will finally know Me as the LORD. (Hosea 2:20 NLT)

> For I know whom I have believed. (2 Timothy 1:12 ESV)

> Yes, everything else is worthless when compared with the infinite value of knowing Christ Jesus my Lord. (Philippians 3:8 NLT)

Then the way you live will always honor and please the Lord, and your lives will produce every kind of good fruit. All the while, you will grow as you learn to know God better and better. (Colossians 1:10 NLT)

WHAT DO YOU THINK? (ADVANCED)
Why do you think it matters to God whether people want to know Him personally?

The chapter "Knowing God through Christian Practices" provides a brief description of practices that will help you know God better and mature as a follower of Jesus. Regularly engaging in these will enable you to experience the presence of God more fully in your life. Learning to live by the Spirit is also vital to knowing God better.

God Wants an Eternal Relationship with You

God is not a distant, detached force at work in the universe, existing in complacency toward you. Instead, He created you to have an eternal relationship with Him. He wants you to know Him, not just know about Him. He wants to have fellowship with you and for you to experience Him and His reality in your life.

The following illustrates how each person of the Trinity of God desires a personal relationship with you.

Father God. He wants such a close relationship with believers that He calls them His children.

> For all who are led by the Spirit of God are sons of God. For you did not receive the spirit of slavery to fall back into fear, but you have received the Spirit of adoption as sons, by whom we cry, "Abba! Father!" The Spirit himself bears witness with our spirit that we are children of God, and if children, then heirs—heirs of God and fellow heirs with Christ, provided we suffer with him in order that we may also be glorified with him. (Romans 8:14-17 ESV)

Jesus Christ. He also wants a close relationship with His followers, so He calls them His *friends* and *brothers* (and sisters).

> I no longer call you slaves, because a master doesn't confide in His slaves. Now you are My friends, since I have told you everything the Father told Me. (John 15:15 NLT)

And stretching out his hand toward his disciples, he said, "Here are my mother and my brothers!" (Matthew 12:49 ESV)

Holy Spirit. He is the Teacher, Guide, and Helper for the followers of Jesus. In the following verses, the Greek word translated as Helper means one called alongside to help. The word denotes the continual close relationship of the Holy Spirit within every believer.

I will ask the Father, and He will give you another Helper, that He may be with you forever; that is the Spirit of truth, whom the world cannot receive, because it doesn't see Him or know Him, but you know Him because He abides with you and will be in you. (John 14:16-17 NASB)

PERSONAL APPLICATION

How would having a personal relationship with each person of God strengthen your faith in them? Which person of God do you know the least, and why is this so?

Anyone Can Communicate with God

I asked a former Bible study classmate when and how often he talked with God. I asked if praying formally to God once a day was the only time he spoke with Him. He emphatically responded that he was always talking to God throughout his day. Many people erroneously believe you only communicate with God through an occasional formal prayer. The Bible doesn't support this idea. You can pray formally and spontaneously talk to the Father, Jesus, and the Holy Spirit whenever you want.

NOTE: You don't need a priest, pastor, or anyone else to talk to God for you. Each person of God wants you to talk to them yourself. But be aware some people erroneously say you can talk to God or the dead through mediums or other occult practices. People who do this may find themselves communicating with demons instead.

Be an active listener. Communication with God, as with people, requires active listening. You must be intent on understanding what He wants to say to you.

Following is a short description of how to be an active listener when communicating with God:

- Listen intently to what He is saying (often this is the Holy Spirit speaking to your mind)

- Strive to understand the meaning and purpose of what He is saying

- Verify it is God speaking to you (For example, does this align with the Bible and the character of God?)

- Once verified, trust what God is saying to you is true and for your benefit

- Apply what He says, so it changes your heart and life

Following are some scriptures that indicate the importance of actively listening to God:

> Then He *[Jesus]* added, "*Pay close attention to what you hear. The closer you listen, the more understanding you will be given.*" (Mark 4:24 NLT, author's emphasis)

> Understand this, my dear brothers and sisters: You must all be quick to listen, slow to speak, and slow to get angry. (James 1:19 NLT)

> Therefore, as the Holy Spirit says, "Today, if you hear his voice, do not harden your hearts as in the rebellion, on the day of testing in the wilderness." (Hebrews 3:7-8 ESV)

Many Ways to Communicate with Him

Following are some common ways you can communicate with each person of God:

- **Praying** at a set time of day in a more formal and structured manner; prayer is often, but not limited to the Father God

- **Talking** spontaneously with no set time; can be to the Father, Jesus, or the Holy Spirit

- **Reading the Bible** includes studying, meditating, and praying scripture; as you do these, talk to God about His word (remember, His word is living and active)

- **Singing** can be speaking to God through songs

- **Worshiping** is a form of speaking to God as you humbly tune your heart and mind to Him; can be done in a church worship service, or any other time

You may find God (usually the Holy Spirit) responding to you as you engage in the above. You may hear His voice, have a thought from Him, or experience an impression about something. These are only a few ways He may respond to you.

PERSONAL APPLICATION

Which of these ways to communicate with God do you do regularly? Which do you need to do more of?

Requests of God in Prayer

Praise God, worship Him, and be grateful to Him in prayer. Then, ask Him in prayer for what you believe is best. But remember, He is not your personal assistant who lives to serve you. Rather, you live to serve Him. Keep this in mind as you determine what to pray for.

The Father God's responses to prayer may be any of the following:

- **Yes.** When God responds with Yes, He will do it according to His will, purpose, timing, and plans. But His answer may not exactly be what you asked for.

- **No.** If His response is No, it is because He knows what's best for you.

- **Wait (not now, but later).** If you sense His answer is Wait, it may be because He is waiting for you to do something first before you are ready to receive His response.

He may not respond. For reasons only He knows, He sometimes doesn't answer. His knowledge and ways of doing things are far beyond our understanding. You must simply trust in His loving kindness and goodness when this occurs.

> "My thoughts are nothing like your thoughts," says the LORD. "And My ways are far beyond anything you could imagine." (Isaiah 55:8 NLT)

Other times He may not answer because your heart is not right with Him. Perhaps, there is something you must repent of before He answers.

And when they cry out, God does not answer because of their pride. (Job 35:12 NLT)

If I had not confessed the sin in my heart, the Lord would not have listened. (Psalms 66:18 NLT)

And even when you ask, you don't get it because your motives are all wrong—you want only what will give you pleasure. (James 4:3 NLT)

Where is the heart? There have been times in prayer when I felt I was just talking at God, not with Him. They were just words. When I realize this, I ask the Father to forgive me. I then start over and try to focus on Him and speak from my heart. When I do so, I often sense His presence more than otherwise.

PERSONAL APPLICATION

Why doesn't God always give you what you request of Him?

Ending your prayers. Always end your prayer as Jesus did (Matthew 26:42) with something like the following, "Not my will, but your will be done." Remember that the Father knows what's best for you. He knows who else will be impacted by His response. He has a plan for your life that may not include the answers you desire. Finally, conclude your prayer with "in the name of Jesus Christ." He is your Savior through whom you are granted access to talk directly to the Father.

NOTE: By the way, the name of Jesus Christ is more than a label on a visitor's badge. It represents who He is as God.

Jesus' model for prayer. The disciples of Jesus asked Him to teach them how to pray to the Father. He responded with the following model for prayer:

Pray, then, in this way: "Our Father who is in heaven, Hallowed be Your name.

Your kingdom come. Your will be done, On earth as it is in heaven. Give us this day our daily bread. And forgive us our debts, as we also have forgiven our debtors. And do not lead us into temptation, but deliver us from evil. [For Yours is the kingdom and the power and the glory forever. Amen.]" (Matthew 6:9-13 NASB)

Jesus continues His teaching on prayer by stating the importance of forgiveness. If you don't forgive others for their offenses against you, the Father God will not forgive you for your sins and transgressions either. Therefore, God may not answer prayers when there is a lack of forgiveness toward others.

> For if you forgive others their trespasses, your heavenly Father will also forgive you, but if you do not forgive others their trespasses, neither will your Father forgive your trespasses. (Matthew 6:14-15 ESV)

NOTE: Sin is self-centered behavior. Rebellion is another word for sin since it's resistance to God's will and purpose.

Another model. My wife, Linda, and I sometimes also use the following model in our more structured morning prayers. You may find this helpful in developing your own approach to prayer. We often address our prayer to the Father, Jesus, and the Holy Spirit (since they are all God).

- Praise and exalt God for who He is and what He does (Psalms 150)
- Thank Him for what He has already done
- Intercede for the needs and welfare of others
- Petition Him for what we would like Him to do
- State our fears, concerns, frustrations, and confusion, and ask Him to bring relief, recovery, and His peace
- Conclude with a statement like the following, "Not my will, but your will be done" – and then end with "in the name of Jesus Christ"

WHAT DO YOU THINK?
What's the value of using a model for prayer? Why can it become a hindrance in communicating to God from the heart?

A story about not being honest with God in prayer. I was teaching a class on spiritual gifts to some leaders of a small church. We got off topic and began to discuss prayer. Several said they are sometimes angry with God and want to tell Him so. While others said a person should never express anger toward God. They thought this was sinful and disrespectful since He is Almighty God who can do no wrong. I responded by saying that people can't hide their emotions from God. He always knows how we feel about everything and everyone. I reminded them that God highly regarded King

David, who often cried out to Him with strong emotions, including anger, fear, worry, and despair.

> O my people, trust in Him at all times. Pour out your heart to Him, for God is our refuge. (Psalms 62:8 NLT)

> Solomon replied, "You showed faithful love to Your servant my father, David, because he was honest and true and faithful to You." (1 Kings 3:6 NLT)

Following are several scriptures about David's honesty in expressing his emotions to God:

> David was angry because the LORD's anger had burst out against Uzzah. (2 Samuel 6:8 NLT)

> I prayed to the LORD, and He answered me. He freed me from all my fears. (Psalms 34:4 NLT)

> In my anxiety I cried out to You, "These people are all liars!" (Psalms 116:11 NLT)

Always honor God. Of course, you need to honor your loving Father God, who is God Almighty. This may mean repenting of thinking or saying things that disrespect Him. Being honest is foundational to having a healthy personal relationship with God (and people). Never fear God will be angry with you because you are upset and express your emotions to Him.

Your Prayers Matter

Be persistent and intently pray as if you are the only person praying for another person or situation because this may be true. Don't wait for or rely on the prayers of others. No one else may be praying for this, so your prayers matter. Even if others are praying, your prayers are unique and are cherished by the Father.

PRACTICE IT
When will you have your next talk with the Father God, Jesus Christ, and the Holy Spirit? Why should you communicate during the day as well as in the morning or at night? How will continual conversations with God change your perspectives on His involvement in your life? How will it strengthen your faith in Him?

As you persist in communicating with each person of the Trinity, you will discover a new attitude of your heart toward them. Your sense of having a personal relationship, rather than a distant one, will be enhanced. So, you can see why it's important to discipline yourself to reap these eternal rewards with God.

9

God Communicates in Incredible Ways

I describe some of my communication experiences with God in this book. Many of these were dialogues with the Father, Jesus, or the Holy Spirit. This entire chapter describes such conversations with each person of God. Please don't just read these stories. Study them and ask the Holy Spirit to help you learn what He wants through them.

WHAT DO YOU THINK? (ADVANCED)
Why do you think your faith and trust in God can be strengthened through true stories like the following?

Prophecy about My Life (and It Includes You)

This story is about the Father God communicating a prophecy about my future.

NOTE: A true prophecy from God comes from the Holy Spirit. It is not a figment of a person's imagination or of human origin. And if it is from God, it will come true. Therefore, one definition of prophecy is that it is an inspired utterance given to a person by the Holy Spirit. There is additional information about prophecy in the Glossary.

Above all, you must realize that no prophecy in Scripture ever came from the prophet's own understanding, or from human initiative. No, those prophets were moved by the Holy Spirit, and they spoke from God. (2 Peter 1:20-21 NLT)

WHAT DO YOU THINK?
Why do you think many people don't believe in prophecies?

The story. In 1982, the Father God spoke (by the Holy Spirit) the following prophecy through my pastor: **"I will send you far, far away, and you will be a blessing to many people!"** As I was praying about it, the Holy Spirit gave me the thought that I would also meet my future wife in a place far, far away.

Where was this "far, far away" place? Soon (in 1983) changes in my job took me from California to Orlando, Florida. The Holy Spirit indicated that Orlando was the start of the "far, far away" **places of prophecy** (notice the plural – places). This was where I would start to be a "blessing to many people." In early 1984, I began teaching an adult Sunday School class in the singles department of a large church. I was involved in other church activities and later began to disciple a small group of men. Many of my new friends told me I was a blessing to them. This blessing was the Holy Spirit's work as I followed His guidance.

Who were the "many people?" Since then, I have continued to teach adult Sunday School classes as well as Bible studies and home groups. In addition, I have developed and supervised various adult ministries for multiple churches. Thus, I have served "many people" over the years since 1984. As a result, many individuals have told me I was a blessing to their faith and life with God.

WHAT DO YOU THINK?
I began writing this book in October 2020. Remember, the Holy Spirit said, "Our book will change people's lives." If He has impacted your life because you read this book, then don't you think you were on God's mind long before I wrote it?

Prophecy included meeting my wife. The Holy Spirit prompted Linda to attend the same church at the same time I did in Orlando. This was not a coincidence. It was the Father's plan. We both became involved in different adult Sunday School classes in the singles department. The Holy Spirit began to draw our attention to each other at various Singles events. Soon we were dating and quickly realized God had brought us together for Christian marriage. We constantly prayed about this, wanting God's will and not our own. He confirmed this in several ways, and so I proposed to her. We were married in September 1984.

PERSONAL APPLICATION

When have you experienced a prophecy from God that came true? How did you know it was from God? How did you feel when it came true?

But I panicked – what is love? The next day after the proposal, I was driving down a major thoroughfare in Altamonte Springs, Florida. Suddenly I panicked! I realized I didn't know anything about how to love a Christian wife. I didn't know what a Christian marriage and love should be like. Many of the non-Christian marriages I had seen ended in divorce. Why would mine be different?

I started to cry in desperation and then started to pray. I asked God for help. The Holy Spirit prompted me to turn on the car radio and turn the dial. I stopped when I heard James Dobson on the Focus on the Family radio program. He had a guest panel that day and they were discussing what I needed to know – how a Christian should love their spouse. I will never forget James Dobson saying that people might be surprised to know that he didn't wake up every morning feeling love for his wife of many decades. His radio program listeners knew he loved his wife dearly, so how could he say this? However, everyone on the panel agreed with him that lasting love is not about a feeling. Instead, it's a life-long commitment to the spouse. It's a firm resolution to stay together and work through life's inevitable problems. Feelings come and go. Too many couples "fall in love" and then "fall out of love," often resulting in divorce. I thanked God for helping me understand how He wanted me to love Linda! That was the beginning of our thirty-eight-plus years of Christian marriage.

PERSONAL APPLICATION

When have you panicked when you realized you did something you didn't think you were ready for? Assuming it was indeed God's will, did you pray and ask Him to help you understand it and give you the faith to move forward? If not, how might this have helped?

Jesus Christ Appears to My Mother in a Coma

Jesus compared Himself to a shepherd who protected and cared for his flock. In the following verse, Jesus said His followers would recognize His voice just as sheep also recognize the voice of their shepherd:

> The doorkeeper opens the door for him, and the sheep hear his voice. He calls his own sheep by name and leads them out. (John 10:3 NET)

PERSONAL APPLICATION

When have you heard the voice of Jesus as He led you and cared for you? Why does it not matter whether He spoke directly to you or through the Holy Spirit?

The story. My mother had developed a low tolerance to many chemical substances, including tobacco smoke, auto exhaust, perfume, insecticide, carpet, and various synthetic materials. Exposure to even small amounts would cause a reaction that could render her unconscious or in a semi-comatose state for hours or days.

In early 1976, my sister flew mom to a clinic in the mid-west specializing in these types of severe sensitivities. Mom spent several months in the clinic and seemed to be progressing. However, she took a turn for the worse and went back into a coma. The head doctor called and asked me to come to take her home to die. There was no hope for her since her body was too weak from fighting these debilitating health problems for so long.

PERSONAL APPLICATION

When have you received news that you or a loved one would die soon? How did you feel? How did this news affect your attitude and faith in God?

When I arrived several days later, my mother was awake and talkative. What happened? Well, Jesus Christ appeared to her while she was in the coma. He awakened her in the middle of the night, and they talked for a while. He told her she would not die at that time because He had not finished His plan for her. After He left, she wrote down the time He appeared and what He said to her.

WHAT DO YOU THINK?

Why is this a prophecy?

The morning nurse found mom back in the coma and saw the note on her nightstand. She recognized mom's handwriting and told the doctors about it. No one could understand what had happened. That afternoon the head doctor told mom (she was still in a coma) that he had been reading about a new treatment for these environmental sensitivities. He knew she could understand him even in her coma, so he asked her to blink once if she wanted to try the treatment or twice if she didn't want to. She blinked once, of course, and within a day, she was sitting up in her bed.

WHAT DO YOU THINK?

Why was this a miraculous intervention by Jesus?

She will die on the plane! I worked as a Ramp Serviceman for an airline company in undergraduate and graduate school. So, I arranged with the airline for special care for mom for boarding, in-flight, and disembarking the plane. They allowed me to create a makeshift tent of cotton sheets around our three seats. First, though, I covered the seats and the back of those in front of us with tin foil to prevent synthetic fabric emissions from entering the tent. They would have likely put her back into a coma while in flight.

Before we left, the head doctor told me mom wouldn't survive the flight home. She was too weak and would die in flight. But remember, the Lord said this was not the time for her to die. So she didn't die on this flight in 1976! Instead, she went home to be with the Lord thirty years later, in 2006.

WHAT DO YOU THINK? (ADVANCED)

Why do you think it could have been the Holy Spirit living within my mother that strengthened her so she would not die on the flight?

Answer. You will see later in this book that the Father God has a plan for each of His children's lives. The indwelling Holy Spirit helps believers carry out the Father's plans.

The Holy Spirit Spoke in the Night

When the Holy Spirit wants a believer to know something, He will communicate in various ways. For example, He can put an impression on a person's heart about something. These will not be words but rather a sense of what He wants or doesn't want. Likewise, he can put thoughts into the mind or speak audible words in the mind. We see the latter in the following verse:

> While they were serving the Lord and fasting, the Holy Spirit said, "Set apart for me Barnabas and Saul for the work to which I have called them." (Acts 13:2 NET)

The following verses say the Father and Jesus sent the Holy Spirit to live within believers. And that He would relay what He has heard from them.

When the Spirit of truth comes, He will guide you into all truth. He will not speak on His own but will tell you what He has heard. He will tell you about the future. He will bring Me glory by telling you whatever He receives from Me. All that belongs to the Father is Mine; this is why I said, "The Spirit will tell you whatever He receives from Me." (John 16:13-15 NLT)

PERSONAL APPLICATION
Describe a situation when the Holy Spirit communicated to your mind with words or thoughts. How did you respond to Him?

The story. On Friday, Feb 21, 2020, I had a routine outpatient treatment to reduce my enlarged nasal passages. The goal was to improve my breathing at night due to Obstructive Sleep Apnea. Unfortunately, I had a medication reaction later in the treatment that rendered me unconscious and unresponsive. As I began to come to, there was just blackness. It was nothingness.

My physical senses returned slowly. I first began to see a slight glimmer of light. Then, the light in the room slowly grew more visible, and I started to make out fuzzy images of the doctor and several nurses standing around me. Next, I began to hear their voices as if they were faintly far away. Their voices gradually became more distinct, and I began to understand what they were saying. They were asking me if I could hear them. At this point, I could not respond. I still could not move my body or speak. Shortly though, I could feel a nurse's hand on my arm. Then I began to be able to move my fingers slightly.

After a while, I could formulate thoughts, but my mind was in a cloud that prevented clear thinking. I started to pray and quote all the scripture I could remember. I was uncertain whether I was speaking out loud or quietly to myself. However, I was soon able to respond to the doctor with short answers. So he asked if I wanted him to complete the procedure in the remaining nostril. Because I became unconscious, he hadn't been able to finish his work there. I told him yes because I didn't intend to return to do this again! I was starting to regain most of my physical senses by this time. The medications also triggered a severe migraine headache. My wife and I were there another two hours after the procedure, waiting for the migraine to subside enough for her to drive us home.

It was not over. However, the ordeal was not over. I awoke in a semi-conscious state that Friday night, experiencing the same blackness and inability to move or function. After a few minutes, I could think and said anxiously in my thoughts, "Holy Spirit, where are you? I can't see you in this darkness."

I immediately heard the voice of the Holy Spirit in my mind say, "I AM HERE! I AM ALWAYS WITH YOU!"

WHAT DO YOU THINK?
What was God's purpose in allowing this to occur? How do you think it affected my faith and trust in God to care for me in a terrible situation?

The following Bible verse says the Father God gave the Holy Spirit to live within a born-again believer as His guarantee of eternal life with Him. This means the Holy Spirit will never leave a believer.

> He has identified us as His own by placing the Holy Spirit in our hearts
> as the first installment that guarantees everything He has promised us.
> (2 Corinthians 1:22 NLT)

Your experiences may be different. These are some of my experiences and those of others in communicating with God. Yours may be similar or different.

NOTE: Your communication with God will improve over time as you persist and seek to know Him better.

PERSONAL APPLICATION
Why do you think each person of God wants you to experience them in regular communications?

Sometimes you initiate the communication, and sometimes God does. Communication with Him will always include knowing Him and His will. The two chapters, "Knowing and Doing God's Will," describe how God may communicate to let you know Him and His will.

10

Life Is Not Random; God Has a Plan

By now, I hope you believe in the existence of God as He describes Himself in the Bible.

WHAT DO YOU THINK?

But what about your life? Do you believe it's nothing more than a series of random events? Is it a series of coincidences and your reactions? In the end, how much eternal value do you achieve from a life like that?

You've seen in this book that God loves you, cares about you immensely and wants an eternal relationship with you. But is there even more? Yes, He has a purpose and plan for you!

There Is a Purpose for Your Life

You hear some people ask the following questions: "What's the purpose of life? or "Why am I here?" In this book, you will learn that God created you to be a unique person because He wants your life to be full of meaning and purpose. You will see that God has a purpose for your life that no one else can fulfill. He created you like no other person. Only you can do what He has planned for you.

People have essentially two purposes in life. The first is for every person. The second is unique for each person.

First: God has a universal purpose for everyone that includes knowing and worshiping Him:

> And *I will give them one heart and one purpose: to worship Me forever*, for their own good and for the good of all their descendants. (Jeremiah 32:39 NLT, author's emphasis)

> *His purpose was for the nations to seek after God* and perhaps feel their way toward Him and find Him—though He is not far from any one of us. (Acts 17:27 NLT, author's emphasis)

Second: God has a unique purpose for each person:

> I cry out to God Most High, to *God who will fulfill His purpose for me*. (Psalms 57:2 NLT, author's emphasis)

> But you, Timothy, certainly *know what I teach, and how I live, and what my purpose in life is*. You know my faith, my patience, my love, and my endurance. (2 Timothy 3:10 NLT, author's emphasis)

PERSONAL APPLICATION
Do you want to know God's purpose for you in this world? What's your answer to the age-old question, "What's the meaning of my life?"

You will find meaning in your life when you allow God to show you His purpose for you. Then you must decide to follow it.

NOTE: God's purpose for my life (the author) is to know Him and help others know Him. Therefore, one primary reason for my writing this book is to help you come to know Him (or know Him better if you are already a follower of Jesus).

I'm Going to Do What I Want!

All human beings have the right and ability to make their own decisions. This is referred to as free will. Self-will results from exercising free will in opposition to God's will. We can see God gave Adam and Eve free will to make their own decisions in the Garden of Eden (Genesis 2:15-17). However, they used self-will to choose to disobey God (Genesis 3:1-6). God can do anything. This is referred to as God's sovereign will.

He doesn't override people's free will. However, He can create circumstances and work in ways that people may choose His will instead of their own. He does this when He makes a plan for a person's life.

WHAT DO YOU THINK?

Since God has a unique purpose for your life, why would He also have a unique plan?

God's Plan Always Fulfills His Purpose

God's plan and will are always based on His purpose for your life. The Apostle Paul is an example. In Ephesians 1:1, the Apostle says about himself: *Paul, an apostle of Christ Jesus by the will of God.* God's purpose for Paul's life was to be an Apostle at that time and place. You can read about God's plan and how He used Paul as an Apostle in the New Testament book of Acts, chapters 9-28.

God's plan is for non-believers to become His children. Before God created the world, He planned to adopt people into His eternal family.

> Even before He made the world, God loved us and chose us in Christ to be holy and without fault in His eyes. God decided in advance to adopt us into His own family by bringing us to Himself through Jesus Christ. This is what He wanted to do, and it gave Him great pleasure. (Ephesians 1:4-5 NLT)

> For He chose us in advance, and He makes everything work out according to His plan. (Ephesians 1:11 NLT)

WHAT DO YOU THINK?

Why does the Father God take *great pleasure* when a person commits their life to Jesus Christ? Why can a person's self-will hinder this?

God's plan for believers includes their entire life. God formed His plan for believers before they were born and became a follower of Jesus. And that plan comprises their entire life.

> You saw me before I was born. Every day of my life was recorded in Your book. Every moment was laid out before a single day had passed. (Psalm 139:16 NLT)

> The LORD will work out His plans for my life—for Your faithful love,
> O LORD, endures forever. (Psalm 138:8 NLT)

God's plan for believers is to live a holy life. This means it's a life set apart by God for His purposes.

> For God saved us and called us to live a holy life. He did this, not because we deserved it, but because that was His plan from before the beginning of time—to show us His grace through Christ Jesus. (2 Timothy 1:9 NLT)

When believers allow the Father God to work in their life, everything that happens (good or bad) can be used by Him to fulfill His purpose and plans.

> "And we know that in all things God works for the good of those who love him, who have been called according to his purpose." (Romans 8:28 NIV)

> "For I know the plans I have for you," says the LORD. "They are plans for good and not for disaster, to give you a future and a hope." (Jeremiah 29:11 NLT)

PRACTICE IT
If you want to know His plan, why not ask Him to show it to you now?

God's Plan Is Like a Cross-Country Race

A cross-country race is an example of how I believe God plans a person's life. These races have markers and signposts that reveal the direction to stay on course. For example, one marker may indicate to turn right, while the next may say to go straight ahead. The Holy Spirit provides markers and signposts to direct believers throughout their lives, enabling them to know and follow the Father's plan. Each of these requires a decision to obey or disobey God, to follow His plan or not. But, of course, every follower of Jesus can and will make decisions that lead them off God's plan.

The following verses describe God's plan as a race and warn self-will can lead believers off course and away from God's plan:

> Therefore, since we are surrounded by such a huge crowd of witnesses to the life of faith, let us strip off every weight that slows us down, especially the sin that so easily trips us up. And let us run with endurance the race

God has set before us. We do this by keeping our eyes on Jesus, the champion who initiates and perfects our faith. (Hebrews 12:1-2 NLT)

My cross-country race example: About 1988, in Michigan, I spent several months training to run a one-mile cross-country fun run. I planned to do the very best I could in the race. I arrived a little late and saw several hundred people already packed together to start the race. So, I was at the back and behind all of those who mostly planned to walk the one-mile course. As I weaved in and out of the pack of people, I could see the signposts ahead that marked out the course. I stayed within the boundaries of the race and finished in eighth place out of several hundred people. I had done my best and ran the race according to the plan.

PERSONAL APPLICATION
What are some markers, some decision points that help identify His plan for you? Did you follow His will for each of them? Why does God redirect your life to get you back on track with His plan if you don't make the right choices?

The LORD says, "I will guide you along the best pathway for your life.
I will advise you and watch over you." (Psalm 32:8 NLT)

If Jesus Christ is your Savior and Lord, the Holy Spirit will help you navigate life's difficulties. Throughout life's challenges, keep your faith and trust in Him. And remember that the Father God has a plan for your life according to His purposes for you alone. You are not an accident but were born into this time and place to become a child of the Father.

You Would Not Be the Person You Are Today Without Your Past

On December 21, 2020, I was thinking about my life and all that has happened when I heard the Holy Spirit say with words in my mind, "You couldn't be writing this book if you had not gone through what you did."

The following day He said, "You would not be the person you are today without your past."

I realized He was telling me I was more beneficial in God's Kingdom now because of my past seasons.

You have your own path (God's unique plan). Each person travels a different path in life. Seek Him, His Kingdom, and His will for your life. If you are a follower of Jesus, the Holy Spirit lives within you. He will guide, teach, and help you. Expect it and look for His hand in your life.

PART B

CHANGE IS NEEDED IN YOUR LIFE

11

The Good News Is about God's Love

Who do you love? Think about the people you love. How much do you love them? Do they love you as much in return? What could they do that would cause you to stop loving them? If your love for them decreases when they treat you poorly, your love is conditional. Unwillingness to forgive may expose this conditional love.

> Forgive anyone who offends you. Remember, the Lord forgave you, so you must forgive others. (Colossians 3:13 NET)

> Beloved, if God so loved us, we also ought to love one another. (1 John 4:11 ESV)

Story of conditional love. The following story indicates that forgiveness is critical to God healing a broken heart. It may take years, but He will heal the heart when He is asked to help.

> He heals the brokenhearted and binds up their wounds. (Psalms 147:3 ESV)

The story. It's about a formerly married couple I once knew. I always enjoyed visiting with their family. They seemed to love and appreciate each other. They would laugh and share funny stories about their life. But that all changed when he confessed that he had an affair with a friend of hers. Even though he was remorseful and asked her for forgiveness, she told him she would never forgive him. She became bitter, spiteful, and angry. He soon moved out of what had seemingly been a wonderful, peaceful home. Unfortunately, since they were not followers of Jesus Christ, they didn't ask Him to heal their broken hearts, so the scars remained.

PERSONAL APPLICATION

Describe your own story about experiencing conditional love from someone. How did you respond to this? How would you respond differently now?

God Loves You Unconditionally

Unlike conditional human love, God's love is unconditional. Nothing you can ever do or say will change how much and deeply He will ALWAYS love you!

> And may you have the power to understand, as all God's people should, how wide, how long, how high, and how deep His love is. (Ephesians 3:18 NLT)

God has always known everything about you and still loves you unconditionally.

> *O LORD, You have examined my heart and know everything about me.* You know when I sit down or stand up. You know my thoughts even when I'm far away. You see me when I travel and when I rest at home. You know everything I do. You know what I am going to say even before I say it, LORD. You go before me and follow me. You place Your hand of blessing on my head. Such knowledge is too wonderful for me, too great for me to understand! (Psalms 139:1-6 NLT, author's emphasis)

PERSONAL APPLICATION

Describe when you experienced the Father's unconditional love, even when you didn't deserve it. How did that make you feel? Do you have a closer personal relationship with Him as a result?

God's love is sacrificial. The following verse says the Father God demonstrated His sacrificial love for you by sending His Son, Jesus Christ, to die a horrible death on the cross for your sins. Jesus' resurrection from the dead is proof of this love and the eternal life God offers.

> In this is love, not that we have loved God but that he loved us and sent his Son to be the propitiation for our sins. (1 John 4:10 ESV)

If you still doubt His unconditional, sacrificial love for you, read the following words from the Bible:

> Who is the one who will condemn? Christ is the one who died (and more than that, he was raised), who is at the right hand of God, and who also is interceding for us. Who will separate us from the love of Christ? Will trouble, or distress, or persecution, or famine, or nakedness, or danger, or sword?... For I am convinced that neither death, nor life, nor angels, nor heavenly rulers, nor things that are present, nor things to come, nor powers, nor height, nor depth, nor anything else in creation will be able to separate us from the love of God in Christ Jesus our Lord. (Romans 8:34-39 NET)

NOTE: Following are definitions of several Greek words translated as the English word *love* in the New Testament. The best way (without a Bible dictionary) to know which Greek word is used is to understand the context of the verses associated with the word *love*.

Human forms of love:

- **Erōs:** Romantic love; or erotic desire
- **Philia:** Brotherly love; friendship
- **Storgē:** Familial love; affection for one's family, country, or team

God's only form of love:

- **Agapē:** Unconditional, sacrificial love. This is God's love for people.

WHAT DO YOU THINK?
Why is experiencing God's unconditional love so much better than even the sincerest human love?

The Good News Proves God's Unconditional Love

The Good News is the Gospel of Jesus Christ, demonstrating God's unconditional, sacrificial love. Jesus preached the Good News when He was on earth. Why? Because He wants everyone to be saved and spend eternity with Him.

> Now after John was arrested, Jesus came into Galilee, proclaiming the gospel of God, and saying, "The time is fulfilled, and the kingdom of God is at hand; repent and believe in the gospel." (Mark 1:14-15 ESV)

What is this Good News? The following verses provide a simple description of this Good News that saves you:

> Let me now remind you, dear brothers and sisters, of the Good News I preached to you before . . . . It is this Good News that saves you if you continue to believe the message I told you . . . *Christ died for our sins, just as the Scriptures said. He was buried, and He was raised from the dead on the third day, just as the Scriptures said.* (1 Corinthians 15:1-4 NLT, author's emphasis)

Three Elements of the Good News

You discover the Good News in both the Old and New Testaments of the Bible. It occurs in the Old Testament as prophecies later fulfilled in the New Testament.

Following are Old Testament prophecies that predict the three elements of the Good News. These prophecies were all fulfilled, as you will see in their related New Testament scriptures.

1. *Christ died for our sins, just as the Scriptures said.*

Old Testament Prophecy:

> But He was pierced for our rebellion, crushed for our sins. He was beaten so we could be whole . . . . Yet the LORD laid on Him the sins of us all. (Isaiah 53:5-6 NLT)

New Testament Fulfillment:

> Christ suffered for our sins once for all time. He never sinned, but He died for sinners to bring you safely home to God. He suffered physical death, but He was raised to life in the Spirit. (1 Peter 3:18 NLT)

2. *He was buried,*

Old Testament Prophecy:

> But He was buried like a criminal; He was put in a rich man's grave. (Isiah 53:9 NLT)

New Testament Fulfillment:

> Afterward Joseph of Arimathea, who had been a secret disciple of Jesus (because he feared the Jewish leaders), asked Pilate for permission to take down Jesus' body. When Pilate gave permission, Joseph came and took the body away. With him came Nicodemus, the man who had come to Jesus at night. He brought about seventy-five pounds of perfumed ointment made from myrrh and aloes. Following Jewish burial custom, they wrapped Jesus' body with the spices in long sheets of linen cloth. (John 19:38-40 NLT

Jesus Christ was dead! Notice in the above verses that the disciples knew that Jesus was dead. They removed His dead body from the cross, took it to a *rich man's grave* (Joseph of Arimathea), and wrapped it up in linen cloth with burial spices. If Jesus were still alive, they wouldn't have done this.

WHAT DO YOU THINK?
Why is biblical evidence that Jesus actually died essential to the message of the Good News?

3. *And He was raised from the dead on the third day, just as the Scriptures said.*

Old Testament Prophecy:

> Because you will not abandon me to the realm of the dead, nor will you let your faithful one see decay. (Psalms 16:10 NLT)

New Testament Fulfillment:

> On the first day of the week, very early in the morning, the women took the spices they had prepared and went to the tomb. They found the stone rolled away from the tomb, but when they entered, they did not find the body of the Lord Jesus. While they were wondering about

this, suddenly two men in clothes that gleamed like lightning stood beside them. In their fright the women bowed down with their faces to the ground, but the men said to them, "Why do you look for the living among the dead? He is not here; he has risen!" (Luke 24:1-6 NIV)

If you responded to the Good News, the Gospel message about Jesus, your faith in God rests securely on this eternal, unconditional love. If not, please read the chapter "Prayer to Know God" to help you understand how to start an eternal relationship with God.

WHAT DO YOU THINK?
How would you explain this Good News to someone who never heard about Jesus and salvation through Him?

Jesus' Unconditional Love – I Must Love My Father, But I Couldn't

This next story underscores the reality that sometimes only God can help you love someone unconditionally. It demonstrates the power of forgiveness to help heal a broken heart. As you will see, His healing and restoration took years but culminated in the salvation of the one person I hated, my own father. For nothing is impossible with God!

Abandonment and abuse. My father abandoned my mother, sister, and me and moved to the state of Washington when I was about six years old. He didn't support our family financially or in any other way after he moved. When I was nine, he convinced us that he wanted us to be a family. My sister and I were thrilled at the prospect of having our father back in our lives. However, after we moved from California to Washington, we seldom saw him. He seemed to only want us nearby so he could occasionally see my sister and me at his convenience.

Our mother went to work to provide for our daily needs. However, our father would come by when he needed money and take ours to spend on his girlfriends and drinking buddies. Because of this, we were often without heat and electricity, sometimes even when it was below freezing with several feet of snow on the ground. We often went hungry while he caroused. The "last straw" was when he took mom into our bedroom one day, and I heard a muffled scream as he hit her. When I opened the bedroom door crying, I saw mom with her mouth bleeding. I began to yell hysterically and scream at him that I hated him and never wanted to see him again! We left immediately after this and returned to where our home would again be in California.

Our mother sacrificed her life for us, while our father sacrificed us for himself. This was the start of many years of anger and hatred for my father. My damaged feelings were deep. Even when he tried to visit me later in life, I refused to see him. As they say today, "He was dead to me!"

WHAT DO YOU THINK?

What does it mean when a person says someone is dead to them? What would their feelings likely be?

But my father was not dead to God! Later in life, I was driving and telling God how much I hated my father and that I would never see him again. By this time, I had committed my heart to Jesus Christ. I heard Jesus speak in my mind and say I needed to forgive him and love him. I responded rather abruptly out loud and told Him it was impossible for me to ever love my father. At this, He said that He would help me love him with His love. He would be faithful to do this, so He wanted me to start spending time with my father. I was apprehensive but wanted to obey the Lord.

PERSONAL APPLICATION

When have you forced yourself to obey God when you absolutely didn't want to? What were your thoughts about God that helped you do this?

The Holy Spirit began to change my heart. Jesus was keeping His promise. Over the next several years, I would go up to Washington to visit my father, or he would come down to California. Sometimes we would go to college football games, dig clams on Puget Sound's beaches, or go out to dinner. It was subtle, but I noticed I was beginning to have a love for him. It was God's unconditional love that was slowly growing in me. This is the love Jesus promised to give me. Only through Christ's love could forgiveness and healing begin and grow in my heart.

> Don't copy the behavior and customs of this world, but let God transform you into a new person by changing the way you think. Then you will learn to know God's will for you, which is good and pleasing and perfect. (Romans 12:2 NLT)

My father is in Heaven with His Savior. I had my first health breakdown in 1976. (More about this at the end of this book.) Two doctors told me I would never be able to work again. However, God healed me in 1983. One evening after this healing, my father called. (He told me previously he had cancer throughout his body. This included a massive tumor wrapped around his spine that created constant, severe pain.) He asked me how I was doing, so I told him God healed me the day before. I could hear him begin to sob. I knew then that the Holy Spirit had prepared my father's heart for God's eternal Kingdom. I told him about God's love for him and that God wanted him to be with Him forever. I asked him if he wanted Jesus Christ to be his Savior and Lord. Still sobbing, he said he did. That night the father I had hated for so many years entered the Kingdom of God. My father chose to respond to the Good News about God's unconditional love for him. He did so because I was willing to allow my Savior and Lord to heal my wounded heart.

PERSONAL APPLICATION
Is there someone in your past who has hurt you deeply? Perhaps someone you now even hate. Are the wounds so deep that you know you can never love the person on your own? Do you sense Jesus asking you to allow Him to love the person unconditionally through you?

NOTE: Sometimes, it's impossible to spend time with this person due to distance, death, or their unwillingness. Nevertheless, you can still forgive them in your heart as an act of will. If they are alive, you can pray for healing of the relationship and for God's love to grow in your heart. God is everywhere. Distance doesn't matter to Him.

Some People Reject the Good News and God's Unconditional Love

I have heard people make the following statements to rationalize why they reject the Good News. Since no one knows when they will die, delaying the decision is the same as rejecting God's free offer of salvation.

NOTE: Once a person's physical body dies, it's too late to be saved from the eternal consequences of rejecting Jesus (Luke 16:19-31).

Following are some common rationalizations with my short counter-response:

- I am too busy. I'll do it later. (There may not be a "later." You don't know when you will die.)

- I was baptized as a baby. (Baptism doesn't save a child or adult.)

- I have always been a Christian. (No one has always been a Christian. It's a decision each person makes in response to the Good News.)

- I was raised in a Christian home. (Parents can't cause their children to be saved. Each person must make their own decision about Christ.)

- I am not good enough for God. (No one is good enough. God wants you to come to Him just as you are.)

- God will accept me into Heaven because I'm a good person. (No one can ever be perfect enough to earn their way into Heaven. That's why Jesus died.)

- There are many paths to God. Christianity is just one of them. (Jesus said that no one could come to God except through Him.)

WHAT DO YOU THINK?

Which of these have you heard people say about why accepting God's unconditional love can wait? Which do you think is the most common excuse for rejecting Jesus Christ?

Answer. From my experience, the most common reason is some people think they can earn their salvation. They feel that if they treat others well, God will accept them. This thinking, however, focuses only on how they treat and interact with people. It ignores their lack of relationship and interaction with God. People are saved only by responding to the Good News about Jesus Christ.

PERSONAL APPLICATION

Do you believe the Good News, the Gospel of Jesus Christ? If you only understand it with your mind but don't believe it in your heart, is it Good News for you? If you are already a follower of Jesus, does knowing the Good News strengthen your faith and trust in the God of the Bible?

The Gospel, the Good News, is about God's unconditional, sacrificial love for you. In the next chapter, you will learn that everyone needs to be rescued, but many will refuse God's free gift of eternal life with Him.

12

Everyone Needs to Be Rescued

Being rescued means someone intervened to save you. Following is my story about being rescued from certain death as a child.

I was rescued from drowning at eight years old. One sweltering summer day, a friend and I were wading in the forbidden irrigation ditch across the road from our houses. (I didn't know how to swim.) As we approached the bridge, a friend of his stopped on the bridge to talk to him. My friend was standing on the side of the ditch. However, I continued to wade in the middle of the widening and deepening ditch. All at once, the bottom was gone, and I plunged straight down several feet over my head. Surprised, I paddled back up to the surface, only to sink again for the second time. The third time I went down, my short life flashed before my eyes in color as if I was watching a movie—a very short movie! My friend saw what was happening, reached over, grabbed my hair, and pulled me up to the surface and toward the bank where it was shallow, saving me from drowning.

WHAT DO YOU THINK?
How do you think God was involved in this near-death experience? I was seconds away from "meeting my maker," as some say.

As you've read previously, God has a plan and purpose for the lives of those who become followers of Jesus. In this case, my dying at this point in my life was obviously not part of His plan. Instead, I believe He somehow caused my friend to become aware of my dire situation and rescue me.

Do You Want to Be Rescued?

Do you NEED to be rescued, to be saved? Yes, everyone does. But a better question might be, do you WANT to be rescued? Some people don't.

NOTE: By the way, I use the words "rescued" and "saved" as synonyms throughout this book.

Jesus says there are five types of people who need Him, but only one wants Him. Following are the five types from the Bible. Jesus explains the first four types in His parable about the farmer planting seeds (Matthew 13:18-23). He describes the fifth type in Matthew 7:21-23. I have added notes to help describe these types of people and their responses to hearing about Jesus Christ as their Savior.

God's Living Word and People's Hearts

Jesus explained that His parable about the farmer sowing seeds was about God's word being heard by people. In the following verses, He uses a person's heart as the place where God's word must be received and believed.

Type One (Hard hearts): People whose hearts are hardened to God. His word has no meaning or importance to them.

> The seed that fell on the footpath represents those who hear the message about the Kingdom and don't understand it. Then the evil one comes and snatches away the seed that was planted in their hearts. (Matthew 13:19 NLT)

WHAT DO YOU THINK?

Why does the following verse indicate this same type of heart?

> **Satan, who is the god of this world, has blinded the minds of those who don't believe**. They are unable to see the glorious light of the Good News. They don't understand this message about the glory of Christ, who is the exact likeness of God. (2 Corinthians 4:4 NLT, author's emphasis)

Type Two (Shallow hearts): People whose hearts are shallow toward God. They have outward indications of being a Christian but have little true belief and faith in

Him. So they quickly fall away from their weak faith in Christ when problems and difficulties occur in their lives.

> The seed on the rocky soil represents those who hear the message and immediately receive it with joy. But since they don't have deep roots, they don't last long. They fall away as soon as they have problems or are persecuted for believing God's word. (Matthew 13:20-21 NLT)

Type Three (Worldly hearts): People whose hearts are congested by their focus on living a worldly life. Their thoughts, ambitions, and personal plans leave little room in their hearts and lives for Jesus. These also fall away quickly because they put success and acquiring wealth above an eternal relationship with Jesus Christ.

> The seed that fell among the thorns represents those who hear God's word, but all too quickly the message is crowded out by the worries of this life and the lure of wealth, so no fruit is produced. (Matthew 13:22 NLT)

Type Four (Responsive hearts): **People whose hearts are prepared and ready to receive Jesus Christ as their Savior and Lord**. Their faith in Him remains steadfast, no matter the problems and challenges of life.

> The seed that fell on good soil represents those who truly hear and understand God's word and produce a harvest of thirty, sixty, or even a hundred times as much as had been planted! (Matthew 13:23 NLT)

She was educated in Christian schools. She was a lovely Asian woman who was intelligent and personable. She told me she was educated in Christian schools all her life until college. She knew the Bible and could quote scripture. When I was rescued later, I told her about it. Her heart was prepared, so she recognized that she also needed to be saved. So, you see, attending church all your life, having a Christian education, or anything other than responding to the Good News about Jesus does not save a person.

Type Five (Deceived hearts): Jesus describes the fifth type of person in Matthew 7:21-23. Some people believe they are a Christian because the Holy Spirit has done supernatural actions through them. However, their hearts were full of self-exultation. They were happy to be used by God but for their personal benefit. Jesus knew their hearts and that He was not their Savior and Lord.

Not everyone who says to Me, "Lord, Lord," will enter the kingdom of heaven, but he who does the will of My Father who is in heaven will enter. Many will say to Me on that day, "Lord, Lord, did we not prophesy in Your name, and in Your name cast out demons, and in Your name perform many miracles?" And then I will declare to them, "I never knew you; depart from me, you who practice lawlessness." (Matthew 7:21-23 NASB)

PERSONAL APPLICATION

Which of these five types of people describes you? What hinders you from having a heart that accepts Jesus?

I hope you have chosen or will choose the responsive heart that receives and honors Jesus as Savior and Lord.

Rescued from What?

God's offer of rescue is about His faithful love because love is part of who He is.

Oh give thanks to the LORD, for he is good; for his steadfast love endures forever! (Psalms 118:1 ESV)

It's about His desire for you to be with Him eternally through His Son, Jesus Christ. The following section is not an easy read. It can turn people off to God if they see Him as an angry God waiting to punish them.

PERSONAL APPLICATION

How do you view God? Is He an angry or vindictive God waiting to punish you for wrongdoing? Or do you see Him as a loving and compassionate Father? How does your view of God affect your willingness to give your life to Him through Jesus Christ?

As you have seen and will see throughout this book, God's nature is loving and compassionate. He wants everyone to be saved and no one to be eternally condemned! That is why this section is in the book.

> The Lord is not slow concerning his promise, as some regard slowness, but is being patient toward you, because he does not wish for any to perish but for all to come to repentance. (2 Peter 3:9 NET)

Rescued from eternal separation from God. There is a terrible, eternal fate for those who haven't accepted Jesus Christ as their Savior and Lord. This fate is eternal condemnation. Every person is born into this state of condemnation due to the sin of Adam in the Garden of Eden.

> Yes, Adam's one sin brings condemnation for everyone, but Christ's one act of righteousness brings a right relationship with God and new life for everyone. (Romans 5:18 NLT)

> The one who believes in him is not condemned. The one who does not believe has been condemned already, because he has not believed in the name of the one and only Son of God. (John 3:18 NET)

This condemnation results in eternal separation from God. This eternal separation from God is referred to in the Bible as the *second death* (Revelation 20:6, 21:8). Christians sometimes refer to it as "spiritual death" since these people will never experience the presence and love of God for all eternity.

WHAT DO YOU THINK? (ADVANCED)

How can a holy and perfect God accept condemned people who continually sin?

But there is a rescue. The following scriptures state that accepting Jesus Christ is the only way to be rescued from this eternal fate. This is the Good News of God's unconditional love.

> For God loved the world so much that He gave His one and only Son, so that everyone who believes in Him will not perish but have eternal life. (John 3:16 NLT)

> There is salvation in no one else! God has given no other name under heaven by which we must be saved. (Acts 4:12 NLT)

Redemption. No one can be good enough to earn the right to spend eternity with God since God is perfect. This condition of not being perfect is what the Bible refers to as sin.

> As the Scriptures say, "No one is righteous—not even one. No one is truly wise; no one is seeking God." (Romans 3:10-11 NLT)

Jesus Christ (who is perfect) is the Redeemer, which means He paid the price with His death to save all who would accept Him.

> For all have sinned and fall short of the glory of God. But they are justified freely by his grace through the redemption that is in Christ Jesus. (Romans 3:23-24 NET)

> In him we have redemption through his blood, the forgiveness of our offenses, according to the riches of his grace. (Ephesians 1:7 NET)

Accepting Jesus as your Redeemer results in the Father God seeing you with the perfection of Jesus. You will still sin and do things that displease God and will need to repent, but He will always see you as having the perfection of Jesus. This perfection is what God requires for you to enter Heaven.

PERSONAL APPLICATION

If you were to die today, meet Jesus Christ, and He asked you, "Why should My Father allow you into His eternal Heaven?" What would you say?

Repentance. The meaning of this word can be confusing. There is more to repentance than feeling remorse and telling God you are sorry. The Greek word in the Bible for repentance means changing your mind and thinking in the opposite way. To understand this, face one direction, then turn around 180 degrees and face the opposite direction. Biblical repentance involves agreeing with God and doing what He wants instead of what you want. It means you stop what you shouldn't do and start doing what God wants.

WHAT DO YOU THINK? (ADVANCED)

Why do you think the Father God wants repentance before He will forgive and save a person?

The following scripture provides insight into the steps of repentance:

> Instead, let us test and examine our ways. Let us turn back to the LORD. Let us lift our hearts and hands to God in heaven. (Lamentations 3:40-41 NLT)

The next verses describe the need for repentance:

> "Let all the house of Israel therefore know for certain that God has made him both Lord and Christ, this Jesus whom you crucified." Now when they heard this they were cut to the heart, and said to Peter and the rest of the apostles, "Brothers, what shall we do?" And Peter said to them, "Repent and be baptized every one of you in the name of Jesus Christ for the forgiveness of your sins, and you will receive the gift of the Holy Spirit." (Acts 2:36-38 ESV)

NOTE: By the way, a careful study of scripture reveals that water baptism (Acts 2:36-38) doesn't save you. However, it's a way to publicly demonstrate your commitment to Jesus Christ after you are saved.

PERSONAL APPLICATION

Have you been rescued from eternal condemnation? If so, what has this chapter taught you about its significance? What hinders you from believing this Biblical truth and accepting Jesus Christ if not?

In the next chapter, you will see that sometimes being rescued takes many years of the Holy Spirit's work in a person's heart, as it did for me.

13

Rescued: The Father Intervened

Different ways and timing. People come to Jesus Christ in many different ways. For some, it's a quiet moment with God that happens in a few minutes. For others like myself, it takes multiple interventions by the Holy Spirit over a period of time. There is no formula for how this process of rescue occurs. Instead, the Father, Jesus, and the Holy Spirit work with each person to help them understand who Jesus is and why they need Him.

WHAT DO YOU THINK?
Why must God intervene in a person's life to capture their attention, leading to salvation?

Answer: Remember, everyone has self-will that opposes God's will.

How It Started

I committed my life to Jesus Christ in May 1976 and was rescued by God from eternal condemnation and separation from Him. Following is this story.

NOTE: The following is a long, personal story about how God worked in my life to save me. Look for the many biblical truths that can help you learn about salvation and the Father's unwavering, unconditional love.

I was given a critical position that quickly became highly stressful. There were only a few people in our company who could do this job for this account. And I was the one doing it. We would lose the account and significant income if major changes to the customer's operations were not quickly made. When I finished, their operational performances were close to national standards. But I paid the price for this achievement.

I was burned out! The stress was enormous! I worked seven days a week, twelve to eighteen hours a day, for over three months. As a result of the stress, my health began to deteriorate. Then, one late night around midnight, I was having dinner and turned on the TV. I was drawn to a televised Billy Graham crusade. Billy talked about God's love and said that God wanted everyone to go to Heaven to be with Him for eternity. He said that God's love for each of us was so great that He sent His one and only Son to die on the cross for our sins (Romans 8:34-35). As I listened to Billy Graham speak, I began to weep, wondering if God truly loved me.

WHAT DO YOU THINK? (ADVANCED)

Why can severe difficulties cause a person to be more receptive to the Good News about salvation? Why do some people harden their hearts instead of responding to God under these conditions?

I talked to God. The next day was Sunday, so I decided not to work for the first time in months. As I drove in the country with the top off of my sports car, I looked up to Heaven and talked to God. I told Him that if what Billy Graham said about His love for me was true, then I wanted to go to Heaven to be with Him forever. BUT, I told Him, there were some things I didn't view as wrong. I said I would continue to do them unless He told me differently. To be clear, I didn't ask God to forgive me for all my sins. So I didn't ask Jesus Christ to rescue me from the consequences of my sins. This meant I didn't ask Jesus to be my Savior and Lord.

WHAT DO YOU THINK?

Why is repentance needed instead of a sincere desire to be with God in Heaven?

The Father God Spoke Audibly to Me

Now fast-forward several months to April 1976. After I left the stressful account, I started my company's demanding twelve-week Systems Engineering training program in Dallas. For many employees like myself, without any prior training in computer programming, it was a grueling experience. The intensive training and long days meant some of us worked seven days a week, ten to sixteen hours a day. If you failed this training, employment was terminated immediately, so the stakes were high. The problem was, I was already experiencing significant health problems from the previous stressful months of account work. As a result, I couldn't think clearly and was constantly exhausted. It was difficult to concentrate, so I was not doing well in the program.

When the Father God spoke, did I obey? We had time off from our studies midway through the twelve-week program. I called Cindy and asked her to visit Dallas to spend the weekend at Galveston Beach. I went to bed about midnight Wednesday and was dozing off when I heard a voice that filled my bedroom say,

"PAUL, PAUL, WAKE UP!"

I was immediately awake. My bedroom door was closed, and the room had been dark. Now the entire room was filled with the light, the glory, and the voice of the Father God. (When you turn the lights on in a dark room, the corners of the room are never as bright as the areas where the lights are located. However, in this case, the light of God's presence filled every part and corner of the room. There were no dark corners.)

However, when God spoke and told me to wake up, my response was, "WHAT?"

The Father God then said, "DON'T DO WHAT YOU PLAN TO DO!"

I responded again with, "WHAT?"

Again, He said the same thing, "DON'T DO WHAT YOU PLAN TO DO!"

And I responded again with the same word, "WHAT?"

(But I knew what He was talking about.)

His presence, glory, and light faded from the room, and it returned to a natural state of darkness. I went back to sleep as if nothing had happened. Remember, I told God several months earlier I wanted to go to Heaven to be with Him forever. And that unless He showed me differently, there were some things I liked and would continue to do.

This experience in my apartment in Dallas was the start of God's reply to me. In retrospect, I understand a Christian can't have a divided heart. You and I can't love the sinful behaviors of the world and expect God to approve that behavior (1 John 2:15). Instead, He wants us to commit our entire hearts and lives to Him and live in a way that honors Him.

WHAT DO YOU THINK? (ADVANCED)

I said previously that the Holy Spirit communicates most often to us rather than the Father or Jesus. So why do you think the Father chose to speak directly to me and do it in this astonishing audible manner?

The weekend at the beach. I took the top off my sports car, so we could drive down from Dallas to the beach and enjoy the sun and fresh air. However, the trip was miserable. We argued constantly. We were severely sunburned and couldn't touch each other. The trip back to Dallas was equally terrible. A severe thunderstorm began about the time we started for the airport.

Sorrowful Repentance and Salvation

The trip back from the airport was one of the worst experiences of my life. It was raining so hard I could barely see the front of my small car. The lightning lit up the sky all around me. The thunder felt like it was going to burst my eardrums. I started to sob and tell God how sorry I was for disobeying Him. I had pledged a fraternity in college. The actives would say to the pledges that we were "lower than whale ___." (You can use your imagination here.) I kept repeating this to God, telling Him that I was so unworthy of His love. I kept asking Him to forgive me for my blatant and many sins. I was sobbing uncontrollably and could hardly see where I was driving.

My mother and sister had committed their hearts and lives to Jesus Christ the year before. They were constantly telling me about God and Jesus, so as soon as I got home, I called my mother. I was still uncontrollably sobbing as I asked her what was happening to me. She began to rejoice and praise God. I asked her how she could be so joyful when I was so miserable. She told me I was experiencing what the Bible refers to as *sorrowful repentance* (2 Corinthians 7:9). She led me through a prayer of repentance and acceptance of Jesus Christ as my Savior and Lord. This was similar to the prayer in the chapter "Prayer to Know God."

PRACTICE IT
Is the Holy Spirit leading you into sorrowful repentance now, perhaps about how you have lived your life without Jesus Christ? If so, what are you willing to do about it? If you are a follower of Jesus, is the Holy Spirit convicting you of something He wants you to repent of right now? Is He leading you into your own sorrowful repentance?

The next chapter describes what happens when, like me, you are "born-again" after receiving Jesus Christ.

14

"Born-Again" Is Misunderstood

Iwas changed! I was different! I was a *new creation* in Christ Jesus (Galatians 6:15). My classmates the next Monday kept looking at me and talking about how I was different. I could hear them wondering what had happened. When I talked to my roommate later, he asked what changed me so much. After telling him, I led him in a similar prayer of faith in Christ like my mother had done with me.

Born-Again: What It Really Means

My life has never been the same since that day in May 1976 when the Holy Spirit came to live within me. As a result, I have been a born-again follower of Christ for over forty-five years. **Unfortunately, though, many people, including Christians, don't know what born-again means and how it happens**.

Too often, many seem to lack biblical knowledge about the Holy Spirit. And if they don't know who the Holy Spirit is, they likely don't know about being born-again. We just don't hear about Him and our need to be born-again from pastors and Bible study teachers. I also wonder if the term "born-again" is a turn-off for some people? The term may even polarize people within a denomination. I am sure it grieves the Holy Spirit when He sees this division.

WHAT DO YOU THINK?
What are some reasons why people may not understand what born-again means?

When does it happen? A careful study of scripture reveals being born-again occurs when people sincerely ask Jesus Christ to rescue them from their self-centered existence. **Being born-again means the Holy Spirit has come to live within the new Christian's heart.**

> And I will ask the Father, and He will give you another Advocate, who will never leave you. He is the Holy Spirit, who leads into all truth. The world can't receive Him, because it isn't looking for Him and doesn't recognize Him. But you know Him, because He lives with you now and later will be in you. (John 14:16-17 NLT)

Jesus said unless you are *born-again*, you can't enter the Kingdom of Heaven.

> Jesus said, "I tell you the truth, unless you are born-again, you cannot see the Kingdom of God." "What do You mean?" exclaimed Nicodemus. "How can an old man go back into his mother's womb and be born-again?" Jesus replied, "I assure you, no one can enter the Kingdom of God without being born of water and the Spirit. Humans can reproduce only human life, but the Holy Spirit gives birth to spiritual life. So don't be surprised when I say, 'You must be born-again.'" (John 3:3-7 NLT)

People have a physical birth when they are born into this natural world. They have a spiritual birth when they are born-again by the Holy Spirit into the Kingdom of God.

WHAT DO YOU THINK?
What does the following verse say about people who are not born-again?

> You are controlled by the Spirit if you have the Spirit of God living in you. (And remember that those who do not have the Spirit of Christ living in them do not belong to Him at all.) (Romans 8:9 NLT)

A *living hope*. You see in the next verse that new believers are given a *living hope* when they are born-again. This is because they accepted the death and resurrection of Jesus Christ to save them. **This *hope* is an assurance, a certainty, that they will live eternally with God.** It's *living* because the Holy Spirit lives within them to empower and enable them to enjoy life with the Father, Jesus, and Himself.

> Blessed be the God and Father of our Lord Jesus Christ, who according to His great mercy has caused us to be born again to a living hope

through the resurrection of Jesus Christ from the dead. (1 Peter 1:3 NASB)

Born-Again into God's Eternal Family

When a person is born-again, the Father adopts them into His eternal family. Thus, they become a spiritual child of the Father God and a brother of His Son, Jesus.

> And because we are His children, God has sent the Spirit of His Son into our hearts, prompting us to call out, "Abba, Father." (Galatians 4:6 NLT)

> And the King will say, "I tell you the truth, when you did it to one of the least of these My brothers and sisters, you were doing it to Me!" (Matthew 25:40 NLT)

When this occurs, they receive an eternal inheritance as a member of God's family. There is joy and celebration in Heaven because another person will spend eternity with God!

> All praise to God, the Father of our Lord Jesus Christ. It is by His great mercy that we have been born-again, because God raised Jesus Christ from the dead. Now we live with great expectation, and we have a priceless inheritance—an inheritance that is kept in heaven for you, pure and undefiled, beyond the reach of change and decay. (1 Peter 1:3-4 NLT)

What about children? *Jesus said, "Let the children come to Me. Don't stop them! For the Kingdom of Heaven belongs to those who are like these children."* (Matthew 19:14 NLT). This statement alone says much about Jesus' special love and concern for children. Even though scripture doesn't state definitively what God's plan is to save children, I think it's vital to trust His limitless love.

A Biblical Worldview and Being Born-Again

George Barna stated in his 2020 survey report about *America's Dominant Worldview* that less than 30% of adult Americans say they are saved and going to Heaven. Yet only six percent (6%) of adult Americans hold a biblical worldview. People with a biblical worldview strive to follow Jesus Christ and live by biblical principles and truths. They understand that their primary reason for being on earth is to know, love, and serve God with all of their heart.

WHAT DO YOU THINK?

Since it seems many, or most, of these nearly 30% of adult Americans don't actively live their lives for God, why is it likely that most are not born-again followers of Jesus Christ?

Answer: People do what they believe. If they don't live consistently by what they say they believe, they don't really believe it. What people choose to do demonstrates their priorities. And priorities are based on what they believe to be important in their life.

As you saw earlier, Leonardo Blair's article Most adult US Christians don't believe the Holy Spirit is real: study is based on reports from George Barna's *America's Dominant Worldview* survey. Mr. Barna reports that some people are simply religious or church-goers who want the label "Christian." They think it's fashionable to be thought of this way. But have they truly committed their lives to Jesus? Remember Jesus' parable of the sower in the chapter "Everyone Needs to Be Rescued"? From it, you saw that **not everyone who thinks they are a Christian is truly a born-again follower of Jesus.**

The following Personal Application provides a way to examine yourself to know whether you are a born-again follower of Jesus with a biblical worldview.

PERSONAL APPLICATION

Do you strive to live by faith in the God of the Bible through the indwelling life and power of the Holy Spirit? Do you humbly worship the Father God? Are you grateful to His Son, Jesus, because He died and rose again to save you? Do you regularly spend time with God in prayer? Do you attend a Bible study, adult Sunday School class, or home group where you learn the Bible and how to apply it to your life? Do you actively serve others using your spiritual gifts?

Answer: If so, you are a spiritually alive, born-again follower of Jesus Christ living with a Biblical worldview. If not, why is this the case?

Changes After Being Born-Again

The following is a list of some changes that occur after being born-again. They describe what people receive as a new follower of Jesus Christ.

- You are a chosen child of God. *(2 Thessalonians 2:13; Ephesians 1:4)*

- You are rescued and forgiven by God; you are made right with God. *(Romans. 5:9; Colossians 1:14)*

- You are transferred from the devil's domain to Christ's Kingdom. *(Colossians 1:13)*

- You are born-again because the Holy Spirit came to live within you. *(1 Corinthians 3:16; Ephesians 2:22)*

- The Father God and Jesus came with Holy Spirit to live within you. *(John 14:23)*

- The Holy Spirit within you is the Father's guarantee He loves you and wants you to be with Him eternally. *(2 Corinthians 1:21-22)*

- You will always belong to God. *(1 Corinthians 6:20)*

- The Father God adopted you as His child. *(John 1:12; Ephesians 1:5)*

- You can never be separated from God's love. *(Romans 8:35)*

- You can never be condemned for your forgiven sins. *(Romans 8:1,2, 31)*

- Jesus Christ calls you His friend. *(John 15:15)*

- You are one in Spirit with Jesus Christ. *(1 Corinthians 6:17)*

- You are a member of the body of Jesus Christ. *(1 Corinthians 12:27)*

- You have a new nature that is continually being transformed to be like Jesus. *(2 Corinthians 5:17; Galatians 6:15)*

- God calls you a "saint" because you are now blameless in His sight. You have received the perfection of Jesus. *(Ephesians 1:1)*

- You have been given spiritual gifts to serve other people. *(1 Corinthians 12:7; 1 Peter 4:10)*

- God works in all things for the good of those who love Him. *(Romans 8:28)*

- God is at work within you to continually transform you to be more like Jesus Christ. He will do so until you are home in Heaven with Him. *(Philippians 1:6)*

- Your eternal citizenship is now in Heaven. *(Philippians 3:20)*

- You have not been given a spirit of fear but of power, love, and a sound mind. *(2 Timothy 1:7)*

- You may approach your Father God in prayer with confidence, knowing He wants you to do so. *(Ephesians 2:18, 3:12; Hebrews 4:16)*

- Jesus Christ gives you His strength to do what He asks you to do. *(Philippians 4:13)*

- You are a witness to others about what Jesus has done for you. *(John 15:26-27; Acts 1:8; 2 Corinthians 5:17)*

NOTE: The term *saint* is another name for a follower of Jesus Christ (Ephesians 1:1-3). It is derived from a similar Greek word translated as *holy*. Both these terms mean one who is set apart from the world and dedicated to God for His purposes. Therefore, to be a saint has nothing to do with a person being more religious or self-sacrificing. Since every believer is a saint, that idea is contrary to the Bible.

PERSONAL APPLICATION
Which of these changes can you see in yourself if you are a follower of Jesus Christ? If you are not a Christian yet, which of these excite you about becoming one?

It's impossible to consistently live the Christian life without being born-again by the Holy Spirit. But it's not the experience of being born-again that's important. Instead, having an eternal, living relationship with the Father, Jesus, and the Holy Spirit should excite and encourage new believers.

15

Gifted and Empowered by the Spirit

One important change. You have seen that when you commit your life to Jesus Christ as your Savior and Lord, you are born-again. With this spiritual birth, the Holy Spirit gives you abilities empowered by Him to serve others in ways you could not do without Him.

Christians Serve because Jesus Served

Jesus left His *divine privileges* behind in Heaven when He came into this world as the Father's Son and servant for the salvation of all people.

> You must have the same attitude that Christ Jesus had. Though He was God, He did not think of equality with God as something to cling to. Instead, He gave up His divine privileges; He took the humble position of a slave and was born as a human being. (Philippians 2:5-7 NLT)

Since Jesus, the Son of God, came to serve, His followers should have this same attitude.

> Those who are the greatest among you should take the lowest rank, and the leader should be like a servant . . . . For I *[Jesus]* am among you as one who serves. (Luke 12:26-27 NLT, author's emphasis)

Christians serve God and others by using their spiritual gifts, natural talents, experiences, education, and passions. The Holy Spirit can work through these to accomplish the Father's purposes and plans. However, believers need to know and use their spiritual gifts because they are explicitly given to serve others. Whatever is done for Christ will be more successful in building the Kingdom of God if Christians use their spiritual gifts.

WHAT DO YOU THINK?

There are many ways to serve God and people. Why is it necessary for the Holy Spirit to help believers serve people?

What Are Spiritual Gifts?

These are abilities divinely given by the Holy Spirit to every believer when they are born-again. In other words, a believer receives their spiritual gifts at spiritual birth, not physical birth. They are "gifts" because they cannot be earned. They are "spiritual" because the Holy Spirit is their source. People who have not committed their lives to Jesus Christ don't have spiritual gifts because they don't have the Holy Spirit living in them (Romans 8:9). They may have extraordinary natural talents from physical birth and may have developed exceptional skills and capabilities, but these are not spiritual gifts.

The following verse says the Holy Spirit wants you to know about spiritual gifts:

> Now concerning spiritual gifts, brothers, I do not want you to be uninformed. (1 Corinthians 12:1 ESV)

He gives a new believer one or more spiritual gifts to benefit others.

> There are different kinds of spiritual gifts, but the same Spirit is the source of them all. (1 Corinthians 12:4 NLT)

> A spiritual gift is given to each of us so we can help each other. (1 Corinthians 12:7 NLT)

Using your spiritual gifts to help others is part of God's purpose and plan for your life. If you don't use them, you are personally missing out on something He wants. Likewise, the people God intends you to serve are missing out on your benefits and blessings.

NOTE: Some say that several spiritual gifts ceased to exist when the last Apostle died. They believe these particular spiritual gifts were only needed to lay the foundation of the early Christian church. However, this idea is not in the Bible. Nowhere does it identify any of the twenty spiritual gifts as ceasing at any time.

WHAT DO YOU THINK?

Why is it essential for believers to serve using all their abilities, but especially their spiritual gifts?

They loved to serve with their gifts. This wonderful Christian couple cared about people and loved to serve in our church in many ways. They knew their spiritual gifts and sought opportunities to serve and help others. This knowledge enabled them to be more effective in their service. They were an inspiration to many, not just with their willingness to serve but also with their genuine, caring hearts. In addition, they maintained a balanced life with social, family, and other involvements.

The Human Body Analogy and Spiritual Gifts

As an analogy, all born-again believers are referred to as the body of Christ (Ephesians 4:15). As the human body has many parts, so does the body of Christ. Each part of His body is a believer with specific spiritual gifts. Each believer has a purpose in making the body whole. One may be an arm and another an eye. One may have the gift of service and another the gift of mercy, but all believers and their gifts are necessary. When all believers function as they should, they can all have greater physical, mental, emotional, and spiritual health.

> The human body has many parts, but the many parts make up one whole body. So it is with the body of Christ. (1 Corinthians 12:12 NLT)

> He makes the whole body fit together perfectly. As each part does its own special work, it helps the other parts grow, so that the whole body is healthy and growing and full of love. (Ephesians 4:16 NLT)

WHAT DO YOU THINK? (ADVANCED)

If some parts of the human body don't function as they should, why does the entire human body suffer loss? Why is this true when every believer doesn't use their spiritual gifts in the body of Christ?

Understanding the Nature of Spiritual Gifts

The following descriptions help define spiritual gifts and how Christians should use them.

- Spiritual gifts are given by the Holy Spirit so believers can serve to benefit others. *(1 Corinthians 12:7)*

- Some believers (as I do) limit the number of spiritual gifts to the twenty found in the following chapters: Romans 12, 1 Corinthians 12, and Ephesians 4.

- Every Christian is given at least one spiritual gift, but often more. *(1 Peter 4:10)*

- No follower of Christ has all twenty gifts. *(1 Corinthians 12:28-30)*

- All Christians are not given one specific gift. *(1 Corinthians 12:29-30)*

- Jesus Christ holds His followers accountable for how they use their gifts. *(1 Peter 4:10)*

- Spiritual gifts help define the purpose of a believer's life in the body of Christ and God's Kingdom on earth. *(Romans 12:2-8)*

- Spiritual gifts must be used out of Christ's love in the believer's heart to accomplish the Lord's purposes. *(1 Corinthians 13:1-3)*

- Spiritual gifts help build up other believers and the body of Christ in general when used under the influence of the Holy Spirit. *(1 Corinthians 12:27)*

- Groups of believers (such as church congregations) function optimally when all the believers use their spiritual gifts under the influence of the Holy Spirit *(Ephesians 4:11-12, 15-16)*

WHAT DO YOU THINK?
If you could pick only one, which of these is least understood in your church? Why do you think this is so?

Where Spiritual Gifts Are in the Bible

The twenty spiritual gifts are identified in four lists in the Bible: Romans 12:6-8, 1 Corinthians 12:4-11, 1 Corinthians 12:28, and Ephesians 4:11. Some of the gifts are duplicated in the lists. Following is the list of the twenty spiritual gifts:

Service	Gifts of Healing
Exhortation	Miracles
Giving	Faith
Administration	Leadership
Mercy	Helps
Speaking in Tongues	Prophecy
Interpretation of Tongues	Teaching
Word of Wisdom	Evangelist
Word of Knowledge	Pastor
Discernment of Spirits	Apostle

Discovering Your Spiritual Gifts

The best way to determine your spiritual gifts is to complete a spiritual gifts assessment. You can find a number of these on the Internet. However, when you complete an assessment, you may find yourself interested in only a few of the spiritual gifts. Often, believers will have three, four, or even five that seem to fit their personality and thoughts about being involved in helping others. (By the way, some believers may already be using their spiritual gifts and not know it.)

Many spiritual gift assessments include other gifts not found in these four lists. Some of these are natural abilities or talents, such as exceptional musical or athletic abilities. Others, such as the "gift of celibacy" or "gift of poverty," I consider to be a personal gift from God. These personal gifts tend to focus on how the believer lives their life without regard to how they function in the church. Therefore, they will also have spiritual gifts to empower their service for others.

Hindrances to Discovering Your Spiritual Gifts

If you fail to address these hindrances, you may have difficulty discovering your spiritual gifts.

1. Lack of understanding of spiritual gifts.

2. Unresolved sin in your life, especially sins that affect your ability to love and serve God and people. (Sin is rebellion against God.)

3. Lack of involvement with the needs of people (you must be involved).

4. Attempts to imitate spiritual gifts you see at work in other believers you admire.

5. Failure to analyze why certain activities appeal to you and why this may indicate your spiritual gifts.

PERSONAL APPLICATION

Which hindrances are interfering with the discovery of your spiritual gifts? What should you do to eliminate them?

Don't Put the Holy Spirit in a Box

Always be open to the Holy Spirit to use spiritual gifts different from your strongest gifts. God may use you temporarily with other gifts in various ministries and service areas at varying periods during your life for His reasons. He may also want you to grow in your faith and trust in Him or temporarily fill a void left by others in serving people around you.

No church can fully function as Christ intends without every follower of Jesus knowing and using their spiritual gifts. That's why the Holy Spirit gives spiritual gifts to every believer. A church congregation will experience its greatest joy and impact on the community when every believer exercises their spiritual gifts. That is how essential spiritual gifts are to the Kingdom of God on earth!

16

A New Creation in Christ

Another significant change occurs when you are born-again. You become a *new creation*. The Holy Spirit gives you a brand-new nature, a nature that never existed in you before. This new nature now lives alongside your existing old nature.

> Therefore, if anyone is in Christ, the new creation has come. (2 Corinthians 5:17 NIV)

The Greek word for *new* used in the above verse means it's a nature that didn't previously exist in you. The Holy Spirit just doesn't take the existing self-centered old nature, modify it, improve it, or renovate it. If you are a follower of Jesus Christ, you can't live the new Christian life in a way that pleases God with just an improved self-centered old nature. You must be given a new nature that enables you to experience your new spiritual relationship and life with God. Think about it this way. You have a forty-year-old home you decide to improve. You renovated it, so it looks much better than it did before. However, its foundation and framework are still the same old construction. Later you decide to build a brand-new home. It's a new construction that previously never existed. Your new nature is like this newly constructed home.

Believers Have Two Natures

The old and new natures are integral to your being as a new believer. You continue to have a self-centered old nature, but now you also have a Christ-centered new nature. However, you can't live simultaneously by both natures. One nature will always dominate and control your thinking, behaviors, and life.

Since you committed your life to Jesus Christ, you want the Holy Spirit and your new nature to control you. You have a choice, but it is not an easy choice to follow.

Those who live according to the flesh have their minds set on what the flesh desires; but those who live in accordance with the Spirit have their minds set on what the Spirit desires. The mind governed by the flesh is death, but the mind governed by the Spirit is life and peace. The mind governed by the flesh is hostile to God; it does not submit to God's law, nor can it do so.

> "Those who are in the realm of the flesh cannot please God." (Romans 8:5-8 NIV)

NOTE: *Being in the realm of the flesh* is another way of saying people are living by their self-centered old nature.

The old nature is your default nature because you have lived by it your entire life. As such, it is often the first response to life. It will always successfully control you unless you work with the Holy Spirit to retrain yourself to respond by your new nature.

WHAT DO YOU THINK?

Why is a new believer's old nature their default nature that they typically respond with rather than their new nature?

The following verse says you must continually exert a determined effort to obey God and live by your new nature:

> Work hard to show the results of your salvation, obeying God with deep reverence and fear. (Philippians 2:12 NLT)

The Holy Spirit helps you *work hard* to be transformed from your old to your new nature. This transformation occurs over time as you seek His guidance, teaching, and empowerment in your life. You will learn more about this in the next chapter, "Be Transformed by the Spirit."

The Old Nature

When I say your old nature is self-centered, I mean it's focused on what you want, not what God wants. You don't naturally submit to Jesus Christ as the One in charge of your life with your old nature. You always want to be the one in charge. You rely on your judgment and trust your choices instead of the Holy Spirit. Maybe you are the most loving, caring, compassionate, and giving person in the world. However, you are still self-centered and not Christ-centered when you live by your old nature.

> All of us, like sheep, have strayed away. We have left God's paths to follow our own. (Isaiah 53:6 NLT)

> As it is written: "None is righteous, no, not one; no one understands; no one seeks for God." (Romans 3:10-11 ESV)

Toby's old nature led him away from Jesus. Toby and I were good friends. We talked on the phone for hours about Jesus Christ and the Christian life. We encouraged one another in this way. He seemed devout and committed to following Jesus Christ. After completing a post-graduate degree, he was hired by a company in another state. Even though he was busy with his new job and life, we still talked occasionally. Sometime later, he told me he had met a woman he deeply loved. They eventually married, and I heard nothing from him for over a year. When he finally did call, he told me he and his wife decided that Jesus Christ was not real, so Christianity was not relevant. He was no longer going to church or involved in anything Christian.

By the way, I had previously learned that when love stops growing, it starts dying. This seems to be what occurred with Toby's love for Jesus Christ. You feed whichever nature you allow to dominate by your thoughts, desires, and beliefs. Therefore, if you live by the old nature, you ensure its growth and dominance, and the new nature is dormant. Toby allowed his old nature to dominate his priorities, values, and desires. As a result, he lost the interest and love he first had for Jesus Christ (Revelation 2:4-5).

WHAT DO YOU THINK?

Which of Toby's two natures did he follow in rejecting Jesus as his Savior and Lord? After many years of learning about Jesus, why do you think he allowed this to happen?

Will I see Toby in Heaven? Only God knows what is in Toby's heart today.

The New Nature

When you sincerely desire Jesus to be in charge of your life, you want the new nature to lead and control you. You ask the Holy Spirit to guide your decisions, expectations, motives, and behaviors. However, your new nature will never wholly dominate your behavior and life until you go home to Heaven. That's why there are disciplines you must practice regularly that nurture and cause your new nature to grow and mature over your lifetime. Just as a baby needs physical food to help it grow physically over time, you need spiritual food to help you grow spiritually. Spiritual disciplines are described in the chapter "Knowing God through Christian Practices."

PERSONAL APPLICATION

Which nature do you want to control your thinking, values, priorities, and behaviors? How does asking Jesus to be in charge of your life (to be your Lord) affect which nature you choose to live by?

A Personal Testimony

The Holy Spirit will give you opportunities, as He has me, to tell people about how you are different after committing your life to Jesus Christ. (It's a way of saying you are a *new creation* in Christ Jesus.) This is referred to as your "personal testimony." It contrasts your old and new natures and includes the following three parts:

- What I was like before I was rescued (your old nature)
- How I was rescued
- What I am like now with the Holy Spirit living in me (your new nature)

Your testimony should be brief, with no more than two or three sentences for each part. You want it to be concise and relatable. I suggest you ask the Holy Spirit to guide you as you create it. You will likely need to revise it several times. Ask some Christian friends to review it to help you refine it to be impactful for others.

The following verses indicate followers of Jesus should always be prepared to tell their testimony to others:

> But set Christ apart as Lord in your hearts and always be ready to give an answer to anyone who asks about the hope you possess. Yet do it with courtesy and respect, keeping a good conscience. (1 Peter 3:15-16 NET)

Here are two fictitious examples of a personal testimony to give you an idea of how to construct one for yourself.

Fictitious Testimony One

<u>Before:</u> People liked me and told me I was a good person. I loved people and had many friends. I didn't believe I needed God in my life, so I just didn't think about Him.

<u>How I was rescued:</u> A friend invited me to church. The pastor was preaching about why people need to be saved. I knew this didn't apply to me, but I was still curious about what he meant. My friend told me God loved me and wanted me to spend eternity with Him. He led me through a prayer to know God.

<u>Now:</u> I still love people, but now I also love God. So I study the Bible, pray, and meet with other Christians. Now I want to know God better and live a life that pleases Him.

Fictitious Testimony Two

<u>Before:</u> Alcohol helped me forget my problems and feel better about myself. I enjoyed drinking with my friends, so why did I still feel empty on the inside? I was not sure what love was about, but I didn't need God in my life. How could He help me?

<u>How I was rescued:</u> I finally admitted the emptiness and loneliness I felt were real. I wanted peace and joy, so I began to read the New Testament of the Bible. I discovered Jesus Christ and invited Him to be my Savior and Lord.

<u>Now:</u> I don't need alcohol anymore. I have joy and peace in my heart where there was once emptiness and loneliness. Jesus now fills my heart and life with His love for me and others.

Share-Check-Share. I learned this method of communication many years ago. It can apply to any subject but is especially helpful when telling people about your personal testimony. Its purpose is to help you determine if people are interested in what you have to say.

The method: After making your first statement, stop talking to see if they want you to continue on the topic. If they do, then make your next statement. Again, stop to see if they want you to continue. If their words or body language indicate they are not interested, stop talking on that subject and move on to another topic.

For example, someone asks what you did last Sunday. You tell them you went to worship service and your adult Sunday School class. Stop and wait for their response. If they ask for more information about the sermon or what you learned in the class, respond with that information. If they change the subject and talk about something else, you know they are not interested in what you just said. So, move on to another topic. You can't force people to want to hear about God and salvation in Jesus Christ.

IMPORTANT: The Holy Spirit prepares people to hear about Jesus and your life as a follower of His. Some may not yet be ready at a particular time to understand and accept what you have to say. He knows their heart and whether they are ready for the Good News.

PRACTICE IT
Why not take time now to write out your personal testimony? Use the two fictitious testimonies as examples of how to write your own. Then, once you have written and tested it with friends, tell it to someone you think may be interested in it. How did they respond? Did they seem to understand it? Did you use share-check-share to assess their interest? Make changes to your testimony as needed from their responses.

Only by being a *new creation* in Christ Jesus can people enter God's Kingdom. Only then will they have the desire and power to defeat their old nature and live by their new nature. It can be a daily battle, but the result is peace, joy, and a fruitful life with God. In the next chapter, you will learn more about the life-long process of being transformed into the nature of Jesus Christ.

17

Be Transformed by the Spirit

As a follower of Jesus, God gives you a choice about how to live your life. You may allow the Holy Spirit to direct your thinking, motivations, conversations, and behaviors, or you may allow your old nature to control you.

The following verses are a reminder of the consequences of this choice:

> For those who live according to the flesh set their minds on the things of the flesh, but those who live according to the Spirit set their minds on the things of the Spirit. For to set the mind on the flesh is death, but to set the mind on the Spirit is life and peace. For the mind that is set on the flesh is hostile to God, for it does not submit to God's law; indeed, it cannot. Those who are in the flesh cannot please God. (Romans 8:5-8 ESV)

Holy Spirit Can Transform the Heart and Mind

When you commit your life to Jesus Christ, the Holy Spirit comes to live within you. You are born-again. He gives you a new nature that needs to grow over time. This growth produces changes within your mind and heart and is manifested in your outward behavior.

The following verses say you are being *transformed* into Christ's nature:

> But when one turns to the Lord, the veil is removed. Now the Lord is the Spirit, and where the Spirit of the Lord is, there is freedom. And we all, with unveiled face, beholding the glory of the Lord, are being transformed into the same image from one degree of glory to another.

For this comes from the Lord who is the Spirit. (2 Corinthians 3:16-18 ESV)

The English word *transformed* comes from the Greek *metamorphose*. It refers to an ongoing process of progressive change. A caterpillar is an excellent example of metamorphosis. Over time it's transformed into a beautiful butterfly. This is a good analogy of how the Holy Spirit can transform your self-centered, old nature into God's beautiful new nature. These changes occur on the inside (your mind and heart) before they are visible on the outside in your behavior. You already know that outward behavioral changes without inward changes often lapse over time, and you may revert to the previous behaviors of your old nature.

WHAT DO YOU THINK?

What happens if you try to change your outward behavior without cooperating with the Holy Spirit to change your heart and mind first?

The Body Grows Old, but the Soul Is Renewed

In the following verse, the Apostle Paul says that the inner man is renewed even while the physical body grows old. The inner man references the soul or the heart (emotions, will, conscience, thinking) instead of the outer man, which is the physical body. The Holy Spirit is transforming you on the inside. This is your new nature that is changing and maturing.

> Therefore we do not lose heart, but though our outer man is decaying, yet our inner man is being renewed day by day. (2 Corinthians 4:16 NASB)

In the following verse, you see that you can know God's will more clearly when you allow the Holy Spirit to transform you and renew your mind:

> And do not be conformed to this world, but be transformed by the renewing of your mind, so that you may prove what the will of God is, that which is good and acceptable and perfect. (Romans 12:2 NASB)

The Old Nature Must Go

This means you must stop letting your old nature dominate you and start letting your new nature control instead. This can only be accomplished by working with the Holy Spirit within you.

In reference to your former manner of life, you lay aside the old self, which is being corrupted in accordance with the lusts of deceit, and that you be renewed in the spirit of your mind, and put on the new self, which in the likeness of God has been created in righteousness and holiness of the truth. (Ephesians 4:22-24 NASB)

The following verses describe some characteristics of the *old sinful nature*:

But now you must put them all away: anger, wrath, malice, slander, and obscene talk from your mouth. Do not lie to one another, seeing that you have put off the old self with its practices. (Colossians 3:8-9 ESV)

PERSONAL APPLICATION

Do you see any of the above characteristics of the old nature in your behaviors and life? Do you see others not on the list? What are you willing to do about it?

The New Nature Must Mature

As a believer, you can ask the Holy Spirit to help transform you into the new nature of Jesus Christ. In the following verse, *Put on the new self* means you are actively part of this transformative process. The phrase above *is being renewed* indicates this is a continual renewal process.

Put on the new self who is being renewed to a true knowledge according to the image of the One who created him. (Colossians 3:10 NASB)

The following verses describe some of the characteristics of the new nature:

Put on then, as God's chosen ones, holy and beloved, compassionate hearts, kindness, humility, meekness, and patience, bearing with one another and, if one has a complaint against another, forgiving each other; as the Lord has forgiven you, so you also must forgive. And above all these put on love, which binds everything together in perfect harmony. And let the peace of Christ rule in your hearts, to which indeed you were called in one body. And be thankful (Colossians 3:12-15 ESV)

PERSONAL APPLICATION
Which characteristics in the above verses do you see in yourself that reflect your transformed new nature?

Because of this new nature, you can change the way you think by dwelling on the following kinds of thoughts instead of those of the old nature:

> Finally, brethren, whatever is true, whatever is honorable, whatever is right, whatever is pure, whatever is lovely, whatever is of good repute, if there is any excellence and if anything worthy of praise, dwell on these things. (Philippians 4:8 NASB)

Make the Most of Your Short Time on Earth

Spiritual maturity requires sacrificing some of your time to serve and help others. When this is a lifestyle, you learn to trust the Holy Spirit to help you use your time wisely. People have a limited time on earth before they step into Heaven or Hell. Unfortunately, you don't know when your physical life will end. So now is the time to help and serve others.

> How do you know what your life will be like tomorrow? Your life is like the morning fog—it's here a little while, then it's gone. (James 4:14 NLT)

> This is all the more urgent, for you know how late it is; time is running out. Wake up. (Romans 13:11 NLT)

Helping others helps you grow spiritually. Serving and helping by the Holy Spirit to positively impact other people's lives has eternal value to God. In addition, these actions of faith help the believer to grow spiritually. So don't waste time doing things that please your self-centered desires that ultimately have no (earthly or eternal) value to God.

So be careful how you live. Don't live like fools, but like those who are wise.

> *Make the most of every opportunity.* (Ephesians 5:15-16 NLT, author's emphasis)

> Live wisely among those who are not believers, and make the most of every opportunity. (Colossians 4:5 NLT)

WHAT DO YOU THINK?

How can Christians know when an opportunity to help others is from the Holy Spirit?

Answer. The two chapters, "Knowing and Doing God's Will," describe ways to recognize opportunities from God.

Two opportunities to do good. The first story is about how I missed an opportunity to do good for a hurting person. The second story is about how the Father answered my request and gave me a second chance.

The missed opportunity. Traffic on the Golden Gate bridge that morning was slow and congested. I was frustrated because it also took me too long to find a parking spot. As a result, I was late for an important meeting. I was rushing down the block and saw a man leaning his head against a building wall. I heard him weeping and sobbing. By his clothing and appearance, he was obviously homeless. But what could I do? I was already late for my meeting. So, I passed him by with feelings of guilt. I knew I should have stopped to ask how I might help, but I didn't.

> Remember, it is sin to know what you ought to do and then not do it. (James 4:17 NLT)

After my meeting, I went outside, but the man was gone. Later that day, I asked the Father to forgive me for not helping this man. I asked Him to provide me another opportunity to help someone in a similar situation. This missed opportunity taught me about God's priorities and helped me mature as a Christian.

I didn't miss the next opportunity. God was faithful to provide a second opportunity in Orlando, Florida, several years later. As I walked to my car from church on a late Sunday evening, I saw two homeless men standing on the street corner. They were intently discussing something. Perhaps it was where they were going to sleep on this frigid night. I sensed the Holy Spirit wanted me to ask them if I could help. However, I felt evil coming from one of them, but the other seemed like a lost soul. I brought him to my apartment (I was single) for the night. He took a shower, and I gave him clean clothes. I threw his ragged, smelly clothes out. We had dinner and talked for a while. He was nearly illiterate. As I told him about his Savior and Lord, Jesus Christ, it was evident he had heard this before. Even though he prayed to receive Christ, I was unsure he meant it. The next morning, I packed him a lunch, gave him some money, and a warm coat. I dropped him off on I-4 in Orlando, where he said he wanted to hitch a ride back to his home state. That was the last I saw of him. This was an opportunity I didn't miss from the Father to do good to a fellow human being in need.

CAUTION: I do not imply that you should invite every person in need to your home. Let the Holy Spirit guide you in all things! Because you know there are unscrupulous and evil people in this world.

WHAT DO YOU THINK? (ADVANCED)
Why were these two similar opportunities not simply a coincidence? How did helping this second man in need increase my faith in God and develop my spiritual maturity?

Perhaps the following verses provide some insights:

> What good is it, my brothers, if someone says he has faith but does not have works? Can that faith save him? If a brother or sister is poorly clothed and lacking in daily food, and one of you says to them, "Go in peace, be warmed and filled," without giving them the things needed for the body, what good is that? So also faith by itself, if it does not have works, is dead. (James 2:14-17 ESV)

Spiritual growth is a slow process that requires a lifetime of serious commitment and endeavor. So, remember, there is no spiritual growth without change. This starts in the heart and mind and can be observed in outward behavior. This is the transformation by the Spirit from the self-centered old nature into the Christ-centered new nature. This is how followers of Jesus live a life that pleases the Father God.

18

The Battle for Spiritual Maturity

Spiritual growth is difficult because it always involves changes to the heart and life of the believer.

> Rather, speaking the truth in love, we are to grow up in every way into him who is the head, into Christ, from whom the whole body, joined and held together by every joint with which it is equipped, when each part is working properly, makes the body grow so that it builds itself up in love. (Ephesians 4:15-16 ESV)

If the Holy Spirit is not transforming believers, they are not growing spiritually. So every follower of Jesus must be willing to put in the effort and time to grow spiritually.

> So then, brothers and sisters, we are under obligation, not to the flesh, to live according to the flesh (for if you live according to the flesh, you will die), but if by the Spirit you put to death the deeds of the body you will live. (Romans 8:12-13 NET)

Struggles Are Necessary for Spiritual Growth

Life can be hard. Unfortunately, some Christians believe that everything should go well after accepting Jesus as their Savior and Lord. However, Jesus said His followers should expect difficult times in this world:

> I have told you all this so that you may have peace in Me. Here on earth you will have many trials and sorrows. But take heart, because I have overcome the world. (John 16:33 NLT)

The most significant increases in spiritual growth don't occur when everything is going well. Instead, they occur during the problems and difficulties of life.

Faith in God is tested during difficult times. However, believers who ask the Holy Spirit to help can persevere and grow spiritually as a result.

> Count it all joy, my brothers, when you meet trials of various kinds, for you know that the testing of your faith produces steadfastness. And let steadfastness have its full effect, that you may be perfect and complete, lacking in nothing. (James 1:2-4 ESV)

PERSONAL APPLICATION

How have you responded during difficult times in your life? Did you blame God, or did you thank Him because He was with you and helped you persevere? How did your reactions affect your attitude toward God?

Seek God during difficulties. Instead of being anxious or angry, believers can experience God's peace in their hearts amid life's difficulties. Sensing and responding to this need to spend more time with God can accelerate spiritual growth for Christians. This is because they learn to depend on the Father's provisions, the Lord's authority, and the Holy Spirit's help when their own efforts fail. Many believers spend more time in prayer, studying the Bible, and talking with trusted Christian friends during difficult times.

God is faithful. The following scripture says the Father God is faithful to enable believers (through the indwelling Holy Spirit) to endure difficulties. He wants them to increase their trust in His love and presence in every situation.

> No trial has overtaken you that is not faced by others. And God is faithful: He will not let you be tried beyond what you are able to bear, but with the trial will also provide a way out so that you may be able to endure it. (1 Corinthians 10:13 NET)

Come to Jesus for rest. Jesus invites His followers to come to Him to receive His rest. He gives His peace, comfort, and grace to persevere (through His Spirit) to enable His followers to find rest in their perseverance.

> Come to me, all who labor and are heavy laden, and I will give you rest. Take my yoke upon you, and learn from me, for I am gentle and lowly in heart, and you will find rest for your souls. For my yoke is easy, and my burden is light. (Matthew 11:28-30 ESV)

WHAT DO YOU THINK?

When times are difficult, why does Jesus ask His followers to come to Him? What does He give them? What is it about His nature that causes Him to do this for His brothers and sisters?

It Was All I Had, and I Didn't Trust God

There was a large health food store in our area that carried fresh, organic produce and other products. One day in the summer of 1977, I was there with all the money I had. We were nearly out of food at home. I was in the back of the store looking to see what I could buy to optimize my $20 for food. As I looked up, I noticed three men dressed like homeless people getting off a boxcar on the railroad tracks across the street. One of them seemed to be telling the others where to go. They split up and came across the street. The one in charge came into the health food store and began talking with the store owner. I could see his face and hear him asking for work, sweeping the floors, anything he could do to earn money for food. The owner told him he didn't have any work and asked him to leave. At this, the Holy Spirit spoke to me (in my thoughts) and told me to give him the $20 I had in my wallet. I argued with the Holy Spirit (in my thoughts) and told him I would not do it since this was all the money I had for food. As soon as I said this in my mind, the man turned and looked at me with great sadness on his face. The thought came to me that these three men were angels (in human form) and that **God had sent the one to test my trust in Him to provide during this difficult period**. As soon as I realized this, I looked up and saw the man was gone from the store. I went outside and couldn't find the three of them anywhere. They had disappeared.

This lesson reminds me that God can intervene in a person's life to demonstrate the need to trust Him in all circumstances. Of course, there will be occasions when you fail Him as I did, but there are other times when you will respond in faith and trust.

PERSONAL APPLICATION

What lesson for your own life can you take from this story?

Spiritual Maturity Comes from the Holy Spirit

Spiritual maturity develops over time through the transformational work of the Holy Spirit. It doesn't develop from living by the culture's standards, morality, values, and norms. These will change over time as society changes.

In the following verses, you see that the believer's wisdom doesn't come from the world's wisdom and perspectives. Instead, it's supernatural wisdom that helps believers mature spiritually.

Yet when I am among mature believers, I do speak with words of wisdom, but not the kind of wisdom that belongs to this world or to the rulers of this world, who are soon forgotten. . . . But it was to us that God revealed these things by His Spirit. For His Spirit searches out everything and shows us God's deep secrets.

> Yet among the mature we do impart wisdom, although it is not a wisdom of this age or of the rulers of this age, who are doomed to pass away. . . . But, as it is written, "What no eye has seen, nor ear heard, nor the heart of man imagined, what God has prepared for those who love him"—these things God has revealed to us through the Spirit. For the Spirit searches everything, even the depths of God. (1 Corinthians 2:6-10 ESV)

The following verses say that spiritual maturity develops as believers train themselves to learn and apply God's word:

> For someone who lives on milk is still an infant and doesn't know how to do what is right. Solid food is for those who are mature, who through training have the skill to recognize the difference between right and wrong. (Hebrews 5:13-14 NLT)

WHAT DO YOU THINK?
What do believers need to do to train themselves to grow spiritually?

When believers learn and apply God's word to their thinking, motives, heart, and behavior, it transforms and equips them to serve people more effectively.

> Every scripture is inspired by God and useful for teaching, for reproof, for correction, and for training in righteousness, that the person dedicated to God may be capable and equipped for every good work. (2 Timothy 3:16-17 NET)

Spiritual Maturity Requires the Father's Training

Parents. Good parents have the life-long well-being of their children at heart. Therefore, they use training to correct their behavior, so the children learn to do what is right and avoid doing what is wrong.

> Since we respected our earthly fathers who disciplined us, shouldn't we submit even more to the discipline of the Father of our spirits, and live forever? For our earthly fathers disciplined us for a few years, doing the best they knew how. (Hebrews 12:9-10 NLT)

The Greek word used above for *discipline* means to train, instruct, chasten, or correct. It references teaching a child to behave in acceptable ways, so they learn to do what is right all their life.

> Train a child in the way that he should go, and when he is old he will not turn from it. (Proverbs 6 NET)

This learning to do what is right is a life-long process of transformation that requires continual effort and time. It's not easy, but the rewards are eternal.

Father God. He corrects and trains His *own children* to know and do what is right.

> As you endure this divine discipline, remember that God is treating you as His own children. Who ever heard of a child who is never disciplined by its father? (Hebrews 12:7 NLT)

PERSONAL APPLICATION

Describe when the Father God disciplined you for disobedience. How did this result in learning to live in ways that please Him?

The Father's purpose is to help His children learn to behave in ways that please Him. In the next verse, we see that the *right living* believers develop results in peace in their hearts.

> No discipline is enjoyable while it is happening—it's painful! But afterward there will be a peaceful harvest of right living for those who are trained in this way. (Hebrews 12:11 NLT)

In the following verse, you see that *God's discipline is always good for us*. To *share in His holiness* refers to the spiritual maturity that results from our learning to obey Him.

> But God's discipline is always good for us, so that we might share in His holiness. (Hebrews 12:10 NLT)

WHAT DO YOU THINK? (ADVANCED)

Some people had parents who didn't discipline them with loving hearts. So why might it be more difficult for them to accept the truth that the Father God's discipline comes out of His heart of love for them?

There is no fear of punishment when the Father corrects His children. This is because they know He always does it out of His eternal, unconditional love.

> So we have come to know and to believe the love that God has for us. God is love, and whoever abides in love abides in God, and God abides in him. By this is love perfected with us, so that we may have confidence for the day of judgment, because as he is so also are we in this world. There is no fear in love, but perfect love casts out fear. For fear has to do with punishment, and whoever fears has not been perfected in love. (1 John 4:16-18 ESV))

PERSONAL APPLICATION

Why are you willing to allow the Father to correct and train you for your earthly and eternal benefit? Why should you ask the Holy Spirit to help you change your heart and behavior first, so you don't have to undergo the Father's discipline?

Our puppy's story. Our puppy, Ellie, was nine weeks old when we got her. She had previously lived in a kennel. Therefore, it wasn't long before we caught her squatting to go pee on our carpet. This wasn't acceptable behavior, so we scolded her and put her outside. She had not previously been trained to know that this was unacceptable. But she wanted to please us, so she quickly learned to go to the back door when she needed to go potty.

Sometimes, like Ellie, believers also don't know what's right and wrong in the Father God's eyes. This is why they should ask the Holy Spirit to help them learn and do what is right. Then, when this happens, the Father does not need to discipline them.

Spiritual growth takes effort and time. It's a slow, lifelong process of being transformed to be more like Jesus Christ. But in the end, faithful believers will hear the Father God say to them, "Well done, and good and faithful servant" (Matthew 25:21).

19

When Love Stops Growing, It Starts Dying

Spiritual Growth Produces Fruit

I come from a farming background. My grandparents on my mother's side had a small farm. Besides occasionally raising sheep or hogs, they mainly relied on fruit trees for their livelihood – apricot and olive, as well as some almond trees. I witnessed firsthand how fruit grows over time. You can't rush the slow growth of fruit. These trees needed to be nourished to develop healthy fruit. This is also true of the spiritual fruit in a Christian's life. Like the fruit from our trees, spiritual fruit is the product of healthy spiritual growth.

A believer who is growing spiritually will increasingly exhibit the following characteristics of the Holy Spirit, referred to as "the fruit of the Spirit," or spiritual fruit.

> But the fruit of the Spirit is love, joy, peace, patience, kindness, goodness, faithfulness, gentleness, self-control. (Galatians 5:22-23 ESV)

PERSONAL APPLICATION
Why will you develop more spiritual fruit as you know God better? Which of the nine fruits of the Spirit above do you see growing in your life?

This spiritual fruit comes from the new nature controlled by the Holy Spirit. That's why it's the fruit of the Spirit. It's visible in the various ways a believer lives.

> Then the way you live will always honor and please the Lord, and *your lives will produce every kind of good fruit*. All the while, you will grow as you learn to know God better and better. (Colossians 1:10 NLT, author's emphasis)

The following describes practical ways spiritual fruit is produced from spiritual growth:

- The old nature has to go, and the new nature has to develop. Believers have a lot to unlearn. The old habits of thinking, speaking, and behaving are contrary to the character of Jesus Christ.

- There is no spiritual growth and fruit without change, and change can be scary. Letting go of familiar, comfortable old habits takes determination and the help of the Holy Spirit.

- New habits that demonstrate Christ-like character take time to develop. These new habits are rooted in the transformed new nature. This is just like the fruit trees on my grandfather's farm that needed to establish deep, strong roots before they were able to produce lasting good fruit.

Love Is a Fruit of the Spirit, but Can It Die?

Before Linda and I were allowed to be married in our church, we were required to participate in a pre-marriage course led by a church pastor. It was practical, covering topics that might later lead to a problematic marriage. It included such topics as financial management, getting along with in-laws, preferred leisure time activities, and so on. The pastor made a statement I had never heard before, **"When love stops growing, it starts dying."** Since then, I have thought about this many times. I see its applicability to all relationships, including a relationship with God. When love for your spouse or God stops growing, it inevitably starts dying. Love never stands still. It never remains the same.

WHAT DO YOU THINK?
Why must the love of God constantly grow (or it will die) in the hearts of believers just as it must for spouses?

The following verses say that God's love in a believer's heart is the greatest fruit of their spiritual life:

> Above all, clothe yourselves with love, which binds us all together in perfect harmony. (Colossians 3:14 NLT)

> Three things will last forever—faith, hope, and love—and the greatest of these is love. (1 Corinthians 13:13 NLT)

PERSONAL APPLICATION

Do you love God? If so, what are you doing to nourish that love to help you love Him more and continually mature as a follower of Jesus Christ?

How do believers neglect the Holy Spirit? The following verse says that believers can *quench* the activity of the Holy Spirit by neglecting to live by His presence, influences, and power. This quenching causes the Spirit's fruit, including love, to diminish and start dying in born-again followers of Christ.

> Do not quench the Spirit. (1 Thessalonians 5:19 NASB)

The Greek word translated *quench* refers to extinguishing something, as one would pour water on a fire to put it out. It can also mean neglecting to supply the fire with the fuel needed. In other words, neglecting to live a disciplined life controlled by the Spirit will quench His activity within the believer.

WHAT DO YOU THINK?

If the Spirit is constantly quenched, why would the fruit of the Spirit (Galatians 5:22-23) within the believer wither and possibly die?

The following verse about grieving the Holy Spirit has the same effect on His ability to impart spiritual life and manifest His spiritual fruit in believers who neglect Him:

> Do not grieve the Holy Spirit of God, by whom you were sealed for the day of redemption. (Ephesians 4:30 NASB)

The Greek word for *grieve* can mean to sadden or make sorrowful. So quenching and grieving the Holy Spirit can result in Him withdrawing His influences and working within believers. Their spiritual life and love for God wither as they strive to live by their self-centered old nature. Their new nature is thwarted and becomes less expressive as they slip further into their old ways of thinking and behaving. As a result, their lives may have little eternal value to God (1 Corinthians 3:11-15).

Grieving and quenching the Holy Spirit is not the same as not having Him in a person's heart. You will learn about baby Christians in the next chapter. Some have not allowed the Holy Spirit to teach, guide, and empower them to live a life pleasing to the Father but are still saved. I think this implies that some born-again believers can quench and grieve the Holy Spirit and not lose their salvation. Only God knows what's in a person's heart.

Can a Christian Lose Their Salvation?

This question has been asked many times by faithful followers of Jesus Christ. When it arises in a group of believers, there are usually strong opinions to support both yes and no answers. This section aims to help you understand the dynamics that may revolve around an answer to this.

God's word in the human heart. Remember the parable in Matthew 13:18-23 where Jesus uses a person's heart as the place where God's word should be received and believed. The following two hearts, I think, represent people who appeared to be Christians but turned away from Him when their faith was tested. Their turning away indicates they never committed their hearts and lives to Jesus as their Savior and Lord. Therefore, they were never born-again followers of Jesus. People can't lose what they never had.

Type Two (Shallow hearts): People whose hearts are shallow toward God. They have outward indications of being a Christian but have little true belief and faith in Him. So, they quickly fall away from their weak faith in Christ when problems and difficulties occur in their lives.

> The seed on the rocky soil represents those who hear the message and immediately receive it with joy. But since they don't have deep roots, they don't last long. They fall away as soon as they have problems or are persecuted for believing God's word. (Matthew 13:20-21 NLT)

Type Three (Worldly hearts): People whose hearts are congested by their focus on living a worldly life. Their thoughts, ambitions, and personal plans leave little room in their hearts and lives for Jesus. These also fall away quickly because they put success and acquiring wealth above an eternal relationship with Jesus Christ.

> The seed that fell among the thorns represents those who hear God's word, but all too quickly the message is crowded out by the worries

of this life and the lure of wealth, so no fruit is produced. (Matthew 13:22 NLT)

They experience God but still turn away. These people regularly attend church and are likely involved in church activities. They experience the presence and power of the Holy Spirit. They seem to have repented of their sins and been saved. Yet, they ultimately still turn away and reject Jesus as their Savior and Lord. The following verses are a chilling indictment of the consequences of this outright rejection of truth:

> For it is impossible to bring back to repentance those who were once enlightened—those who have experienced the good things of heaven and shared in the Holy Spirit, who have tasted the goodness of the word of God and the power of the age to come—and who then turn away from God. It is impossible to bring such people back to repentance; by rejecting the Son of God, they themselves are nailing Him to the cross once again and holding Him up to public shame. . . . Dear friends, even though we are talking this way, we really don't believe it applies to you. We are confident that you are meant for better things, things that come with salvation. (Hebrews 6:4-9 NLT)

There are different opinions about the proper interpretation of these verses. Some firmly believe they represent born-again believers who lost their salvation. Others (as I do) believe verse nine indicates these people were never born-again followers of Jesus Christ.

WHAT DO YOU THINK? (ADVANCED)
It seems to me the writer of the book of Hebrews says in verse nine that he doesn't believe true followers of Jesus will reject and turn away from Him. So why do you agree or disagree that they could lose their salvation?

We each need to study the scriptures and ask the Holy Spirit to help us understand His answer to the question, "Can a born-again Christian lose their salvation?" When I consider the above scriptures, my conclusion is that there are people in most churches who say they are a Christian but don't demonstrate this reality in their lives. Their hearts don't seem to be transformed. When difficulties arrive (as they will), they walk away from Jesus. Their appearance of being born-again followers of His is absent. I don't believe these people were saved. Again, I would say, how can they lose what they never had?

Well, you might ask, what about other people who are undoubtedly born-again followers of Jesus? Can they lose their salvation? Will the Holy Spirit unseal and leave a born-again believer He has sealed as a guarantee of eternal life with God (2 Corinthians 1:21-22; Ephesians 4:30)? Remember that in the chapter "God Communicates in Incredible Ways," during that difficulty when I couldn't sense the Holy Spirit in me, He said to me, "I am here. I am always with you." At His Great Commission's conclusion, Jesus said, *I am with you always, to the end of the age* (Matthew 28:20 NET).

So, I don't believe a born-again follower of Jesus Christ will lose their salvation. Their love for God will continue to grow and produce spiritual fruit as they discipline themselves to keep Him of utmost importance. The chapter "Knowing God through Christian Practices" provides more information about these essential disciplines. Life is full of difficulties, so ask the Holy Spirit to use these times to help you trust the Father and rely on the Spirit to enable you to persevere in your faith, hope, and love.

20

Allow the Holy Spirit to Control You

Do Thoughts Affect Spiritual Growth?

What do your thoughts have to do with maturing as a Christian? Do you have a habit of thinking in the wrong ways? Perhaps you hide these thoughts in a secret place in your heart and never speak about them to others or even God. But, of course, He knows everything, as you see in the following verses:

> Nothing is hidden that will not be revealed, and nothing is secret that will not be made known. (Luke 12:2 NET)

> Nothing in all creation is hidden from God. Everything is naked and exposed before His eyes, and He is the One to whom we are accountable. (Hebrews 4:13 NLT)

The following verse says people are not slaves to their thoughts and desires:

> Those who are dominated by the sinful nature think about sinful things, but those who are controlled by the Holy Spirit think about things that please the Spirit. (Romans 8:5 NLT)

WHAT DO YOU THINK?
What things can a believer think about that please the Spirit of God within them?

Let the Holy Spirit Control Your Mind

The following verse says to let the Holy Spirit change the way you think and behave by transforming your mind:

> And do not be conformed to this world, but be transformed by the renewing of your mind. (Romans 12:2 NASB)

Changing the way you think is not easy. It's a daily effort that requires the help of the Holy Spirit to persevere.

You must stop living out of your old self-centered nature and start living out of your Christ-centered new nature.

> That, in reference to your former manner of life, you lay aside the old self, which is being corrupted in accordance with the lusts of deceit, and that you be renewed in the spirit of your mind, and put on the new self, which in the likeness of God has been created in righteousness and holiness of the truth. (Ephesians 4:22-24 NASB)

If you are a born-again follower of Jesus Christ, you have the Holy Spirit living in you. He is there to teach and help you throughout your life. Ask Him to help with your old nature's unwanted thoughts and desires. Repent, if needed, and work with the Holy Spirit to be transformed by His love and power.

But what if you want to keep some of these thoughts and desires? Even though God says they are sinful, what if they are still precious to you? They are yours to enjoy, correct?

WHAT DO YOU THINK?
Why don't believers have a right to think anything they like?

Perhaps the following verses will help believers understand that they gave up their right to be in charge of their lives when they committed themselves to Jesus as Savior and Lord.

> Or do you not know that your body is a temple of the Holy Spirit within you, whom you have from God? You are not your own, for you were bought with a price. So glorify God in your body. (1 Corinthians 6:19-20 ESV))

Jesus did not die and rise from the dead so people could pick and choose what they believe and how they behave. Instead, as the following story indicates, He did so because He wanted their entire heart and life.

Jesus, My Heart Is Yours (except for this)

Robert Boyd Munger wrote a booklet titled My Heart - Christ's Home in 1954, updated in 1986. The premise is that when you commit your life to Jesus Christ, **you are inviting Him to live in all your heart, not just parts of it.**

> Then Christ will make His home in your hearts as you trust in Him. (Ephesians 3:17 NLT)

> Look! I stand at the door and knock. If you hear My voice and open the door, I will come in, and we will share a meal together as friends. (Revelation 3:20 NLT)

In his fictional story, Robert Munger uses the analogy of a home and its rooms to represent various places in a believer's heart. He tells Jesus that he wants Him to feel at home, living comfortably everywhere in his heart. Then, he shows Jesus around the rooms of his heart, describing what he and Jesus can do together in each room. He is comfortable being with Jesus in these rooms. He has nothing to hide, nothing about which to worry.

But the door to one tiny room is closed and locked. In his story, Robert has hidden some things there about which he is ashamed. They are thoughts and desires from his past he doesn't want to give up. (Of course, these are from his self-centered old nature.)

PERSONAL APPLICATION

Are there aspects of your old ways of life you want to continue to enjoy, even though you know they are wrong? Why do you erroneously think they can be part of your new life as a born-again Christian living under the Lordship of Jesus Christ?

Robert Munger says that when you love Jesus and want Him to be in charge of your life as your Lord, you must relinquish everything that hinders this life-long commitment. This includes the passing pleasures of life (Hebrews 11:25).

When some thoughts and desires of the old nature are too difficult to let go of on your own, Jesus wants you to ask Him for help. The following verse says that He wants to set you free to enjoy the abundant life you can have with Him fully:

> I have come so that they may have life, and may have it abundantly. (John 10:10 NET)

Baby Christians and Spiritual Maturity

Baby Christians have not matured as followers of Jesus Christ. We find two types identified in the Bible.

Type One (New Christians)

These are people who recently committed their lives to Jesus Christ. They are born-again and are just starting their journey as maturing followers of His.

> Like newborn babies, you must crave pure spiritual milk so that you will grow into a full experience of salvation. Cry out for this nourishment, now that you have had a taste of the Lord's kindness. (1 Peter 2:2-3 NLT)

I was a new Christian and hungry for God's living word. After I committed my life to Jesus Christ, I found I had an unquenchable thirst to know God and the Bible. I was disabled, so I had time to spend six or more hours a day immersed in the Bible for two years. I slowly studied as I read through the entire Bible several times. I wrote cross-references to scriptures of the same topic, for instance, salvation and faith. My breadth and depth of knowledge increased better than if I had just read the Bible. I wanted to know the truth, and I wanted to know the God of truth.

Perhaps you are a new believer in Jesus Christ and wonder what you should be doing to know Him better and live the life He desires. Please read the chapter "Knowing God through Christian Practices" to learn more about essential disciplines for spiritual growth.

Type Two (Perpetual baby Christians)

These are people who were born-again sometime in the past. However, they have stopped, or perhaps never started, disciplining themselves to live a life worthy of their eternal relationship with God. They hold onto the old ways of life perhaps without realizing that they likely include sins and rebellion against God. They may keep the door to a secret closet of their heart closed and locked as you just read. They don't want Jesus or people to know the hidden sins they wish to continue to enjoy.

We pleaded with you, encouraged you, and urged you to live your lives in a way that God would consider worthy. For He called you to share in His Kingdom and glory. (1 Thessalonians 2:12 NLT)

The following verses describe perpetual baby Christians:

There is much more we would like to say about this, but it is difficult to explain, especially since you are spiritually dull and don't seem to listen. You have been believers so long now that you ought to be teaching others. Instead, you need someone to teach you again the basic things about God's word. You are like babies who need milk and cannot eat solid food. For someone who lives on milk is still an infant and doesn't know how to do what is right. (Hebrews 5:11-13 NLT)

Dear brothers and sisters, when I was with you I couldn't talk to you as I would to spiritual people. I had to talk as though you belonged to this world or as though you were infants in the Christian life. I had to feed you with milk, not with solid food, because you weren't ready for anything stronger. And you still aren't ready, for you are still controlled by your sinful nature. (1 Corinthians 3:1-3 NLT)

One way to recognize perpetual baby Christians is by their behavior. In the above verses, the Apostle Paul says they behave like non-Christians.

WHAT DO YOU THINK?
Are they still trying to fit in with the lifestyles of their non-believing friends? Are their values the same as those of their culture, instead of the Bible? What do they do with their life, time, and money? Do they spend these mostly on themselves?

When you see these perpetual baby Christians in the church, you may notice they are often not paying attention. They are there but not really interested. Perhaps they grew up in church but became bored with it. Maybe they've never experienced solid teachings from the Bible in worship service, Sunday School, or Bible studies. Whatever their reasons, they are not engaged in learning and maturing. Being a mature follower of Jesus Christ is just not important to them.

They asked, "Why do we have to study the Bible?" This couple attended an adult Sunday School class I was teaching. They had attended this church and class for many years. However, they only engaged in the class discussion if I asked them a direct question. Their answers were often not well thought out. Their interest in coming seemed to be more for social opportunities. They occasionally attended a weekly Bible study group. On one occasion, this couple asked something like the following, "Why do we have to study the Bible?" They seemed to value fellowship with their long-time friends more than the spiritual growth offered by God's living word.

According to the following scripture, some perpetual baby Christians may be saved, but their life has little eternal value to God. Oh, they will be in Heaven, but they will miss out on some wonderful eternal rewards that could have been theirs.

> For no man can lay a foundation other than the one which is laid, which is Jesus Christ. Now if any man builds on the foundation with gold, silver, precious stones, wood, hay, straw, each man's work will become evident; for the day will show it because it is to be revealed with fire, and the fire itself will test the quality of each man's work. If any man's work which he has built on it remains, he will receive a reward. If any man's work is burned up, he will suffer loss; but he himself will be saved, yet so as through fire. (1 Corinthians 3:11-15 NASB)

Only God knows a person's heart. I earnestly desire to see perpetual baby Christians experience the God of the Bible in ways they can't imagine. Jesus came to earth, lived, suffered, died, and rose again for their salvation and eternal life with Him. He wants them to experience a lifetime of joy and peace of heart that occurs only by living for Him. God is the only one who knows the eternal value of a person's heart and life.

What about your heart and life? Are you a follower of Jesus who earnestly seeks to know God and live your life with Him? Are you actively maturing as a Christian, or are you a perpetual baby Christian?

PERSONAL APPLICATION

Where are your heart and mind focused during the day? What do you spend your time thinking about? Do you have attitudes or habits you don't want the Lord Jesus to be in charge of? If so, why are the temporary pleasures of life worth the eternal ramifications of disobedience to God?

The Holy Spirit can help you put these old ways to death so you can live by your new nature in Christ. But you must be willing to allow Him to do so.

21

Life Is Wasted without God's Love

When you consider how to treat people, what phrase comes to your mind? Perhaps, "Treat others as you wish to be treated." Or "Treat others as they have treated you." Jesus answered this basic question about human relations when He was asked what the most important commandment was.

> "Teacher, which is the great commandment in the Law?" And he said to him, "You shall love the Lord your God with all your heart and with all your soul and with all your mind. This is the great and first commandment. And a second is like it: You shall love your neighbor as yourself." (Matthew 22:36-39 ESV)

So then, loving God with all your being also means sincerely and deeply loving people. This is God's unconditional, sacrificial love (*agape*) given by the Holy Spirit at spiritual birth.

WHAT DO YOU THINK?
Why can't non-believers have this kind of love for God and people?

Jesus says people demonstrate love for Him by doing what He says. Therefore, living in ways that reflect obedience to Jesus demonstrates they are maturing as His followers.

> Those who accept My commandments and obey them are the ones who love Me. And because they love Me, My Father will love them.

And I will love them and reveal Myself to each of them. (John 14:21 NLT)

The Apostle Paul says a life without love for others has no eternal value to God. It is a wasted life.

> If I speak in the tongues of men and of angels, but have not love, I am a noisy gong or a clanging cymbal. And if I have prophetic powers, and understand all mysteries and all knowledge, and if I have all faith, so as to remove mountains, but have not love, I am nothing. If I give away all I have, and if I deliver up my body to be burned, but have not love, I gain nothing. (1 Corinthians 13:1-3 ESV)

"You Must Be a Heathen!"

As you saw in the chapter "The Battle for Spiritual Maturity," God's love is one of the fruits of the Holy Spirit's work in maturing believers. Christians exhibit their spiritual maturity through their behavior. For example, do they demonstrate Jesus Christ's love in the ways they treat people? Maturing believers are careful to behave in a manner that pleases God.

> Therefore be imitators of God, as beloved children. And walk in love, as Christ loved us and gave himself up for us, a fragrant offering and sacrifice to God. (Ephesians 5:1-2 ESV)

The following story demonstrates a lack of Christ's love and spiritual maturity by the offending couple.

> **The restaurant.** A good friend and his wife were at a restaurant after church on Sunday. They were sitting diagonally across from another couple. A waitress approached the other couple and asked to take their order.
>
> The conversation went something like the following:
>
> The man said to the waitress, "You must be a heathen!" His wife was smiling in approval as he said this.
>
> His accusation hurt the waitress, so she asked the man why he said this.
>
> He replied, "You are working on the Sabbath!"

After the couple left, my friend asked the waitress about the conversation. She said she didn't know why he would say something like that. She was a Christian and went to church regularly. She took her child to Sunday School every Sunday. This young woman was offended and hurt by the accusation!

Spiritual maturity grows as the Holy Spirit gradually transforms believers into the character of Jesus Christ. Since Jesus is God, His intrinsic nature is love. Therefore, spiritually mature Christians will have Christ's love in their hearts as part of their new nature.

WHAT DO YOU THINK?

Why did the couple's prideful and demeaning comments show their lack of Christ's love and spiritual maturity?

Biblical Errors and Hypocrisy

Following are several biblical errors I believe this couple made in their attitude toward the waitress. All of these indicate a lack of Christ's unconditional, sacrificial love for people as well as their lack of spiritual maturity.

Error #1 – Ignorance of the Bible

Let's start by providing a biblical fact – The Sabbath is Saturday (7th day of the week), not Sunday (1st day of the week).

> So God blessed the seventh day and made it holy, because on it God rested from all his work that he had done in creation. (Genesis 2:3 ESV)

> Keeping the Sabbath on Saturday is one of six hundred and thirteen Old Testament commandments required of the nation of Israel. The death and resurrection of Jesus removed this requirement for all people, including Israel and Christians (Romans 6:14-15; Ephesians 2:8-9).

However, there is a spiritual principle that people should rest one day a week from work activities. The Apostle Paul says people may freely choose the best day for rest.

> In the same way, some think one day is more holy than another day, while others think every day is alike. You should each be fully convinced that whichever day you choose is acceptable. (Romans 14:5 NLT)

Error #2 – Lack of Christ's love

The following verses describe characteristics of Christ's love for people. How many of these did this couple fail to demonstrate? For example, were they kind, or instead proud and rude?

> Love is patient and kind; love does not envy or boast; it is not arrogant or rude. It does not insist on its own way; it is not irritable or resentful; it does not rejoice at wrongdoing, but rejoices with the truth. Love bears all things, believes all things, hopes all things, endures all things. (1 Corinthians 13:4-7 ESV)

Error #3 – Judgmental Attitude

Judgmentalism can mean being overly critical of others, typically with a condemning attitude. God makes it clear we are not to judge other people.

> Judge not, that you be not judged. For with the judgment you pronounce you will be judged, and with the measure you use it will be measured to you. (Matthew 7:1-2 ESV)

Error #4 – Hypocrisy

They were eating lunch at a restaurant on Sunday. Who did they think would cook the food and wait on them? They violated their own religious code of moral conduct by requiring others to serve them on Sunday.

Only God knows the true heart of a person. Jesus is the judge, so He will hold everyone accountable for their behavior.

PERSONAL APPLICATION

Suppose you had been there and overheard this couple demeaning the waitress. Would their behavior cause you to be inclined to become a Christian if you weren't one already? Would you have been embarrassed for the waitress if you were a Christian?

I would have. This couple didn't behave like disciples of Jesus Christ and children of God.

The Cult Group: They Chose Poison Over Love

Living and maturing as a follower of Jesus Christ can include unforeseen events. For example, you may encounter resistance and even danger from your spiritual enemy (the devil and his demons), especially when entering their territory. Love is not part of the fallen, corrupted nature of the devil and his demons. Instead, they are consumed with hate for God and His people. Therefore, they will always try to use people to express this hatred. The following story is an example of this.

We were on "their beach." My mother and I lived in Hawaii for several years. She had a health breakdown just before I did. Our doctors said the fresh salt air would help us recover. We lived in several places on or near a beach while there during that time. Near the end of our stay, we moved at night into a caretaker's cottage near the beach in the back of a large mansion. The following morning, I saw about a dozen young women dancing on the beach in the early sunlight in thin see-through dresses. An older man and his wife shortly came down to the beach to introduce themselves. After a brief conversation, his wife told me her husband had been a successful surgeon. However, he retired because he didn't like having his hands in blood all the time. As a result, they moved to Hawaii and became vegetarians. They told me about their religious beliefs. So I told them about Jesus Christ's love and eternal life. But they angrily left the beach. I had confronted not only them but also the deceiving spirits (demons) who were misleading them.

WHAT DO YOU THINK? (ADVANCED)

Why do the devil, his demons, and even people they deceive hate the truth about Jesus Christ? Why do they also hate those who tell the truth about salvation and God's love?

The following scriptures describe the devil and his demons as liars and deceivers:

> This great dragon—the ancient serpent called the devil, or Satan, the one deceiving the whole world—was thrown down to the earth with all his angels. (Revelation 12:9 NLT)

> For you are the children of your father the devil, and you love to do the evil things he does. He was a murderer from the beginning. He has always hated the truth, because there is no truth in him. When he lies, it is consistent with his character; for he is a liar and the father of lies. So when I *[Jesus]* tell the truth, you just naturally don't believe Me! (John 8:44-45 NLT, author's emphasis)

Later I discovered many people were living with this couple in the large mansion. The owner of the property told me he was renting only to the couple. When he confronted the couple, they denied it, saying the others were just friends who visited occasionally. This was not true. These other people clearly lived there.

The Poisoning!

Long story short, they didn't like Christians living on "their beach." I didn't realize at first that the neighbors by our cottage were part of this cult group. We had been purchasing organic fruits and goat milk from them. One afternoon I came back from errands and was hot and tired. I quickly drank eight or ten ounces of cold goat milk we recently purchased from them. Almost immediately, I began to feel like I was going to pass out. I knew what to do and began to feel better in a few hours. It seemed evident our neighbors had poisoned the goat milk.

Several days later, when I felt better, I went to the Honolulu Police Department and met with a detective to tell him what happened. My story sounded absurd, so he didn't believe me. However, after I made a pest of myself over several visits, he agreed to have the goat milk tested for poison. About two weeks later, he came to our cottage to say they found Diazinon in the goat milk. Diazinon is a poison commonly used in the 1970s and 1980s for pest control. Unfortunately, the test could only detect its presence, not the concentration in the milk. When he interviewed our neighbor, he said it was apparent she had prepared her cover story. When he questioned her about the poison in the goat milk, she said they use Diazinon for insect control around the farm where they raised the goats. Therefore, it was impossible to prove she had intentionally poisoned me, though both the detective and I knew she had done so.

I reported this incident to the owner of the property. It turned out he was already planning to evict the doctor and his wife. Other neighbors had complained about seeing many people, especially young girls coming and going from the house. He came to believe it was a cult group living there.

The detective was a strong Christian and had become a friend. He would stop by to visit, and I went to church with him on several occasions. When I told him about the eviction, he encouraged us to move to the other side of the island where the cult group couldn't find us. He was concerned about reprisals since they would certainly blame us for being evicted. He provided a police escort as we moved out of the area.

WHAT DO YOU THINK?
Why can situations of rejection and even hate by others be opportunities to trust God and mature in the Christian faith?

The following verses say that anyone who doesn't love (with God's agape love) doesn't know God. Therefore, if you are a follower of Jesus, make every effort to demonstrate Christ's unconditional, sacrificial love to others.

> Beloved, let us love one another, for love is from God, and whoever loves has been born of God and knows God. Anyone who does not love does not know God, because God is love. (1 John 4:7-8 ESV)

> God instructs His children, *Let all that you do be done in love* (1 Corinthians 16:14 ESV).

PART C

DEVELOP NEW HABITS TO KNOW GOD

22

Knowing God through the Bible

The Bible is just another book about religion written by people – correct? By now, you know the answer is a resounding NO! It's the living word of God written by the Holy Spirit to change people's hearts and lives. People begin to know God as they read and study His word.

"It's Just a Book, Harvey!"

Many years before I committed my life to Jesus Christ, I had frequent discussions with Harvey about the Bible. He was a coworker who read the Bible every opportunity he had at breaks and lunch. I was a college student and thought I knew much more about life than this older Christian man. I asked him why he only read the Bible at work. He told me it was because the Bible was God's word. On one occasion, when he was reading it, I told him it was just a book like any other with words in black ink on white paper. I could take him to the university library and show him thousands of books just like it. I didn't believe the Bible was anything more than this. Of course, I had no idea people could discover God by reading and studying it.

> For the word of God is living and active, sharper than any two-edged sword, piercing to the division of soul and of spirit, of joints and of marrow, and discerning the thoughts and intentions of the heart. (Hebrews 4:12 ESV)

Now I know the Bible is so much more than ink on paper. It is indeed the living word of God because it is the living God's word.

WHAT DO YOU THINK?

What makes the Bible living and not just another book of black ink on white paper?

Most Read Book in the World.

Jennifer Polland wrote an article in the Business Insider Australia edition on December 28, 2012. She said writer James Chapman created a list of the most read and sold books in the world over the last fifty years. The Bible far outsold all other books.

WHAT DO YOU THINK?

Why do you think so many people have purchased the Bible over the last fifty years? If it is just black ink on white paper, do you think it would be the world's best-selling book (ever)?

The Holy Spirit Wrote the Bible for You

God, the Holy Spirit, wrote the entire Bible through the people He chose for this task. Every scripture in the Bible is the inspired word of God that you can learn and benefit from.

> All Scripture is breathed out by God and profitable for teaching, for reproof, for correction, and for training in righteousness, that the man of God may be complete, equipped for every good work. (2 Timothy 3:16-17 ESV)

As a result, the Bible is divinely inspired. It doesn't come from the intelligence or imagination of people. This inspiration includes verses some people choose not to believe. They think certain verses of the Bible are no longer applicable in this modern world. They say people today are far more sophisticated than those who lived several thousand years ago when the Bible was written. However, since all scripture came from God, it's all still relevant today for all people.

Where to start in the Bible. If you are new to the Bible, I strongly encourage you to start your learning about God with the books of the New Testament. In particular, I suggest starting with the four gospel books about the life of Jesus Christ on earth at His first coming (Matthew, Mark, Luke, and John). Then the book of the Acts of the Apostles. The books of Romans, Hebrews, and Revelation can be difficult to understand. I suggest delaying these until you feel you know Jesus and the life of a Christian from the other New Testament books (Corinthians, Galatians through Jude).

You may want to spend several years using the following learning methods before launching into the Old Testament. Once you have developed a personal relationship with each person of the Trinity, start learning the Old Testament with the books of Genesis, Exodus, Psalms, and Proverbs. Then, add the other books as you learn more about God and His people Israel. View God as He interacts with Israel from your New Testament perspective. This is especially true of Him as Almighty God (*El Shaddai*), who you also know as *Abba*, your heavenly Father. Look also for Jesus as the Savior and Lord and the Holy Spirit as the Helper, Teacher, and Guide. Identify the work of the Holy Spirit in the lives of Israel. Without Him, there would be no Old Testament books.

INFORMATION: The Old Testament books of the Bible were primarily written in what is now an ancient Hebrew language. The New Testament books were written in what is now an ancient Greek language. A few words in the Old and New Testaments were written in other languages, such as Aramaic. Unfortunately, there are no surviving original manuscripts of the Bible today. Still, we do have ancient copies of these original manuscripts.

Biblical scholars and translators have done significant research and analysis of these copies over hundreds of years. They have compared existing copies of a particular book of the Bible for similarities and differences. The translations into English and other languages are based on this extensive research. As a result, you can be confident the Bible is God's word as He wants it to be known to you today.

How to know God through the Bible. Following are some of the ways you can learn to know God through the Bible:

- Reading scripture
- Studying scripture
- Meditating upon scripture
- Praying scripture
- Applying scripture

"It's not fair that we have to think on a test!" I taught college for several years. This class had one hundred forty-four students, many of whom didn't seem interested in learning. The size of the class forced me to give the midterm exam with multiple-choice, true/false, and fill-in-the-blank questions. And there were a lot of these. Each question was written to evaluate their learning. After the midterm exam, three students disagreed with the answer to a particular multiple-choice question. I told them that to determine the correct answer, they needed to carefully think about what the question was asking and then carefully think about the alternative answers. One of them responded with anger and said, "It's not fair that we have to think on a test!" WOW! It's not fair to ask students to learn by thinking!

WHAT DO YOU THINK?

Why is thinking about God necessary to learn about Him and know Him?

Reading Scripture

Reading portions of the Bible is something you can do daily. In scripture, you find hope, encouragement, faith to persevere, promises, prophecies, and so much more.

> Such things were written in the Scriptures long ago to teach us. And the Scriptures give us hope and encouragement as we wait patiently for God's promises to be fulfilled. (Romans 15:4 NLT)

Since the Bible is not merely human words, reading it can help you grow spiritually as a follower of Jesus.

> Therefore, we never stop thanking God that when you received His message from us, you didn't think of our words as mere human ideas. You accepted what we said as the very word of God—which, of course, it is. And this word continues to work in you who believe. (1 Thessalonians 2:13 NLT)

Read the Bible five minutes a day. My mother and sister committed their lives to Jesus before I did. My mother would periodically ask me to start reading the Bible for five minutes a day. I agreed to this only because I wanted her to stop asking me about it. However, I was working long and stressful hours and wasn't getting enough rest. I tried but would fall asleep before the five minutes ended. Eventually, though, I began to be able to read longer and found I was indeed learning about God and the Christian life. Later, what I had learned was important in my decision to commit my life to Jesus Christ.

I encourage you to read the Bible daily. God's word is alive and active, so the Holy Spirit can use it in your life.

PERSONAL APPLICATION
What are some circumstances under which reading the Bible is best for you? How could a daily Bible reading plan help you discipline yourself to do this?

Memorization and the Bible. Memorization is something we all need to do throughout life. However, it does not engage the brain in a way that promotes understanding. Understanding is what learning is about, not just memorization of facts. I hope you memorize but also spend time reading about God and the life He has for you as a follower of Jesus.

Studying Scripture

Studying the Bible is different from reading it. It's a slower process because you spend more time and effort understanding what the Holy Spirit is saying in the verses. This enables you to focus more on the nature and actions of God in the scripture.

> I will study Your commandments and reflect on Your ways. I will delight in Your decrees and not forget Your word . . . . Open my eyes to see the wonderful truths in Your instructions. (Psalms 119:15-18 NLT)

> Help me understand the meaning of Your commandments, and I will meditate on Your wonderful deeds. (Psalms 119:27 NLT)

Inductive Bible study. This approach will help improve your understanding of scripture. It involves three techniques: Observation, Interpretation, and Application.

Observation

This is about determining the facts. As you read the scripture, ask yourself the five Ws and H questions. **Who** is it about? **What** is it about? **When** did it, or will it, occur? **Where** did it, or will it, happen? **Why** is it being said? And **How** will it happen?

Interpretation

Answers the question, "What do these verses mean?"

Application
Answers the question, "What do these verses mean to me personally?" Or "How can I apply the biblical facts or principles to my life?"

PERSONAL APPLICATION
What can you do differently in your life to allocate extended time to study the Bible?

Biblical precepts. These are biblical facts that don't vary by circumstance. They are specific, black and white, with no variation of interpretation. One everyday precept is: "Speed limit 45 MPH." The following verse is an example of a biblical precept:

> Therefore, having been justified by faith, we have peace with God through our Lord Jesus Christ. (Romans 5:1 NASB)

Spiritual principles. Many verses in the Bible provide a spiritual principle that can be applied to multiple situations in life. They provide a general guideline that can be applied to various situations. One principle is: "Proceed with caution." A spiritual principle will not violate the original scripture's nature, intent, or purpose. For example, the following is a verse about living by a spiritual principle:

> Peace and mercy to all who follow this rule. (Galatians 6:16 NIV)

WHAT DO YOU THINK? (ADVANCED)
How can understanding spiritual principles enable believers to develop a well-rounded view of God?

What is your goal in studying the Bible? Have you competed in a sport, such as baseball, golf, cricket, or soccer? When you compete in a sport, you have a goal. So likewise, it is helpful to have a goal, something you want to accomplish when studying the Bible. This gives you focus. As you have seen in this book, one important goal is to know God as He describes Himself in the Bible.

Search the scriptures to find the truth. Sometimes, you need to search the scriptures to better understand a Bible verse or topic. You want to learn as much as you can about the topic of that verse. If you don't do this, you may have limited and insufficient knowledge that prevents you from understanding and applying it correctly to your life.

Now the Berean Jews were of more noble character than those in Thessalonica, for they received the message with great eagerness and examined the Scriptures every day to see if what Paul said was true. As a result, many of them believed. (Acts 17:11-12 NIV)

There Are Mysteries in the Bible

There are some verses and topics in the Bible that are simply a mystery. A mystery in the Bible is something for which God has partially concealed the complete meaning or even hidden the entire meaning. In 1 Corinthians 2:7, the Apostle Paul writes the following, *No, the wisdom we speak of is the mystery of God—His plan that was previously hidden* (NLT). An example of a mystery in the Bible would be the nature of the Trinity of God discussed earlier in the book. It isn't possible to understand with our limited human minds how three separate persons of God can at the same time be one God. Therefore, your response to a biblical mystery requires faith in God as the one who knows all things (since He created everything).

Sometimes you may need to speculate and develop a conclusion. This can lead to further understanding but can also be incorrect. Recognizing and admitting this to others is important, so they don't misunderstand scripture. Statements that begin with "I think," "I believe," or "My understanding" will let others know this is your opinion based on your thoughtful study of the Bible. People can then choose to develop their own conclusion or accept yours as possibly correct.

Meditating on Scripture

The word for *meditate* in the following verse means pondering or conversing with oneself:

> I meditate on your precepts and consider your ways. (Psalm 119:15 NIV)

Meditating on a verse helps you remember and understand its meaning. As a result, you can more accurately apply it to your life.

> Finally, brethren, whatever is true, whatever is honorable, whatever is right, whatever is pure, whatever is lovely, whatever is of good repute, if there is any excellence and if anything worthy of praise, dwell on these things. (Philippians 4:8 NIV)

In the above verse, *dwell on* means to consider, take into account, weigh, or meditate on something. Meditating on scripture is another essential method for knowing God.

PERSONAL APPLICATION

How would you describe your thought process when you meditate on scripture? Why can the Holy Spirit help you develop a more profound knowledge of God through it?

NOTE: Christian meditation does not involve emptying the mind. On the contrary, it consists in filling the mind with the word of God. Its focus is on God and not on oneself or a meaningless chant (Matthew 6:7). Christians can't learn about and know God with an empty mind. Instead, their mind must be full of scripture about who He is and what He does.

Praying Scripture

Praying Bible verses means reading and speaking them back to God (out loud, if you prefer) with an attitude of humility. The purpose is to allow the passage's meaning to inspire your thoughts, so they become your conversation with God. Therefore, select verses that have significance to you. They can be verses praising God for who He is and what He has done or verses representing a need or concern. You can use any scripture to talk to God and learn to know Him in this way.

PRACTICE IT

You might want to practice this now by praying the following scripture back to God (for yourself or someone else).

> I do not cease to give thanks for you when I remember you in my prayers. I pray that the God of our Lord Jesus Christ, the glorious Father, will give you spiritual wisdom and revelation in your growing knowledge of him, – since the eyes of your heart have been enlightened – so that you can know what is the hope of his calling, what is the wealth of his glorious inheritance in the saints, and what is the incomparable greatness of his power toward us who believe, as displayed in the exercise of his immense strength. (Ephesians 1:16-19 NET)

Following are examples of more scriptures to pray back to God:

- Ephesians 3:14-19
- Philippians 1:9-11
- Colossians 1:9-14
- 1 Thessalonians 3:11-13
- Hebrews 13:20-21
- Revelation 4:8, 11; 5:9-10, 12-14

In addition to praying specific Bible verses, there are many prayers in the Bible that you can use as your own prayer to Him. You can find many of these in the Old Testament book of Psalms. One way to categorize these prayers follows. I have included two Bible passages with each of these as examples.

- Praise, worship, and honor God (Psalm 104:1-24; Psalm 145:1-7)
- Thanksgiving for all God has done (1 Chronicles 29:10-15; Psalm 28:6-7)
- Confession of sin with a humble heart toward God (Psalm 19:12; Psalm 119:169-176)
- Petitions for everyday needs (Hebrews 4:16; Matthew 6:33)
- Petitions for unusual and significant events (Psalm 104:24-30; Psalm 139:7-12)
- Request for guidance and direction in life (Psalm 25:1-5; Psalm 43:3-4)

The next chapter is about applying what you learn from scripture. If you don't use it for yourself and allow it to change you, what eternal value does it have for you?

23

Knowing God through the Bible: Applying Scripture

Remember that God's living word can change your heart, mind, and behavior if you let it.

> As I learn Your righteous regulations, I will thank You by living as I should! (Psalms 119:7 NLT)

> Give me understanding and I will obey Your instructions; I will put them into practice with all my heart. (Psalms 119:34 NLT)

Applying the meaning of scripture to your relationship with God can help you know Him better. You can see aspects of His intrinsic nature, majesty, and greatness you didn't know before.

The application of scripture is also an essential means of spiritual growth for Christians. The Holy Spirit can use it to transform the old nature into the new nature of Jesus Christ. Therefore, if you are not changing through the Holy Spirit, you are not growing spiritually.

> Do not conform to the pattern of this world, but be transformed by the renewing of your mind. (Romans 12:2 NIV)

> But don't just listen to God's word. You must do what it says. Otherwise, you are only fooling yourselves. (James 1:22 NLT)

> All Scripture is breathed out by God and profitable for teaching, for reproof, for correction, and for training in righteousness, that the man

of God may be complete, equipped for every good work. (2 Timothy 3:16-17 ESV)

PERSONAL APPLICATION

Why should you ask the Holy Spirit to help you apply scripture to change your thinking, priorities, behaviors, and lifestyle based on His word? What barriers prevent you from being willing for Him to do this?

Learning Is Easier with a Study Bible

There are many types of Bibles available. For example, some are better for reading, while others are better suited for studying. In addition, Bibles are available in printed and electronic formats.

Bible resource libraries. Before the advent of electronic Bibles and associated electronic study resources, everything was in printed format. Serious Bible students could have a physical library with multiple bookshelves of various printed Bibles and study aids. Today these resources are available in electronic form. A typical Bible resource library may include various Bible versions, concordances, Bible atlases (maps), commentaries, Bible dictionaries, handbooks of Bible times and customs, and ebooks by renowned Christians.

Printed study Bibles typically contain the following in addition to text:

- Introduction to each book of the Bible (May include date written, author, themes, key verses, and more).

- Notes within the text to explain the meaning or application of a verse.

- Cross-references to other verses in the Bible about the same topic.

- Back of the study Bible may contain the following:

  o Concordance (alphabetic list of words that include portions of applicable verse with the word).

  o Bible atlas (maps) of ancient and modern Israel and surrounding regions.

- Some translations indicate the words spoken by Jesus Christ in red font.

Electronic study Bibles can provide even more resources to enhance your Bible study.

WHAT DO YOU THINK? (ADVANCED)
What are some ways an electronic resource library can help you learn to apply scripture?

My Use of Electronic Resource Libraries

I use e-Sword on my computer and MySword on my Android tablet and cell phone for their electronic resource libraries for all my studies of the Bible, including writing this book. Nearly all the resources are free from these websites. However, I have paid a small subscription fee for a few I wanted to include in my collection. You will notice in this book that I use several different Bible versions. This is easy to do since I can compare the multiple versions of the same verse to see which one best renders the meaning for this book. I also review multiple Bible commentaries to determine which offers the most straightforward understanding of the verse. Bible dictionaries provide definitions of Greek and Hebrew words to help me accurately describe a word in a verse. These are invaluable, easy-to-use electronic resource libraries I downloaded years ago. I don't have to use the Internet to use them, which also saves steps. And I learn much more about the verse or topic because of my use of them. So, they are both productivity and learning tools.

Some electronic Bibles that include resource libraries with which I am familiar follow:

- For Windows computers: e-Sword, Bible Gateway, and Olive Tree. Following is the website address to download the free Windows e-Sword Bible resource library: https://www.e-sword.net

- For Apple iPads and iPhones: e-Sword HD and Olive Tree. Following is the website address to download the free iPad/iPhone e-Sword HD Bible resource library: https://www.e-sword.net/ipad/

- For Android smartphones and tablets: MySword, e-Sword, Bible Gateway, and Olive Tree. Following is the website address to download the free Andriod MySword Bible resource library: https://mysword-Bible.info/download-mysword/mysword

---

PRACTICE IT

Use the concordance in your printed or electronic Bible to practice finding one scripture for each of the following topics:

Faith

Hope

Love

Go to the scripture for each of these in your Bible, find a note of explanation or application, and write it down. Next, write down a verse that is cross-referenced for the scripture. It's easier than you think once you train yourself to do it. You will discover that you are learning, remembering, and applying much more of God's living word.

How about a Bible for both reading and studying? If you are considering a Bible for both reading and Bible study, I recommend the New Living Translation (NLT). It's written for people who want an easy-to-understand yet accurate translation of the Bible. It is appropriate for anyone, including new and maturing Believers.

PERSONAL APPLICATION

Why is now an excellent time to start knowing God better through the Bible? What do you need to decrease or stop to enable you to do this?

Nothing is more vital in life than knowing God as He describes Himself in the Bible. Your communications and life experiences with the Father, Jesus, and the Holy Spirit will be enriched beyond your imagination as you do this.

24

Knowing and Doing God's Will

God's will for us is to love Him and people. God's nature is love, so He wants His children to live a life of love. Jesus expressed this in the following verse when asked what the greatest Old Testament commandment was:

> "Teacher, which commandment in the law is the greatest?" Jesus said to him, "'Love the Lord your God with all your heart, with all your soul, and with all your mind.' This is the first and greatest commandment. The second is like it: 'Love your neighbor as yourself.'" (Matthew 22:36-39 NET)

As you seek to know God's will in your life, remember His will is always based on His love.

You Will Experience God's Reality More in Your Life

God will reveal His will to you because He wants you to know and do it. As you follow His will, you experience Him in ways you may not have thought possible. This is because the Holy Spirit was sent so you can experience Him as your Helper, Guide, and Teacher. He will help you navigate life and make decisions according to the Father's will. In Matthew 6:10, Jesus says to pray for God's will to be done: *Our Father in heaven, may Your name be kept holy. May Your Kingdom come soon. May Your will be done on earth, as it is in heaven* (NLT).

WHAT DO YOU THINK?
Why can doing God's will strengthen your faith in Him?

Be Intentional about Knowing and Doing God's Will

The Apostle Paul says to be thoughtful, not thoughtless in your desire to know and do God's will. This determined focus will aid you in understanding what God wants.

> Don't act thoughtlessly, but understand what the Lord wants you to do. (Ephesians 5:17 NLT)

You need to allow the Holy Spirit to *transform* the way you think so you can know God's will better.

> Don't copy the behavior and customs of this world, but let God transform you into a new person by changing the way you think. Then you will learn to know God's will for you, which is good and pleasing and perfect. (Romans 12:2 NLT)

The Father works within you through His Spirit to enable you to have the desire and ability to know and do His will.

> For it is God who works in you to will and to act in order to fulfill his good purpose. (Philippians 2:13 NIV)

She Believed All Her Thoughts Were from God

Many years ago, Linda and I knew a Christian woman who said every thought she had was from God. She said that this was because she had sincerely given her mind and thoughts completely to God. She would routinely tell people that God had told her His will for them about a particular situation in their life. Her intentions were good since I believe she genuinely wanted to be helpful to people. However, she failed to understand that she had a self-centered old nature that could lead her astray from God's will for her and others.

IMPORTANT: There are many ways to be fooled into thinking you know and are doing God's will. For example, your self-centered thoughts and imaginations can be a source of deception. Other well-meaning or not-so-well-meaning people can mislead you. The enemy of your soul (the devil and his demons) will always try to deceive you with thoughts contrary to God's will.

WHAT DO YOU THINK?

What are some ways even faithful followers of Jesus Christ can be fooled about God's will for their lives?

Remedy from God. The Holy Spirit is the *Spirit of Truth*, so ask Him to reveal deceptions and show you the truth, especially when you are in doubt.

God Often Uses Multiple Ways to Reveal His Will

I have discovered God frequently reveals His will through multiple avenues. For example, you may sense the Holy Spirit wants you to do something for a person. Then, you unexpectedly meet the person at the grocery store. Finally, the Holy Spirit may put a thought of encouragement into your mind the person needs at that time.

The following story includes multiple means by which the Holy Spirit guided me to know the Lord's will for a significant situation in my life.

The Lord Prepared Him to Guide Me

Through the Holy Spirit, the Lord told this new friend how I would respond to a job transfer. I planned to go back to my account in San Francisco, but the Lord's plan was for me to go somewhere else. You read the story about this prophetic job transfer to Orlando, FL in the chapter "God Communicates in Incredible Ways." So why did I rebel? Well, I wasn't thinking about the future. I was only thinking about the present and doing what I thought was best for me. I prayed that night, felt the conviction of the Holy Spirit, and the Lord confirmed I was to go elsewhere. I felt the peace of God in this decision. I apologized to my manager and happily moved forward, following the Holy Spirit.

PERSONAL APPLICATION

What circumstances, people, or influences have led you astray from God's will in your life?

Each Person of God May Communicate with You

The Father God. You may never hear the audible voice of the Father. This doesn't seem to be a typical experience for Christians today. I have only experienced this once in my forty-five years as a follower of Jesus. I wrote about this earlier regarding my salvation experience in the chapter "Rescued: The Father Intervened."

The following verses are an exception when the Father spoke audibly from Heaven when Jesus was on earth:

> Now in those days Jesus came from Nazareth in Galilee and was baptized by John in the Jordan River. And just as Jesus was coming up out of the water, he saw the heavens splitting apart and the Spirit descending on him like a dove. And a voice came from heaven: "You are my one dear Son; in you I take great delight." (Mark 1:9-11 NET)

Jesus Christ. As you see in the following verse, Jesus spoke audibly from Heaven to Saul during his salvation experience:

> "Who are You, lord?" Saul asked. And the voice replied, "I am Jesus, the one you are persecuting!" (Acts 9:5 NLT)

NOTE: Saul was the Apostle Paul's Jewish name before he committed his life to Jesus Christ.

Holy Spirit. As you know, the Father and Jesus sent the Holy Spirit to live within every born-again believer. He was sent to be the primary means by which they would teach, guide, and communicate with believers (John 16:13-15). **Most of the time, it will be the Holy Spirit communicating the will of the Father and Jesus for your life.** Following are some examples of this:

> So I say, let the Holy Spirit guide your lives. (Galatians 5:16 NLT)

> For David himself, speaking under the inspiration of the Holy Spirit. (Mark 12:36 NLT)

> Meanwhile, as Peter was puzzling over the vision, the Holy Spirit said to him, "Three men have come looking for you." (Acts 10:19 NLT)

> Then the Spirit said to Philip, "Go over and join this chariot." (Acts 8:29 NET)

> While they were serving the Lord and fasting, the Holy Spirit said, "Set apart for me Barnabas and Saul for the work to which I have called them." (Acts 13:2 NET)

The Holy Spirit is a person of God, yet a spirit that exists everywhere. As such, He doesn't have a physical body as Jesus did while He was on earth. Therefore, when He communicates with people, it's always internal, such as to their minds or hearts.

WHAT DO YOU THINK?
Why can't the Holy Spirit speak audibly to a person's ears, as Jesus and the Father did in the above verses?

In the next chapter, you will discover various ways the Holy Spirit reveals God's will.

25

Know and Do God's Will: Guidance

External Means of Guidance

The Holy Spirit may provide external **experiences** to help you know God's will. These may include the following external means:

Counsel of Others

He may confirm the Father's will through someone else. Be sure their words align with the Bible, the character of God, and that you have peace from the Holy Spirit.

> Plans go wrong for lack of advice; many advisers bring success. (Proverbs 15:22 NLT)

Circumstances

He may orchestrate circumstances so that your decision becomes obvious. He can close doors He doesn't want you to go through and open others to guide you. Sometimes circumstances may dictate there is only one viable choice to make.

> When I came to the city of Troas to preach the Good News of Christ, the Lord opened a door of opportunity for me. (2 Corinthians 2:12 NLT)

PERSONAL APPLICATION
What's an example of an external means when you experienced the Holy Spirit guiding you to know the Father's will?

Internal Means of Guidance

The Holy Spirit may communicate the Father's will in **ways not obvious to others**. These may include the following internal means:

Your Will

He may give you the desire (and ability) necessary to do something God wants.

> For God is working in you, giving you the desire and the power to do what pleases Him. (Philippians 2:13 NLT)

> *My God placed it on my heart* to gather the leaders, the officials, and the ordinary people so they could be enrolled on the basis of genealogy. (Nehemiah 7:5 NLT, author's emphasis)

Your Emotions

He may give you certain emotions or feelings to help you know God's will. Sometimes it may be a feeling of God's peace or joy deep within you that you can't explain.

> Then you will experience God's peace, which exceeds anything we can understand. His peace will guard your hearts and minds as you live in Christ Jesus. (Philippians 4:7 NLT)

You may have a sense of firm conviction to say or do something. However, this is not the same as feeling forced against your will since God does not typically violate your free will. The Apostle Paul describes this feeling with the word *bound* in the following verse:

> And now, behold, bound by the Spirit, I am on my way to Jerusalem, not knowing what will happen to me there. (Acts 20:22 NASB)

Of course, not all emotions are from God. You have feelings that come from yourself and life experiences.

WHAT DO YOU THINK?
If something feels harsh or judgmental, why is it not from the Holy Spirit? Why is it from the enemy of your soul? Why do you think that as you mature as a follower of Christ, you can learn to discern the source of your feelings?

Your Mind

He may enable you to understand something, so it's just common sense. It just seems like the reasonable, logical thing to do.

> Foolishness brings joy to those with no sense; a sensible person stays on the right path. (Proverbs 15:21 NLT)

Your Conscience

He may give you a sense of what is right and wrong. For example, there may be an uneasiness about something because it's wrong. The Holy Spirit may impress upon you that something is wrong to stop you from doing or saying it.

> Even Gentiles, who do not have God's written law, show that they know His law when they instinctively obey it, even without having heard it. They demonstrate that God's law is written in their hearts, for their own conscience and thoughts either accuse them or tell them they are doing right. (Romans 2:14-15 NLT)

He said everyone knows right from wrong. This person would argue that understanding right from wrong was common sense, so no one needed to be taught it. He said that people were born with this knowledge from God.

I believe God does give every person an intuitive sense of right and wrong. But this God-given guidance mechanism can be overridden by teachings and culture. People can be taught to believe something is right when it is actually wrong. Since people and their cultures are not perfect, a person's inborn sense of right and wrong can develop contrary to God's intentions (1 Corinthians 8:10). If in doubt, always look it up in your guidebook of truth, the Bible. The saying, "Let your conscience be your guide," is misleading. Instead, ask the Holy Spirit to be your guide (Romans 9:1).

WHAT DO YOU THINK?

The existence of conscience is part of human nature. God has given every person a conscience with the ability to discern right from wrong. So, how can it develop contrary to the will of God?

Your Spirit

The Holy Spirit may speak directly to your spirit without speaking words to your mind (1 Corinthians 14:14). Sometimes, it's a sense that you may express as "I know that I know."

But it was to us that God revealed these things by His Spirit. For His Spirit searches out everything and shows us God's deep secrets. . . . When we tell you these things, we do not use words that come from human wisdom. Instead, we speak words given to us by the Spirit, using the Spirit's words to explain spiritual truths.

> But, as it is written, "What no eye has seen, nor ear heard, nor the heart of man imagined, what God has prepared for those who love him"—these things God has revealed to us through the Spirit. For the Spirit searches everything, even the depths of God. . . . And we impart this in words not taught by human wisdom but taught by the Spirit, interpreting spiritual truths to those who are spiritual. (1 Corinthians 2:9-13 ESV)

Guidance from the Bible

The Holy Spirit wrote the Bible through faithful men of God. It's, therefore, the living word of God. The Holy Spirit will communicate God's will and teach you as you read, study, meditate on, pray, and apply the Bible.

> Let the word of Christ richly dwell within you, with all wisdom teaching and admonishing one another with psalms and hymns and spiritual songs, singing with thankfulness in your hearts to God. (Colossians 3:16 NASB)

How the Holy Spirit Guided Me

In the previous chapter, I related the story of how God sent a Christian man to guide me (through the Holy Spirit) to the Father's will. I can see the following means of guidance in this story:

- Council – of another follower of Jesus.
- Circumstance – The end of this training required a change. In this case, I was either going back to where I was from or somewhere else. God used this circumstance to direct me elsewhere.

- My conscience – The Holy Spirit convicted me of my sin of self-will.

- My will – was changed by the Holy Spirit.

- My emotions – I felt the peace of God when I chose to follow His direction.

The Father provides many ways to know His will. If you ask Him, He will reveal it.

PERSONAL APPLICATION
Which of the above ways do you need to be more aware of to recognize God's will? How can the Holy Spirit help you identify the will of the Father and Jesus?

You will learn by experience to identify the many ways God reveals His will. The more you live out of your new nature with the Holy Spirit, the more clearly you will recognize God's will.

26

Knowing God through Christian Practices

As you read earlier, it takes effort and time to mature as a follower of Jesus Christ. In this chapter, you will learn that regular spiritual practices help you with this spiritual growth. These are sometimes referred to as spiritual or Christian disciplines. You will see that you must train yourself to do these, so they become a way of life, a habit. Your sense of closeness with God and fellowship with other believers will be enhanced as you do so.

Training the body and mind. The Apostle Paul describes training the body and mind for spiritual purposes as similar to what an athlete would do. Athletes have a goal in mind, and so should you as you train yourself for spiritual growth and living by the Spirit. When you do this, you discipline your old nature's natural desires, attitudes, and behaviors to develop Christian habits.

> Every athlete exercises self-control in all things. . . . But I discipline my body and keep it under control, lest after preaching to others I myself should be disqualified. (1 Corinthians 9:25-27 ESV)

> Physical training is good, but training for godliness is much better, promising benefits in this life and in the life to come. (1 Timothy 4:8 NLT)

My example with football training. The summer temperatures were in the 90s when we started our practices for high school football. Naturally, none of us wanted to be out in the heat running sprints, doing calisthenics, hitting tackling dummies, and running offensive and defensive plays. So, why did we discipline our bodies and minds this way for weeks before we played our first football game? The answer: Our goal was to compete in the games to the best of our abilities. And we wanted to win, of course.

PERSONAL APPLICATION

When have you trained yourself through personal discipline to do something you wanted?

Spiritual Practices with God

Christianity is not just about religious doctrine. It's about a spiritual life that the Holy Spirit is continually transforming. The practice of spiritual disciplines pleases the Father and Jesus because they enable you to experience the awesomeness of their presence. However, deciding to do these disciplines and then actually doing them can be quite different. Success requires you to train your mind and body, even when you don't want to (as we did with football). Such training may sometimes entail disciplining yourself to forgo things less beneficial to your eternal life.

NOTE: The word *discipline* used in this chapter might be confusing. Spiritual disciplines are not about being chastised by God for wrongdoing. They are also not about developing legalistic rituals to earn God's love and blessings. Far from it! Instead, they are about choosing to develop spiritually healthy habits that enable you to draw closer to God. They are about learning to experience His presence, joy, and love in ways you may not have imagined.

I discussed some of the following disciplines in the chapter "Knowing God through the Bible." Meditation, prayer, and Bible study are presented here from the perspective and value of being spiritual disciplines that require regular practice.

Meditation

Christian meditation differs from what people often think meditation is. Instead, it involves listening to or reading scripture and thinking about the meaning of the verses. You may decide to memorize the Bible verses while considering their meaning and importance to you. Meditation may involve focusing on and thinking about who God is, His majesty and glory, and His loving-kindness. You may consider what He has done in your life and how you see Him at work in it.

NOTE: As you read earlier, meditation doesn't involve emptying your mind and chanting meaningless words (Matthew 6:7). That is the opposite of Christian meditation, where the mind is actively engaged.

PERSONAL APPLICATION
Why do you think God is pleased when you spend time meditating upon Him?

Following are several verses about meditating upon God:

> I meditate on your precepts and consider your ways. (Psalm 119:15 NIV)

> Finally, brethren, whatever is true, whatever is honorable, whatever is right, whatever is pure, whatever is lovely, whatever is of good repute, if there is any excellence and if anything worthy of praise, dwell on these things. (Philippians 4:8 NIV)

Prayer

Prayer is essential to the Christian life of faith and love for God. It's a primary means to communicate directly with each person of God. I believe it's of utmost importance because it can bring you into the spiritual presence of the Father God and Jesus who are in Heaven. In addition, the Holy Spirit can change you through prayer. (I discussed prayer and communication with God in some detail in an earlier chapter, "Imagine Never Talking to Someone You Love."

Following are some verses about prayer and talking to God:

> First of all, then, I urge that requests, prayers, intercessions, and thanks be offered on behalf of all people. (1 Timothy 2:1 NET)

> Do not be anxious about anything. Instead, in every situation, through prayer and petition with thanksgiving, tell your requests to God. (Philippians 4:6 NET)

> Call on me in prayer and I will answer you. I will show you great and mysterious things which you still do not know about. (Jeremiah 33:3 NET)

WHAT DO YOU THINK?

Why can regularly praying and talking to each person of God help believers develop a more personal relationship with them?

Fasting

Fasting in the Bible often (but not always) refers to abstaining from food for spiritual purposes. You may decide to fast, or God may call you to do so for His purposes. The purposes may vary, but the focus in fasting is always on God (not on yourself and what you want from Him). It's done voluntarily on any day for any period of time. And you decide what you will abstain from during the fast.

> I continued fasting and praying before the God of heaven. (Nehemiah 1:4 NET)

> When they had appointed elders for them in the various churches, with prayer and fasting they entrusted them to the protection of the Lord in whom they had believed. (Acts 14:23 NET)

PERSONAL APPLICATION

What would you abstain from during a spiritual fast - food (never water), alcohol, entertainment (such as TV), or eating out?

Our story about fasting and prayer. Our adult Sunday School department decided to spend a day and night in fasting and prayer. We spent Saturday day on our own, fasting in whatever way we each felt we could do. We spent that night together as an opportunity for further spiritual growth. The pastor for single adults agreed to lead the all-night activities. The Saturday night was exhilarating as we prayed for many people and circumstances. We had ample time for fellowship throughout the night as well as times for singing and worship of God. The next morning many of us went to a local restaurant for breakfast. (Notice the word "breakfast" means to break a fast.) We were energized as we discussed what we experienced from God during our night of fasting, prayer, worship, and fellowship.

Study

Among other things, the Bible is about relationships. It's about the relationships between God and believers and between believers. Therefore, God wants you to search the Bible, examine it closely, and study it to know Him and how to live the Christian life. The two chapters, "Knowing God through the Bible," have more information about the value and benefits of studying the Bible.

> These Jews were more open-minded than those in Thessalonica, for they eagerly received the message, *examining the scriptures carefully every day to see if these things were so.* (Acts 17:11 NET, author's emphasis)

WHAT DO YOU THINK?

Why can studying the Bible regularly with the Holy Spirit's help enable believers to learn about the kind of life that pleases the Father?

He listened to the Bible daily. My friend worked a job where he could use a headset and listen to the dramatized Bible. Over the years, his knowledge of the Bible increased significantly, and his personal relationship with God was enhanced. If you have the opportunity to do this safely, it can do the same for you.

Spiritual Practices with Other Believers

To please God, you must live like a biblical Christian. To do this, you must be involved with other believers. Following are some Christian practices that help you better know God and other believers better. They enable you to live as Jesus Christ Himself did while on earth.

WHAT DO YOU THINK?

If God is kept first in the heart, how can focusing on others help believers love God and people more?

Submission

This is about having a humble heart toward God and people. First and foremost, followers of Jesus are to submit their hearts and lives to God, to know Him, and do His will.

> Submit yourselves, then, to God. (James 4:7 NIV)

In the next verse, Jesus says submission is about denying your self-centered desires to serve and follow Him:

> Then Jesus said to his disciples, "If anyone wants to become my follower, he must deny himself, take up his cross, and follow me." (Matthew 16:24 NET)

Following are some verses about submission to other believers. This doesn't imply you should submit to anyone who wants to cause you harm.

> Instead of being motivated by selfish ambition or vanity, each of you should, in humility, be moved to treat one another as more important than yourself. (Philippians 2:3 NET)

> Submit to one another out of reverence for Christ. (Ephesians 5:21 NIV)

PERSONAL APPLICATION

Some people are more difficult to love and respect. In what ways could you submit to them to demonstrate love without compromising Christ-like values and integrity as a follower of Jesus?

Confession

Confession of sin is essential for a healthy spiritual life with God and other believers. There is a confession of sin to God as well as a confession of sin to people. When you commit your life to Christ and confess your sins to the Father God, you receive eternal and complete forgiveness. However, you break fellowship with God when you sin in a situation. He desires to forgive you so you can continually experience Him. Therefore, you should always acknowledge your situational sins to the Father as soon as the Holy Spirit makes you aware of them. If these sins involve others, you acknowledge the wrong to them and ask them to forgive you.

Following are some verses about confessing your sins to God:

> I acknowledged my sin to You, And my iniquity I did not hide; I said, "I will confess my transgressions to the LORD." (Psalms 32:5 NASB)

> But if we confess our sins to Him, He is faithful and just to forgive us our sins and to cleanse us from all wickedness. (1 John 1:9 NLT)

The next verse is about confessing your sins to other believers:

> Confess your sins to each other and pray for each other so that you may be healed. The earnest prayer of a righteous person has great power and produces wonderful results. (James 5:16 NLT)

I suggest that if you sin in ways people observe, you should confess these sins to them and ask for their forgiveness. However, if the sins are in your thoughts alone, confess these to God alone and ask for His forgiveness only. Otherwise, you may unnecessarily and irreparably damage your relationship with the other people.

WHAT DO YOU THINK?

If you sin in your thoughts without it showing in your behavior toward people, why may it not be wise to tell people about these sinful thoughts? Why may this damage your relationship?

Service

The Father asks you to serve with humility and love toward Him and people. Service is a mindset that enables you to recognize needs and joyfully respond to help with the love of Christ. Service is about what you can do for others, not what you want them to do for you. It's about listening and responding to the Holy Spirit to guide you where and whom to serve.

> All of you, serve each other in humility, for "God opposes the proud but favors the humble." (1 Peter 5:5 NLT)

> Use your freedom to serve one another in love. (Galatians 5:13 NLT)

> Because the service of this ministry is not only providing for the needs of the saints but is also overflowing with many thanks to God. (2 Corinthians 9:12 NET)

Since Jesus came to serve, so should His followers.

> For even the Son of Man did not come to be served, but to serve, and to give His life a ransom for many. (Mark 10:45 NASB)

NOTE: Serving others doesn't transform believers' hearts to become more like Jesus. Even non-believers can serve in a church or elsewhere with a desire to do good. When people serve out of human kindness alone, without a desire to demonstrate Christ's love, their service has little to no eternal value to God. The chapter "Be Transformed by the Spirit" contains information about this change process from the old to the new nature.

WHAT DO YOU THINK? (ADVANCED)
Why do you think God wants believers to have a humble attitude and a desire to demonstrate Christ's love when serving others?

Worship

Worship of God comes from the heart as you express love, joy, and gratitude to Him for who He is and what He has done. Praising God is the outpouring of this grateful heart.

> Worship the LORD with joy! Enter his presence with joyful singing! (Psalms 100:2 NET)

> Praise the LORD! Praise God in his sanctuary; praise him in his mighty heavens! Praise him for his mighty deeds; praise him according to his excellent greatness!... Let everything that has breath praise the LORD! Praise the LORD! (Psalms 150 ESV)

True spiritual worship of the Father is based on biblical truth and occurs through the presence of the Holy Spirit.

> God is spirit, and those who worship him must worship in spirit and truth. (John 4:24 ESV)

The following verses say that the people of God are to worship Him continuously.

> And day by day, attending the temple together and breaking bread in their homes, they received their food with glad and generous hearts, praising God and having favor with all the people. (Acts 2:46-47 ESV)

Since we are receiving a Kingdom that is unshakable, let us be thankful and please God by worshiping Him with holy fear and awe. (Hebrews 12:28 NLT)

WHAT DO YOU THINK?
Why can singing be a wonderful way to worship God? Since worship aims to focus on God and His majesty, how does the type of music impact this goal? Why can some music distract the worshiper from this humble focus on Abba, the Father who is Almighty God?

Anointed worship leader. Linda and I attended a large church where we experienced the wonderful presence of the Holy Spirit, His love, and joy as we all sang together in worship. It was truly an experience we looked forward to each Sunday. We realized that the worship leader was called and anointed for this ministry at this time and place. She was the Holy Spirit's instrument through whom He manifested Himself to the congregation. A few years later, she was called into another ministry and no longer led the worship service singing. The next several worship leaders had good hearts and tried their best but just did not have the same powerful anointing for leading worship as she had.

To learn more about spiritual practices. If you want additional detailed information about spiritual disciplines, the following books are good to read: *Celebration of Discipline,* subtitle *The Path to Spiritual Growth,* by Richard J. Foster, and *Spiritual Disciplines Handbook*, subtitle *Practices That Transform Us* by Adele Ahlberg Calhoun.

You Must Practice the Spiritual Disciplines

Followers of Jesus Christ should be actively engaged in all these practices. They should become regular habits. If you are not doing them, I suggest you select several and start with a short amount of time, perhaps ten to fifteen minutes a day. Then, add other disciplines over time until you are regularly experiencing God in all of them. This is not as difficult as it may seem.

PERSONAL APPLICATION
Which of these spiritual disciplines are you currently doing well? Which do you sense the Holy Spirit is asking you to start now? Why do you think these regular habits will help you persevere and mature as a follower of Jesus? Why will they help you know God better?

When you spend time in God's presence and get to know Him better, you will experience a greater sense of assurance of your eternal salvation as a believer. In addition, you will continue to learn more about the character and greatness of God and His love for you.

> As a result, you will discover more meaning and enjoyment of life (John 10:10).

> Draw near to God, and he will draw near to you. (James 4:8 ESV)

> For I am sure that neither death nor life, nor angels nor rulers, nor things present nor things to come, nor powers, nor height nor depth, nor anything else in all creation, will be able to separate us from the love of God in Christ Jesus our Lord (Romans 8:38-39 ESV)

The Father, Jesus, and the Holy Spirit will never leave or forsake you, so learn to enjoy their presence and eternal love each day.

PART D

GOD IS SUPERNATURAL AND STILL DOES MIRACLES

27

The Natural World

The natural world. For the purpose of this book, I describe the natural world as consisting of the earth and everything in it as well as the universe. It's all that exists physically everywhere. This includes the multitude of universal laws that govern it.

The Creation Story in Brief

The following verses summarize God's work in creating the natural world:

> This is the account of the heavens and the earth when they were created, in the day that the LORD God made earth and heaven. Now no shrub of the field was yet in the earth, and no plant of the field had yet sprouted, for the LORD God had not sent rain upon the earth, and there was no man to cultivate the ground. But a mist used to rise from the earth and water the whole surface of the ground. Then the LORD God formed man of dust from the ground, and breathed into his nostrils the breath of life; and man became a living being. The LORD God planted a garden toward the east, in Eden; and there He placed the man whom He had formed. Out of the ground the LORD God caused to grow every tree that is pleasing to the sight and good for food; the tree of life also in the midst of the garden, and the tree of the knowledge of good and evil. (Genesis 2:4-9 NASB)

But where did all this physical material come from? The answer is in the next section.

God Created Everything Out of Nothing

Of course, nothing existed, except God Himself, before creation. Not even the smallest dust particles or invisible matter existed.

The following verse says God, the Creator, existed before He created the earth:

> Before the mountains were born or You gave birth to the earth and the world, Even from everlasting to everlasting, You are God. (Psalm 90:2 NASB)

God created everything out of nothing ("Ex Nihilo"). If you know chemistry, you are familiar with the Periodic Table. No element in the Table existed until God created it. By the way, scientists are still discovering new elements previously unknown to people but known to and created by God.

> By faith we understand that the entire universe was formed at God's command, that what we now see did not come from anything that can be seen. (Hebrews 11:3 NLT)

God not only created the earth out of nothing, but also the sun, moon, and stars.

> God made two great lights—the larger one to govern the day, and the smaller one to govern the night. He also made the stars (Genesis 1:16 NLT).

The creation story describes God's majesty, unique power, and all-encompassing authority to create anything and everything. Thus, the creation of the universe (heavens) points to God and His glory.

> The heavens are telling of the glory of God; And their expanse is declaring the work of His hands. Day to day pours forth speech, And night to night reveals knowledge. (Psalm 19:1-2 NASB)

An important purpose of creation was to provide a suitable natural, physical environment within which people could exist.

> For the LORD is God, and He created the heavens and earth and put everything in place. *He made the world to be lived in, not to be a place of empty chaos.* "I am the LORD," He says, "and there is no other." (Isaiah 45:18 NLT, author's emphasis)

Of course, in doing so, the world was fit for all animal and plant life to live within.

WHAT DO YOU THINK?
What do you find particularly amazing about the natural world in which you live?

The Bible, Science, and the Natural World

Science studies the natural world, whether the earth or the universe. Yet, some people think science and the Bible contradict one another. When scientists study this natural world without bias, they discover God's creation. Therefore, science (without bias) and the Bible are not in conflict. On the contrary, they complement and support one another. Many Bible verses describe aspects of God's natural creation that are now proven scientific facts. This corroboration is further evidence to validate the existence of an intelligent Designer who was the Creator of everything. More and more, our learned scientists confirm what God says about His creation in the Bible with their discoveries.

Science and the Bible. Following are a few scientific disciplines and related facts about the natural world that are found in the Bible. Most of these truths are apparent because we have known them to be true for some time.

- Geology:
  - Fountains (springs) of water exist under the seas – Genesis 7:11
  - The flow of wind currents and their direction – Ecclesiastes 1:6
- Physics:
  - The earth is round – Isaiah 40:22
  - Gravity holds the earth up in space and stars and planets in their places – Job 26:7
- Hematology:
  - The life of people and all animals is in its blood – Leviticus 17:11
- Oceanography:
  - The flow of warm and cold ocean currents – Psalm 8:8

But unfortunately, some scientists don't want to admit they spend their lives studying God's creation. Some pursue their own agenda and bias. And some are blinded to it by *the god of this world* (2 Corinthians 4:4).

What would you say to someone to help them understand that the Bible and
science (without bias) do not contradict one another?

Design of the complex human brain. It's a highly complex component of the
human body that controls every aspect of the human life we humans experience
every moment of every day. For example, did you know that it controls the following
essential functions of human life: Thinking, memory, emotions, touch, motor skills,
vision, breathing, body temperature, and hunger? In addition, it controls all other
functions that regulate the body to keep it balanced and healthy. Without its complex
construction, we human beings would not exist. The following link to the John
Hopkins Medical Center website provides scientific details about this incredible source
of human life:

> https://www.hopkinsmedicine.org/health/conditions-and-diseases/
> anatomy-of-the-brain

Review the scientific information about the brain in this link (and others if you
like). Then, ask yourself how this interdependent complexity of construction and
functioning could have evolved by chance, whether over millions or billions of years.

Why isn't an intelligent Designer the logical conclusion for the brain and human
body's complex existence? Why is any other explanation for their complex
existence unreasonable?

The Bible, atheism, and science. Eric Metaxas recently published a book, *Is
Atheism Dead?*, which addresses this assumed conflict between science and the Bible.
He addresses modern archeological advancements, historical evidence, and testimonies
from scientists as he lays out detailed analyses. His thirty topical chapters clearly and
logically engage readers in the wonder of God as the intelligent Designer of everything.
His chapters include the "Big Bang" theory, the origin of life, the failure of evolution
to explain the world we live in, atheism, and much more. He says that more and more
modern scientific discoveries validate creation and God as its Designer.

God created everything that exists out of nothing. This includes the physical, natural
world that can be seen and the unseen supernatural world. The next chapter describes
the supernatural world (on earth and above) that God created.

28

The Supernatural World

There is something beyond the realm of this physical, natural world. It's the supernatural world, the unseen world around you.

In the verses below, you see God created the natural world (*things we can see*) and the supernatural world (*things we can't see*) through His Son, Jesus Christ.

> He is the image of the invisible God, the firstborn of all creation. For by Him all things were created, both in the heavens and on earth, visible and invisible, whether thrones or dominions or rulers or authorities— all things have been created through Him and for Him. He is before all things, and in Him all things hold together. (Colossians 1:15-17 NASB)

God Is Supernatural, and All He Does Is Supernatural

The term *invisible God* above indicates that God is a supernatural being existing outside of the physical realm. God demonstrates His supernatural nature and powers throughout the Bible, from the first book of Genesis to the last book of Revelation.

WHAT DO YOU THINK?
Why do you think some people refuse to believe in the existence of the supernatural realm? Do you think they are afraid or simply choose to ignore it?

God's supernatural powers on earth. The following are just two examples that clearly show God doing something supernatural to demonstrate His love and power on earth.

Healings. In the following verse, you see Jesus exercising supernatural power to heal people and drive out demons from those possessed by them. Remember that the Holy Spirit's power working within Him actually does the miracles.

> People brought to him all who suffered with various illnesses and afflictions, those who had seizures, paralytics, and those possessed by demons, and he healed them. (Matthew 4:24 NET)

Temple curtain torn by God. When Jesus died on the cross, the Father God supernaturally tore the heavy curtain in the temple that separated the inner chamber (Holy of Holies) from the outer chamber. He did this to signify people could come directly to Him in prayer and communication. They no longer needed a priest to talk to Him for them. The Father wants His children to come directly to Him under all circumstances.

> And behold, the curtain of the temple was torn in two, from top to bottom. And the earth shook, and the rocks were split. (Matthew 27:51 ESV)

WHAT DO YOU THINK?
Why do some people insist they need someone else to talk to the Father God for them? Why is this attitude biblically incorrect as well as demeaning to Jesus and His death for them?

God Supernaturally Responds to Prayer

God is supernatural and displays this in the natural world He created. He works in and through people, circumstances, and anything else to accomplish His purposes.

Following are two stories about how God responded to prayer in a time of need. As you will see, sometimes His power heals, and other times He changes a person's mind and decision.

Severe asthma attack. In the 1990s, I was having frequent asthma problems. On one occasion, I had a severe asthma attack. I was lying in bed, struggling to breathe. I was scared. Linda had her hand on my chest. As she was praying and rubbing my chest, she felt the Lord's hand (she knew it was Him) on her hand in response to her prayers. The asthma immediately left me, and I slept restfully.

Jesus is in Heaven with His Father. So how did He put His hand on Linda's hand to heal me?

Answer. Even though Jesus resides in Heaven, He exists everywhere and is all-powerful and all-knowing. Like the Father and the Holy Spirit, He can do anything, any time, anywhere (Psalm 139:1-10).

What did they want? I was working for an organization that hired me to implement project management and a Project Management Office (PMO). For this story, it is important to know that I implemented all this according to the PMO charter a consultant helped them create earlier. I did nothing of significance for the PMO without their management review and approval. They seemed to value it. But after several years, their attitude changed. So, what happened? What did they want? Well, they said they changed their minds about wanting a PMO and project management. They said they didn't realize what the PMO charter they created would require of them. In the end, I think it was about the success of project management and the PMO. Sometimes success breeds resistance. Before compromises were agreed to, several functional managers convinced the organization's director to lay off my six project managers and myself. The director announced one day that he was seriously considering this and would decide our fate that night.

After dinner that night, I sensed an urgency to pray and ask God to save all our PMO jobs. Due to my age, being laid off meant I would likely find no future employment. I knew I was still four or five years from retirement. Who would hire me at my age for such a short time? After I prayed, I sensed God's peace about whatever would happen. The next day the director announced he had decided to lay us off but changed his mind that night. God answered my prayer by changing the director's mind and decision! It was clear God was not finished with His plan for my working career.

> The king's heart is a stream of water in the hand of the LORD; he turns it wherever he will. (Proverbs 21:1 ESV)

PERSONAL APPLICATION

When has God intervened in your life so you could continue on a path He had you on? What would have happened to you if He had not intervened?

God's Angels Are Supernatural

The Old and New Testaments of the Bible mention the supernatural existence of God's angels many times. From this, you learn they are diverse in their nature and functions. And, of course, they are invisible, so people don't typically see them. Many reside and exercise their supernatural abilities in Heaven, while others do so on earth and outer space (Daniel 10:12-13, 20).

The following verses say God created angels before He created the natural world. The *morning stars* in the verses are the angels of God.

> Where were you when I laid the foundation of the earth? Tell me, if you possess understanding! Who set its measurements – if you know – or who stretched a measuring line across it? On what were its bases set, or who laid its cornerstone – when the morning stars sang in chorus, and all the sons of God shouted for joy? (Job 38:4-7 NET)

God says in scripture there are so many angels people can't count them.

> No, you have come to Mount Zion, to the city of the living God, the heavenly Jerusalem, and to countless thousands of angels in a joyful gathering. (Hebrews 12:22 NLT)

God sends His mighty angels to earth to help people.

> Regarding the angels, He says, "He sends His angels like the winds, His servants like flames of fire." (Hebrews 1:7 NLT)

> Praise the LORD, you angels, you mighty ones who carry out His plans, listening for each of His commands. Yes, praise the LORD, you armies of angels who serve Him and do His will! (Psalms 103:20-21 NLT)

In the Old Testament book of Daniel 8:16-18, 21 and the New Testament book of Luke 1:19, 26, 28, you see God sending His angel Gabriel to communicate His will to people. In Matthew's New Testament book, you see God sending an angel to speak to Joseph, the earthly stepfather of Jesus, to guide and forewarn him (Matthew 1:20-25).

God's angels are mighty warriors referred to as the *armies of Heaven*.

> Praise Him, all His angels! Praise Him, all the armies of heaven! (Psalms 148:2 NLT)

> Suddenly, the angel was joined by a vast host of others—the armies of heaven—praising God and saying, (Luke 2:13 NLT)

These mighty angels of God will come with Jesus in His second coming.

> When the Son of Man comes in his glory and all the angels with him, then he will sit on his glorious throne. (Matthew 25:31 NET)

WHAT DO YOU THINK?

Imagine what this will look like when Jesus returns with His innumerable angels. How would you describe this to someone?

Jesus is superior to angels. God declares that His Son, Jesus Christ, is superior to angels (and the devil and demons, which were once angels).

> Having become as much superior to angels as the name he has inherited is more excellent than theirs. For to which of the angels did God ever say, "You are my Son, today I have begotten you"? Or again, "I will be to him a father, and he shall be to me a son"? And again, when he brings the firstborn into the world, he says, "Let all God's angels worship him." (Hebrews 1:4-6 ESV)

In Colossians 2:16-23, we are told not to worship angels. Even though they are mightier than people, they are not God. Only God deserves to be worshiped (Exodus 20:3-5).

> Therefore no one is to act as your judge in regard to food or drink or in respect to a festival or a new moon or a Sabbath day—things which are a mere shadow of what is to come; but the substance belongs to Christ. Let no one keep defrauding you of your prize by delighting in self-abasement and the worship of the angels, taking his stand on visions he has seen, inflated without cause by his fleshly mind, and not holding fast to the head, from whom the entire body, being supplied and held together by the joints and ligaments, grows with a growth which is from God. (Colossians 2:16-19 NASB)

WHAT DO YOU THINK?

Since God says He has angels, why do some people ignore their existence? Why have others exaggerated their presence and activities? Why should people pray to the Father God and not angels?

Asking the Father to send His angels to help someone. Since the Father God sends His angels to help people, I think it's acceptable to ask Him to do so when there is a need. For example, Linda and I have a friend suffering terribly from cancer throughout his body. In addition, he has many other serious health problems that increase his suffering. His wife is overwhelmed with his care and all the other things she must do. So, Linda and I recently started asking the Father to send His ministering angels to help them during this incredibly difficult time (Hebrews 1:7). We believe it's our responsibility to ask God for what we think is best. But we also ask Him to do what He knows is best – His will and not ours to be done.

Miracles are supernatural interventions by God. In the next chapter, you will see a variety of miracles by God to help His children. These are only a few of the many supernatural interventions by God of which we are aware.

29

Different Kinds of Miracles

Miracles override the natural order of the material world and, therefore, can't be explained by human reasoning. They can only be understood as an act of a gracious God on behalf of people. We know God by His nature is supernatural, so everything He does is supernatural. Miracles, then are supernatural interventions by God in human affairs. They are done according to His divine nature, will, and plan for the benefit of people.

Following are several verses about how God's miracles are beyond human understanding:

> God's voice thunders in marvelous ways; he does great things beyond our understanding. (Job 37:5 NET)

> Pay attention to this, Job. Stop and consider the wonderful miracles of God! (Job 37:14 NLT)

> For as the heavens are higher than the earth, So are My ways higher than your ways And My thoughts than your thoughts. (Isaiah 55:9 NASB)

Jesus Did Many Miracles

Jesus Christ performed many miracles two thousand years ago at his first coming to earth. One important purpose was to prove to the nation of Israel that He was their promised Messiah of the Old Testament. However, most failed to recognize Him even though supernatural miracles were done by Him on many occasions. Just a reminder that every supernatural feat of Jesus was done by the Holy Spirit working in and through Him.

Following is a list of some miracles to illustrate their diversity. Nothing, of course, is impossible for God (Luke 1:37). He can do anything, anywhere, and at any time.

- Turned water into wine (John 2:1-11)
- Without being present in their home, Jesus healed a man's son who was sick and near death (John 4:46-54)
- Caused Peter to catch an enormous amount of fish when he had caught none after fishing all night (Luke 5:1-11)
- Raised a widow's son from the dead (Luke 7:11-17)
- Fed five thousand men with five barley loaves and two fish in an isolated location (count doesn't include the unknown number of wives and children) (Matthew 14:13-21)
- Walked on water (John 6:16-21)
- Delivered a boy from a demon (Luke 9:37-43)

Jesus did much more than is recorded in the four Gospels (Matthew, Mark, Luke, and John). The Apostle John (who wrote the Gospel of John) said the world is not big enough for all the books that could have been written about the things Jesus did while on earth.

> There are many other things that Jesus did. If every one of them were written down, I suppose the whole world would not have room for the books that would be written. (John 21:25 NET)

Jesus' followers performed supernatural feats. After the death, resurrection, and ascension of Jesus (Acts 1:11), His followers performed many of the same miracles, also by the Holy Spirit. For example, the Apostles Peter and Paul and Philip the deacon consistently did so (Acts 3:16, 5:15-16, 8:6-7).

WHAT DO YOU THINK?
Why should people expect supernatural miracles to occur in our modern world? What has changed over the last two thousand years since Jesus lived on earth that would cause miracles to cease?

Linda's Car Pushed Off Track from Oncoming Train

The following is a story about how God supernaturally pushed Linda's stalled car off a railroad track just before an oncoming train would have struck it and killed her and her friends. She was a new Christian at the time. These are her words.

Story. When I was in high school (the mid-1960s), my father purchased a used car from a coworker. It was a convertible! So, I was excited about it, and he graciously allowed me and some friends to take it for a drive. Upon leaving our base housing area (my father was in the Air Force), I came to railroad tracks. The car stalled on the tracks. (Later, dad found out stalling was a common problem with this car.) We were all laughing and not focused on what was happening. I tried to start the car, but it wouldn't start. Then, it slowly and quietly moved off the tracks, like it had been gently pushed. After we cleared the tracks, the car started. A train sped by us moments later. We were stunned! We were so busy talking we didn't realize a train was coming toward us. I remember thinking this had to have been a miracle from God that moved my car to safety.

WHAT DO YOU THINK?

Who do you think pushed Linda's car off the railroad tracks? Did the Father send an angel to be there in advance so he could save her life? Did He somehow reach down from Heaven with a supernatural hand or breath to push her car? Or did the Holy Spirit do it?

Answer. We don't know how the Father did this miracle. We just know that He did it.

White-out and the Holy Spirit's Warning

In March 1993, Linda and I were driving on Interstate 75 to our home in Holly, Michigan, after visiting Grand Blanc. I approached an exit to a country road and considered it instead of staying on the Interstate. A thought immediately came to my mind to take the scenic country road, so I did. We didn't know a white-out snowstorm had just occurred on a seven-mile stretch of Interstate 75 ahead of us near our home. The Holy Spirit led us onto the country road that bypassed the white-out. This storm caused a seventy-five car pileup. One person was killed, and twenty-eight were injured. A person involved in the massive collisions stated people were screaming and crying. Abandoned cars littered this stretch of the Interstate after the storm.

PERSONAL APPLICATION

When did Holy Spirit guide you to prevent a tragedy or save your life?

Fred Was Healed from a Fear of Death

Sometimes the Father allows suffering to come to His children. But, when He does, there is always a divinely inspired purpose. So, His children must not lose faith in Him and never doubt His love.

> Trust in him at all times, O people; pour out your heart before him. (Psalms 62:8 ESV)

> Therefore let those who suffer according to God's will entrust their souls to a faithful Creator while doing good. (1 Peter 4:19 ESV)

The next verse says that even Jesus suffered while He was on earth:

> Jesus said, "The Son of Man must suffer many things and be rejected by the elders and chief priests and scribes, and be killed, and on the third day be raised." (Luke 9:22 ESV)

The following verses say nothing can separate believers from God's love:

> Who shall separate us from the love of Christ? Shall tribulation, or distress, or persecution, or famine, or nakedness, or danger, or sword?... No, in all these things we are more than conquerors through him who loved us. For I am sure that neither death nor life, nor angels nor rulers, nor things present nor things to come, nor powers, nor height nor depth, nor anything else in all creation, will be able to separate us from the love of God in Christ Jesus our Lord. (Romans 8:35-39 ESV)

Story. Occasionally the pastor of our small church in Michigan would ask Jack, another former pastor, and me to accompany him on home visits to pray for sick people. On one occasion, we met Fred, who had just been diagnosed with late-stage lung cancer. Cancer had also spread throughout his body. He was a relatively new Christian and was uncertain about his eternal fate when his physical body died. And, of course, he also wanted to live. The four of us gathered around Fred. We laid our hands on him and began to pray for his physical healing. I had my hands on his chest. It was so hot I could hardly keep my hands on him. All four of us experienced the Holy Spirit flowing through us into Fred's body. We left thinking the Holy Spirit was healing Fred of cancer. But He didn't. Instead, Fred died and went home to Heaven shortly after this. We wondered how we could have been so wrong! What was God's purpose in sending us to pray for Fred if not for physical healing? Later, Fred's wife called our pastor and said Fred went home to the Lord with peace in his heart and confidence about where he was going after death. That, she said, was the purpose of our praying for Fred. It was not for physical healing but an assurance of peace and security in his final days on earth. God's mercy replaced Fred's anxieties and fear with His peace and comfort in his soul. Praise God! He is truly a God of love! He always knows and does what's best for His children.

PERSONAL APPLICATION

When you pray for healing, why should you have confidence in the love of the Father God, Jesus Christ, and the Holy Spirit to do what is best?

> Trust in the LORD with all your heart, and do not lean on your own understanding. (Proverbs 3:5 ESV)

Healing and Faith

You have seen that supernatural healings are certainly miracles of God. The following verse indicates that faith in the Lord Jesus is needed for a sick person to be miraculously healed:

> And the prayer of faith will save the one who is sick, and the Lord will raise him up. (James 5:15 ESV)

The following verse says that miracles will not occur without faith in Jesus to do so:

> And he did not do many miracles there because of their lack of faith. (Matthew 13:58 NIV)

Most of us would desire to see a sick person healed. But is our human compassion the same as having faith in the Lord to heal?

The following verse indicates that our faith must be based on God and not on our desires:

> But when you ask Him, be sure that your faith is in God alone. (James 1:6 NLT)

Two stories. Following are two stories about an inadequate understanding of faith in God to heal.

She will be healed! That was my proclamation to her and her parents. Why would I state this so strongly? I was a new Christian listening to people I respected who said if you have enough faith, Jesus will heal a person. I was convinced of this, and so several friends and I prayed for the daughter. Unfortunately, she was not healed and was despondent. And her parents were very displeased with me for building her hopes up. I was wrong and apologized. I didn't understand biblical faith and healing.

Your faith is weak! Now it was my turn. I was having problems with asthma. A friend of ours told us I lacked the faith needed to be healed. If I just had enough faith, Jesus would heal me. But, by now, I had learned this is not always true.

What is biblical Faith? Both stories revolve around one simple point: Faith in Jesus to heal must be based on the Father's will and not on human desire and compassion. When He heals or doesn't heal, it is because He knows what's best.

Anointing, Laying on Hands, Prayer, and Healings

In November of 2014, Linda and I knew the Lord was calling us out of our current church and into another one. But which church out of the many in our area? Once we entered this next church's front door, we knew this was where the Lord wanted us. And once we entered the classroom for the large adult Sunday School, the Holy Spirit again gave us His peace to know this also was the Lord's plan. This was the first Sunday after their prior teacher of twenty-six years was called to serve in another church. Since they didn't have a replacement teacher, they asked me to teach the class. Linda and I prayed and felt one reason the Lord brought us there was for me to do this.

WHAT DO YOU THINK? (ADVANCED)
Why do you think our arrival the first Sunday after the prior teacher left was the Lord's plan for us, the preceding teacher, and the class? Was it a coincidence, or did the Holy Spirit orchestrate it all?

Prayer for the sick. Later in 2018, I began to sense the Holy Spirit wanted our class to pray for one another during our class meetings. I felt we were to do this by anointing with oil and hands-on prayer for those with any need. Our pastor said an elder didn't need to do this in our denomination and that we could do it ourselves.

The following scripture describes the hands-on anointing and prayer used in our class:

> Are any of you sick? You should call for the elders of the church to come and pray over you, anointing you with oil in the name of the Lord. Such a prayer offered in faith will heal the sick, and the Lord will make you well. (James 5:14-15 NLT)

The Lord healed several people of various physical and emotional health problems due to these anointings and prayers. I remember the following two in particular:

- A woman was healed of chronic depression she had for years
- The son of a couple was healed of total kidney failure (He was on dialysis several days a week)

WHAT DO YOU THINK?
Why is healing the mind and emotions just as much a miracle as healing the body?

Following is what the father said about the miraculous healing of his son with kidney failure:

> Our son was hospitalized for the sudden onset of type 2 diabetes. After many weeks of care in ICU, his condition deteriorated to total kidney failure. When finally out of ICU, he required kidney dialysis 3-4 days a week and months of continued hospitalization. Several months later, he was out of the hospital, although he still needed almost daily outpatient dialysis. After our prayers for him, his kidney function went from 0% to full function in a single week. He had been diagnosed with no hope for kidney recovery after total and long-term kidney failure, so his doctors could only agree it was a miraculous healing.

NOTE: Not everyone we anointed and prayed for was healed. We don't know why, but we accepted the results without losing faith in Jesus Christ to heal and restore.

Yes, God Still Does Miracles Today

Miracles today don't seem to be frequent occurrences. And so, not every Christian may experience supernatural miracles in their life. Moreover, some people may not recognize them as miracles even when they do occur. They may be too busy with life activities or be unaware of the Holy Spirit's work in and around them.

PERSONAL APPLICATION
Has God done some minor or tremendous miracle in your life? Why could you have overlooked or rationalized a miracle because you didn't believe in them?

Sometimes even the little things of life can include a small intervention by God. For nothing is too small or great for the God who created the universe!

Following is another chapter about the supernatural world that exists all around. You will see that the devil and his demons are fallen angels and are very real. However, you will also see that the followers of Jesus Christ don't need to fear them.

30

The Devil and His Demons Are Real

In the chapter "The Supernatural World," you saw that God created an uncountable number of angels (Hebrews 12:22) with a diversity of abilities and responsibilities. And that He created them before He created the natural world (Job 38:4-7). The devil and his followers (demons, evil spirits) were among these angels until they rebelled against the Father God and were kicked out of Heaven.

The following verse indicates that the devil and his demons were on earth by the time God created the Garden of Eden:

> Now the serpent *[the devil]* was more crafty than any other beast of the field that the LORD God had made. (Genesis 3:1 ESV, author's emphasis)

WHAT DO YOU THINK?
Why do you believe there are forces of good and evil at work in the world? Who is behind them?

IMPORTANT: The devil, his demons, and God's angels are eternal, supernatural beings. They are spirits, not human beings. But they do not have the divine nature of El Shaddai, Almighty God. For example, they are not all-powerful (omnipotent) and all-knowing (omniscient). They are not present everywhere at the same time (omnipresent). This also means they cannot see the future even though they are eternal (1 Peter 1:12). They only know what the Father God allows (Luke 8:28-31).

Kicked out of Heaven. The devil and his demons were still angels when they tried to dethrone God and claim Heaven as the throne for the devil. Of course, they lost this battle, and God cast them from Heaven to earth. They became corrupted in their nature and character. As a result, they are sometimes referred to as "fallen angels."

> Then there was war in heaven. Michael and his angels fought against the dragon and his angels. And the dragon lost the battle, and he and his angels were forced out of heaven. This great dragon—the ancient serpent called the devil, or Satan, the one deceiving the whole world—was thrown down to the earth with all his angels. (Revelation 12:7-9 NLT)

Since being cast out of Heaven, the devil and his demons continually try to exercise their destructive influences against people and all of God's creation. They hate everything about His creation since it represents the Almighty God who defeated them. They now exist on the earth, in the sky above, and in what you see as outer space above the earth.

WHAT DO YOU THINK?

What are some reasons the devil and his demons hate people, especially Christians?

Who Is the Devil?

Lucifer was the devil's angelic name. He was one of the highest-ranking angels of God before his rebellion (Isaiah 14:12-15 KJV). Satan has been his proper name since this rebellion. However, he is often referred to as the devil in the Bible.

Following are several names and descriptions of the devil in the Bible:

> So that huge dragon – the ancient serpent, the one called the devil and Satan, who deceives the whole world – was thrown down to the earth, and his angels along with him. (Revelation 12:9 NET)

> Stay alert! Watch out for your great enemy, the devil. He prowls around like a roaring lion, looking for someone to devour. (1 Peter 5:8 NLT)

> He [the devil] was a murderer from the beginning, and does not stand in the truth, because there is no truth in him. When he lies, he speaks out of his own character, for he is a liar and the father of lies. (John 8:44 ESV, author's emphasis)

> Then Jesus was led up by the Spirit into the wilderness to be tempted by the devil. . . . And the tempter came and said to Him *[Jesus]*, "If You are the Son of God, command that these stones become bread." (Matthew 4:1-3 NASB, author's emphasis)

> Then I heard a loud voice in heaven saying, "The salvation and the power and the kingdom of our God, and the ruling authority of his Christ, have now come, because the accuser *[Satan]* of our brothers and sisters, the one who accuses them day and night before our God, has been thrown down." (Revelation 12:10 NET, author's emphasis)

In the following verses, the devil and his demons are described as the spiritual enemies of God's people. By spiritual, I mean they are not physical beings like humans. Instead, they are supernatural beings, spirits, that exist beyond the physical realm. Also, remember that the devil is not equal to God. He is a created being. He is not anything like the sovereign, Almighty God who created everything and reigns supremely!

> Put on the whole armor of God, that you may be able to stand against the schemes of the devil. For we do not wrestle against flesh and blood, but against the rulers, against the authorities, against the cosmic powers over this present darkness, against the spiritual forces of evil in the heavenly places. Therefore take up the whole armor of God, that you may be able to withstand in the evil day, and having done all, to stand firm. (Ephesians 6:11-13 NASB)

Their two primary goals. From my perspective, they have two primary goals, both of which have a destructive intent:

1. Prevent people from being saved through Jesus Christ and spending eternity with God.

    > But even if our gospel is veiled, it is veiled only to those who are perishing, among whom the god of this age has blinded the minds of those who do not believe so they would not see the light of the glorious gospel of Christ, who is the image of God. (2 Corinthians 4:3-4 NET)

    > So listen to the parable of the sower: When anyone hears the word about the kingdom and does not understand it, the evil one comes and snatches what was sown in his heart; this is the seed sown along the path. (Matthew 13:18-19 NET)

2. Distract, discourage, and deceive the followers of Jesus Christ, so they live a defeated life with little eternal value.

> That is why, when I could bear it no longer, I sent Timothy to find out whether your faith was still strong. I was afraid that the tempter had gotten the best of you and that our work had been useless. (1 Thessalonians 3:5 NLT)

> For false christs and false prophets will arise and perform great signs and wonders, so as to lead astray, if possible, even the elect. (Matthew 24:24 ESV)

PERSONAL APPLICATION

Think back over your life. What have you experienced with demons trying to prevent your salvation or discourage your Christian life?

Demon Possessed Teenager and Worship of the Devil

The following story illustrates the first goal of the devil and his demons. We met Rodney and Joyce at church in Michigan in 1986. We developed a close relationship, often having dinner and extensive prayer at each other's homes. Linda and I also became friends with another couple from our church. They had three sons, the youngest of which was in middle school. Without the parent's initial knowledge, he became the leader of a small group of students that met in their basement to worship Satan. At our suggestion in 1989, the parents asked Rodney to intervene and save their son from the demons. When Rodney went down to the basement, the boys gladly showed him their articles of satanic worship. These included parts of a goat they used in their rituals. Rodney was full of the Holy Spirit and mighty in spiritual warfare. In the name of Jesus Christ, he commanded the demons to leave the boys and the house. They quickly went, and the son realized Jesus Christ was superior to the devil and his demons. He prayed with Rodney and asked Jesus to be his Savior and Lord. Much later, when he graduated from college, we heard he was studying to become a pastor. God is supreme and holds all authority and power! The devil is NOT God! A lesson here is that God can rescue and restore what the devil tries to destroy.

Supernatural hedge of protection from God. I believe the following scripture indicates that God has put a hedge of protection in the spiritual realm around every person. The devil and his demons cannot break through this on their own. People must open a supernatural door into their lives that enables them to influence (and even harm) them.

Have you not made a hedge around him and his household and all that he has on every side? You have blessed the work of his hands, and his livestock have increased in the land. (Job 1:10 NET)

CAUTION: Do not engage in activities that open your life in the supernatural realm to demons. Occult practices such as using mediums, Ouija boards, automatic handwriting, and witchcraft are examples of how people can do this.

What can you do? If you have done any of these things, even a long time ago, don't let demons continue to deceive and influence you. Please repent and ask for the Father's forgiveness. Stop doing these demonic practices and ask the Holy Spirit to fill you with His presence, power, and life. Seek other followers of Christ you trust and ask them to pray with and for you until you are entirely free of the demons.

PRACTICE IT
What should you do now if you have exposed yourself to demons through an occult practice?

The chapter "Believers at War" covers more about the devil, his demons, and their destructive actions. But, for now, you must know that Jesus Christ is God and has absolute authority over the devil and his demons. He will set you free if you trust and ask Him.

Demons Believe Jesus Christ Is the Son of God

Since demons exist in the supernatural realm, they know Jesus Christ and who He is. They also know Jesus has absolute authority over them.

And when he came to the other side, to the country of the Gadarenes, two demon-possessed men met him, coming out of the tombs, so fierce that no one could pass that way. And behold, they cried out, "What have you to do with us, O Son of God? Have you come here to torment us before the time?" (Matthew 8:28-29 ESV)

And demons also came out of many, crying, "You are the Son of God!" But he rebuked them and would not allow them to speak, because they knew that he was the Christ. (Luke 4:41 ESV)

Jesus Christ Is Victorious Over Death and the Devil

Jesus Christ voluntarily died on the cross to complete His Father God's promise to provide salvation and eternal life to those who would accept Him as their Savior and Lord. At that time, He also disarmed the devil and his demons, as the following verses indicate:

> And you, who were dead in your trespasses and the uncircumcision of your flesh, God made alive together with him, having forgiven us all our trespasses, by canceling the record of debt that stood against us with its legal demands. This he set aside, nailing it to the cross. He disarmed the rulers and authorities and put them to open shame, by triumphing over them in him. (Colossians 2:13-15 ESV)

> For this purpose the Son of God was revealed: to destroy the works of the devil. (1 John 3:8 NET)

> Since therefore the children share in flesh and blood, he himself likewise partook of the same things, that through death he might destroy the one who has the power of death, that is, the devil, and deliver all those who through fear of death were subject to lifelong slavery. (Hebrews 2:14-15 ESV)

WHAT DO YOU THINK?
Consider what you have just read, and answer the following question: Why don't the followers of Jesus Christ need to fear the devil and his demons, even though this enemy is mighty?

The following verses tell us that the devil and his demon's complete and utter defeat is imminent. Their eternal fate is the *Lake of Fire*, where they will never again be able to persecute the children of God (Revelation 20:10).

> The God of peace will soon crush Satan under your feet. May the grace of our Lord Jesus be with you. (Romans 16:20 NLT)

> Now when the thousand years are finished, . . . the devil who deceived them was thrown into the lake of fire and sulfur, where the beast and the false prophet are too, and they will be tormented there day and night forever and ever. (Revelation 20:7-10 NET)

The Father, Jesus Christ, and the Holy Spirit want believers to live in joy and peace without fear. Therefore, the indwelling Holy Spirit will help believers overcome the inevitable battles with their enemy. They have the authority of Jesus Christ and the power of the Holy Spirit to lead them to victory in this spiritual war.

The next chapter describes other supernatural experiences with demons. It also exposes the lie that purported paranormal sightings are the ghosts of deceased people. And, of course, it reinforces that the followers of Jesus Christ don't need to fear this defeated enemy.

31

Paranormal Sightings – Not "Ghosts" of Dead People

"Ghosts" are not dead people. Some people believe that when a person's body dies, their spirit/soul can linger on earth for a while, sometimes to complete unfinished business or become a guardian angel. You may hear them referred to as ghosts. However, this idea is not accurate and is contrary to the teachings of the Bible. When people physically die, their spirit/soul goes directly to Heaven or Hell. There is no intermediate state where a person's spirit/soul lingers on earth.

Following are several scriptures that indicate what happens to the spirit/soul of a person upon physical death:

> We are of good courage, I say, and prefer rather to be absent from the body and to be at home with the Lord. (2 Corinthians 5:8 NASB)

> But Stephen, full of the Holy Spirit, looked intently toward heaven and saw the glory of God, and Jesus standing at the right hand of God. "Look!" he said. "I see the heavens opened, and the Son of Man standing at the right hand of God!" . . . They continued to stone Stephen while he prayed, "Lord Jesus, receive my spirit!" Then he fell to his knees and cried out with a loud voice, "Lord, do not hold this sin against them!" When he had said this, he died. (Acts 7:55-60 NET)

> Finally, the poor man died and was carried by the angels to be with Abraham. The rich man also died and was buried, and his soul went to the place of the dead. (Luke 16:22-23 NET)

People Can't Talk to the Dead

People who are alive can't communicate with people who have died. However, ghost hunters, psychics, and others profess (usually for a fee) to speak with a deceased friend or relative. Attempts to speak with the dead are against God's will (Leviticus 20:6). If such a communication appears to have occurred, it's a demon doing the communication or a complete fraud.

WHAT DO YOU THINK?

Since people are not ghosts, why are ghost hunters, psychics, and the such potentially exposing themselves to demons?

Stories of Haunted Locations

There are TV shows, and movies about locations and buildings haunted supposedly by ghosts. If the paranormal experience is authentic, they are experiencing demons, not the spirits/souls of people who have died. Demons are deceiving spirits (Revelation 12:9) and sometimes can visually manifest their presence. My friend Rodney could see them because the Holy Spirit had given him the spiritual gift of discernment of spirits.

Remember that the devil and his demons are liars and deceivers all the time! They are always malevolent and never benevolent in their activities.

NOTE: As you will see in these following stories, some demons are territorial (Daniel 10:20). When they claim a specific location, they don't want to leave. In these stories, someone had invited them into these locations through occult or other demonically inspired activities.

Two stories. Following are descriptions of two encounters with demons who had claimed physical locations as their own. I share these as evidence that demons are real and not your friends.

Finding a place for me and my dogs. I waited too long to find a place to rent before my first day at work in San Francisco in 1974. I spent several days looking but couldn't find a furnished apartment that would allow my two dogs. Finally, in the fading sunlight of Saturday evening, I found a furnished house for rent. It was locked, so I could not go inside before renting it.

I moved my few things into the house late Sunday afternoon. The house felt cold and unwelcoming. That evening my two dogs were sitting with me on the couch as I watched TV across the room. Soon they began to see something floating in the air in front of us. They moved their heads in unison as they nervously watched. That first night I felt the evil presence of demons in the bedroom.

That Monday after work, I put the perishable groceries I purchased in the refrigerator and the cans in the cupboard. The next morning all the cans were neatly stacked in a pyramid on the kitchen counter below the cupboard. The demons had done this during the night. This happened on two separate occasions. Later in my stay, I would find things moved around the house from the original location where I had placed them. It became clear these demons claimed this house as their territory and didn't want me there. Well, I didn't want to be there either. However, it was several months before I found another place to rent.

WHAT DO YOU THINK? (ADVANCED)

Why do you think demons are territorial? Why don't they want to leave a place they occupy?

Haunted apartment. In late 1976 I was living temporarily in an apartment in San Francisco. By this time, I was a Christian and familiar with sensing the presence of demons, so I could tell they were in this apartment. The coldness of their evil presence was there every evening when I came back from work. Occasionally, they would let me know this was their territory by moving something around the room. I was reading a book on this particular night and had put it on the end table by the couch where I was sitting. When I came back from the bathroom, the book was on the couch where I had been sitting. It couldn't have fallen from the end table to the couch. When I went to bed, the sense of the demons in the bedroom was more oppressive than it had ever been. So much so that I kneeled by my bed, reading the book of Psalms and praising God out loud. The presence of the demons intensified as I sang and quoted Psalms of praise to our mighty God. Suddenly, I felt compelled by the Holy Spirit to leave. I dressed, packed my belongings, and left the apartment, never to return. Later I realized this occurred because I needed to leave there in order for the next steps in God's plan for my life to start. God can and will use anybody, including the devil and his demons, to accomplish His will for His children.

The following verse says that what others, including demons, mean for evil and harm, God means for good to bring about His intended results:

> You meant evil against me, but God meant it for good in order to bring about this present result. (Genesis 50:20 NASB)

God is greater. If you are a born-again follower of Christ, the following verse says the Holy Spirit living in you is greater than the devil and his demons around you:

> The Spirit who lives in you is greater than the spirit who lives in the world. (1 John 4:4 NLT)

PERSONAL APPLICATION

Describe a situation where you experienced demons that claimed a location as their own. How did you feel, and what did you do? Did you feel victorious or defeated?

The White Witch – She Wanted to Help

Sometimes a person under a demon's influence can have a genuine concern for other people. This comes from their human compassion. (However, demons are not compassionate because they hate people.) Sometimes, these kind people may unknowingly allow the demons to affect someone else's life negatively. Following is an example Linda and I experienced.

The white witch and her garden. In 1997 in Michigan, we met a new neighbor a few houses down from us. She was friendly and wanted to show us her herbal garden. She told us she used them as a white witch in her prayers and practices. We asked her what a white witch was. What did they do? She said that a black witch practiced black magic to bring harm to people. On the other hand, white witches practiced white magic to bring good to people. We also talked a little about my health problems. A few days later, the neighbor brought over a bouquet of herbs she said would help me recover. She said she prayed over them with a spell. We genuinely thanked her for her compassion and kindness. However, we put them in the garage when she left because we felt uneasy about them. It was not the herbs but the spell that concerned us. It seemed this opened a door for demons into our home. A few days later, we threw them out. Another friend, Jack, who had a powerful ministry in spiritual warfare, came over and did spiritual warfare in our home and garage to drive out any remaining presence of demons. There was now peace again in our home and garage. We remained friendly with our white witch neighbor. However, we didn't invite her to our home or go into hers again.

PRACTICE IT

God says witchcraft is evil (2 Chronicles 33:6). If you have practiced witchcraft or been the recipient of it, you must repent to be set free from it. Please do this now to be free from their overt and subtle influences.

NOTE: Herbs are vegetation created by God for good. By themselves, they are not sources of demonic activity. I have used herbs for culinary and medicinal purposes for over forty-five years without inviting demons into my life.

Masters of Disguise

The devil and his demons are masters of disguise. They try to infiltrate anything Christian to deceive unsuspecting people into thinking they are emissaries from God sent to help people.

> And no wonder, for even Satan disguises himself as an angel of light. Therefore it is not surprising his servants also disguise themselves as servants of righteousness, whose end will correspond to their actions. (2 Corinthians 11:14-15 NET)

They can only lie and deceive since truth is not part of their corrupted nature. Oh, sometimes they will say something that is partly true, but it's always a deception.

> He was a murderer from the beginning. He has always hated the truth, because there is no truth in him. When he lies, it is consistent with his character; for he is a liar and the father of lies. (John 8:44 NLT)

PERSONAL APPLICATION

If you are a follower of Jesus Christ, is there something in your heart that causes you to fear demons? If so, why should you ask trusted friends to pray with you?

No fear. In the chapter "Believers at War," you will see that Jesus Christ has absolute authority over the devil and his demons. As a result, there is no need for His followers to fear this spiritual enemy.

32

Be Prepared: Know the Truth

You know about battles and wars between people. People are fighting against other people using military weapons. These are constantly in the media. But did you know there are spiritual battles as well? And that the nature of these battles is about truth?

> Set them apart in the truth; your word is truth. (John 17:17 NET)

The Battleground for Truth Is the Mind and Heart

These battles are primarily fought in the minds and hearts of people. There, the enemy tries to gain a foothold with lies and deceptions to influence thinking, values, and behavior.

> For though we live as human beings, we do not wage war according to human standards, for the weapons of our warfare are not human weapons but are made powerful by God for tearing down strongholds. We tear down arguments (2 Corinthians 10:3-4 NET)

NOTE: Most of these influences are so subtle that many people don't recognize their source.

Test the Spirits to Discern Truth

God warns in the Bible that people, including born-again followers of Jesus Christ, will be exposed to lies and deceptions. The following verses say people must learn to discern truth from error:

> Dear friends, do not believe every spirit, but test the spirits to determine if they are from God, because many false prophets have gone out into the world. By this you know the Spirit of God: Every spirit that confesses Jesus as the Christ who has come in the flesh is from God, but every spirit that refuses to confess Jesus, that spirit is not from God, and this is the spirit of the antichrist, which you have heard is coming, and now is already in the world. (1 John 4:1-3 NET)

Know who you are in Christ. As a follower of Jesus Christ, you are:

- Born-again by the Spirit of God (Ephesians 2:22)
- A chosen child of God (Ephesians 1:4)
- Transferred from the devil's domain into Christ's Kingdom (Colossians 1:13)
- Forgiven for all your sins and will never be condemned by God (Romans 8:1)
- Given power, love, and self-control by God (1 Timothy 1:7)
- Given strength by Jesus to do what He asks of you (Philippians 4:13)

Knowing this about yourself as a believer can help you recognize lies that attempt to undermine your faith in the God who loves you.

Be prepared with God's truth. Following are some preparations to protect the mind and heart with truth:

- Study God's written word, the Bible, to know the truth (John 8:32)
- Apply His words of truth to daily living (James 1:22)
- Consistently meet together to encourage and support one another (Hebrews 10:24-25)
- Pray consistently by the Holy Spirit in everything (Ephesians 6:18-19)

In the next verses, Jesus says to follow His teachings to know the truth:

> Then Jesus said to those Judeans who had believed him, "If you continue to follow my teaching, you are really my disciples and you will know the truth, and the truth will set you free." (John 8:31-32 NET)

Remember to rely on the Holy Spirit. As the *paraclete*, He is the believer's Helper, Teacher, and Guide. He will help them control their thoughts (Romans 8:5-6), where deceptions start.

Deceiving spirits. Demons are trying to deceive people by any possible means, including teaching false Christian beliefs to those who don't know the truth of God.

> The Spirit clearly says that in later times some will abandon the faith and follow deceiving spirits and things taught by demons. (1 Timothy 4:1 NLT)

IMPORTANT: The devil and his demons can't read people's minds. They can only attempt to put thoughts into their minds to influence them (Ezekiel 38:10; Matthew 16:21-23). They are not like God, who knows everything, including the thoughts, desires, and motives of everyone (1 Chronicles 28:9; Luke 6:8; Hebrews 4:12). However, they have been around since people were created, so they know human behavior. They know what can tempt people and cause them to violate even their most fundamental beliefs and values.

WHAT DO YOU THINK?
Why is it not possible for a demon to know what a person is thinking?

Following are several examples from the Bible about how the devil and his demons distort the truth with deceptive thoughts in the minds and hearts of people. As these verses indicate, they often target weak areas of human character.

> But Elymas the magician (for that is the meaning of his name) opposed them, seeking to turn the proconsul away from the faith. But Saul, who was also called Paul, filled with the Holy Spirit, looked intently at him and said, "You son of the devil, you enemy of all righteousness,

full of all deceit and villainy, will you not stop making crooked the straight paths of the Lord? (Acts 13:8-10 ESV)

But a man named Ananias, with his wife Sapphira, sold a piece of property, and with his wife's knowledge he kept back for himself some of the proceeds and brought only a part of it and laid it at the apostles' feet. But Peter said, "Ananias, why has Satan filled your heart to lie to the Holy Spirit and to keep back for yourself part of the proceeds of the land?" (Acts 5:1-3 ESV)

WHAT DO YOU THINK?

What human weaknesses allowed these people to be deceived?

Following is a story about a young woman who was led astray from the truth of God.

Did she abandon truth to follow lies? Our adult Sunday School class was having a social get-together at someone's apartment. We wondered where Crystal was since she usually enjoyed these. Later that evening, she came in just bubbling with exciting news. She had met a spiritual teacher (from an eastern religion) who told her things about her life she thought only God could know. However, this man was led by a deceiving spirit who wanted people to *abandon the faith* in Christ and pursue his form of Godless religion. When I explained this to her privately, she angrily left the party. She didn't come back to our Sunday School class. I don't know whether this was temporary or the end of her relationship with Jesus Christ. Only He knows what's in her heart today.

NOTE: The lies and deceptions of the enemy will violate the truths in the Bible. They will misquote or misuse them. For example, you can see how the devil tried but failed when he tested Jesus' faith in the Father God in Matthew 4:1-11. They will also distort or malign the character of God to turn people away from Him. This can be seen when the devil tempted Adam and Eve to sin against God in the Garden of Eden (Genesis 3:1-5).

Demons Can Deceive Non-believers

People who have not committed their hearts and lives to Jesus Christ function out of their self-centered old nature. Since the Holy Spirit does not dwell within them, they can be deceived more easily by the subtle lies of demons, as the following verses indicate:

> As for you, you were dead in your transgressions and sins, in which you used to live when you followed the ways of this world and of the ruler of the kingdom of the air, the spirit who is now at work in those who are disobedient. (Ephesians 2:1-2 NIV)

> Satan, who is the god of this world, has blinded the minds of those who don't believe. They are unable to see the glorious light of the Good News. They don't understand this message about the glory of Christ, who is the exact likeness of God. (2 Corinthians 4:4 NLT)

> You belong to your father, the devil, and you want to carry out your father's desires. He was a murderer from the beginning, not holding to the truth, for there is no truth in him. When he lies, he speaks his native language, for he is a liar and the father of lies. (John 8:44 NIV)

> For such people are false apostles, deceitful workers, masquerading as apostles of Christ. And no wonder, for Satan himself masquerades as an angel of light. It is not surprising, then, if his servants also masquerade as servants of righteousness. Their end will be what their actions deserve. (2 Corinthians 11:13-15 NIV)

WHAT DO YOU THINK?

What are some ways the devil and his demons use people to pretend to be Christians to deceive and try to lead others away from God?

Demons Can Deceive Believers

Even when believers strive to live the Christian life in ways that please the Father, they can still be deceived. Following are two important examples of how this can occur:

Human motives, not God's motives: Even when believers think they have a person's best interest at heart, they can be saying and doing things that are opposed to what God wants. In the following verse, the Apostle Peter did this when he reprimanded Jesus for saying He would be crucified and raised from the dead:

> But when Jesus turned and looked at his disciples, he rebuked Peter. "Get behind me, Satan!" he said. "You do not have in mind the concerns of God, but merely human concerns." (Mark 8:33 NIV)

As he did with Peter in this verse, the devil can use the good intentions of human compassion to try to disrupt God's plans and purposes.

Lack of forgiveness: A lack of forgiveness is another way believers can be vulnerable to the lies and deceptions of the devil and his demons.

> Anyone you forgive, I also forgive. And what I have forgiven—if there was anything to forgive—I have forgiven in the sight of Christ for your sake, in order that Satan might not outwit us. For we are not unaware of his schemes. (2 Corinthians 2:10-11 NIV)

WHAT DO YOU THINK?

Describe two ways a demon easily deceives some followers of Christ to believe their lies.

The Battle for Truth Is Not with People

Those who follow Jesus Christ must understand that the battle for truth is not against people but against the devil and his demons.

> Finally, be strong in the Lord and in the strength of his might. Put on the whole armor of God, that you may be able to stand against the schemes of the devil. For we do not wrestle against flesh and blood, but against the rulers, against the authorities, against the cosmic powers over this present darkness, against the spiritual forces of evil in the heavenly places. (Ephesians 6:10-12 ESV)

Be Prepared: Wear the Full Armor of God

Followers of Jesus Christ must be prepared and always wear the full armor of God. Therefore, they must be committed to the Lordship of Jesus Christ (1 Peter 3:15) and wear God's whole armor, as identified in Ephesians 6:13-18. If they do so, they can be confident of prevailing against the lies and deceptions of their spiritual enemy.

> Therefore take up the whole armor of God, that you may be able to withstand in the evil day, and having done all, to stand firm. Stand therefore,
>
> having fastened on the **belt of truth**, and
>
> having put on the **breastplate of righteousness**, and,

as shoes for your feet, having put on the readiness given by the **gospel of peace**.

In all circumstances take up the **shield of faith**, with which you can extinguish all the flaming darts of the evil one; and

take the **helmet of salvation**, and

the **sword of the Spirit**, which is the word of God,

praying at all times in the Spirit, with all prayer and supplication. To that end keep alert with all perseverance, making supplication for all the saints. (Ephesians 6:13-18 ESV, author's emphasis)

NOTE: The Apostle Paul, who wrote the New Testament book of Ephesians, used the military armor of a Roman solder to describe how followers of Jesus Christ should be prepared to fight in the supernatural war with the devil and his demons. After he describes the armor, he concludes by urging believers to pray by the Holy Spirit in all things, which includes spiritual warfare.

WHAT DO YOU THINK? (ADVANCED)

Why is it vital for believers to wear the full armor of God, not just parts of it?

Following is a brief explanation of each piece of the armor of God:

Belt of Truth. Knowing and living by truth from the Bible is the foundation for the entire armor of God. Each piece is dependent upon this. Truth is not arbitrary. Rather, it is absolute and found in the Bible. The enemy's most prevalent weapons are deception and lies. God's truth, therefore, enables each piece of the armor of God to be used to counter these falsehoods.

Breastplate of Righteousness. Righteousness protects the spiritual and emotional heart of the believer. It has two meanings that are important. First, born-again believers are made right with God when they accept the death and resurrection of Jesus Christ to rescue them from the consequences of their sins. Second, righteousness is choosing to live in ways that honor God. Therefore, believers must strive to obey God and avoid the sins of the world that can easily entangle them and provide an opening for the enemy's influences.

***Gospel of Peace* as Shoes**. Followers of Jesus have peace with God as a solid foundation in their battles with the enemy. They can stand firm in this peace, knowing the enemy's lies can't change their eternal relationship with God. They must also know the gospel message (1 Corinthians 15:1-4) in order to tell others about the salvation offered by Jesus Christ and this peace with the Father God.

Shield of Faith. Faith in God is not "blind faith." Instead, it's based on the assurance and certainty of the truths in the Bible (Hebrews 11:1-3). Knowing truth enables believers to recognize the enemy's lies and deceptions and provides the basis to respond with faith in God. This faith rests solidly in the knowledge Jesus Christ has all authority over everything and has given this authority to His followers (Luke 10:19). They fight with confidence, knowing Jesus has already won not just the battle but the spiritual war for them.

Helmet of Salvation. Believers must be fully convinced of the eternal salvation they received when they accepted Jesus as their Savior and Lord. This security protects their minds from the enemy, especially those lies that say they are not really saved or that God doesn't love or care about them.

Sword of the Spirit, which is the word of God. The *sword* is words given by the Holy Spirit when they are needed for a specific situation. They are words to be spoken to resist and defeat the particular temptation or deception of the enemy. These words are biblical truths used as a weapon for defense and offense. Often, the Holy Spirit will bring scriptures that were studied, meditated on, and memorized to the minds of believers to use as their swords. Therefore, believers must live close to the Holy Spirit (the *paraclete*) to be responsive when He communicates.

This concludes the Apostle's teaching about how the armor of a Roman soldier represents the spiritual armor for believers in the spiritual battles for truth.

Praying in the Spirit. Since this is a spiritual battle in the mind and heart, not a physical struggle, prayer by the Holy Spirit is essential.

Pray in the Spirit at all times and on every occasion. Stay alert and be persistent in your prayers for all believers everywhere. (Ephesians 6:18 NLT)

Ask the Holy Spirit to help you know what to pray and for His manifested presence and power in these prayers. This kind of prayer does not involve closing your eyes and bowing your head. Rather, this requires you to be alert to the enemy's presence and the Holy Spirit's direction.

WHAT DO YOU THINK?

Prayer is not part of a Roman soldier's armor. Why do you think it should also be used in spiritual warfare?

Beware and be alert. Remember Harvey, my friend from work who read his Bible at break time? Eventually, we became friends, and he invited me to his small farm where he had some cattle. He wanted to show me something in the field but warned me that a young steer (with shortened horns) might sneak up behind us. If my friend wasn't alert to its presence and location, it would come up behind him, put his head and horns between his legs, and lift him off the ground. As we walked, I was alert to its location but soon was caught up in conversation and lost sight of the steer. Then, suddenly, I was being lifted off the ground. You can imagine that it was not a pleasant experience.

Followers of Christ don't need to be constantly looking for indications the enemy is sneaking up on them. If you recall, their typical approach is to put thoughts into the minds of believers. However, they should understand this approach and be alert to the enemy's apparent lies and deceptions.

Receive Jesus's peace, not fear. When believers focus on Jesus, they can receive His gift of peace of mind and heart.

> I am leaving you with a gift—peace of mind and heart. And the peace I give is a gift the world cannot give. So don't be troubled or afraid. (John 14:27 NLT)

> But they overcame him by the blood of the Lamb and by the word of their testimony, and they did not love their lives so much that they were afraid to die. (Revelation 12:11 NET)

Be alert and secure. The following verses say believers must know the truth and be alert and secure in Jesus Christ's love:

> Stay alert! Watch out for your great enemy, the devil. He prowls around like a roaring lion, looking for someone to devour. Stand firm against him, and be strong in your faith. (1 Peter 5:8-9 NLT)

The squirrel and our dogs. A house Linda and I lived in bordered a wooded area. Our two dogs were constantly chasing the many squirrels out of our fenced yard. I noticed one squirrel had begun to run more slowly. As I let our dogs out one day, I saw the squirrel sitting in the middle of our backyard. The dogs ran as fast as they could, barking as loudly as they could to warn the invading squirrel they meant business. However, it didn't run this time. The dogs came to a screeching halt in front of the squirrel. The squirrel looked at them as if to say, "See, I am not afraid of you," and slowly wandered away.

WHAT DO YOU THINK?

How is this story a lesson for believers that they do not need to be afraid of demons when they know the truth of God?

Want more information? *The Invisible War* by Chip Ingram provides well-researched descriptions and examples about this spiritual war, how to use each piece of the armor of God, and how to live without fear because the believer belongs to Jesus Christ. It's a balanced approach to spiritual warfare that demonstrates the authority of Jesus Christ over all the powers of the evil one.

In the next chapter, you will learn specific tactics to defeat the lies and deceptions of the devil and his demons. Even though it's not a common experience for people, you may encounter the presence of demons in a location they claim as their own. (You saw this in a previous chapter.) Believers will learn how to respond with spiritual warfare tactics based on the authority of Jesus Christ and the indwelling power of the Holy Spirit. The devil and demons must submit to Almighty God when the followers of Jesus Christ rely on Him (not themselves) in these encounters.

33

Believers at War

This chapter is for the followers of Jesus Christ who want to know how to defeat their spiritual enemy. You know that most spiritual battles occur in the mind and heart. However, some believers may occasionally be confronted with a spiritual struggle in a specific location. These are sometimes referred to as open spiritual warfare. To be prepared, believers must know truth and biblical tactics that lead to victory.

IMPORTANT: In this book's stories about open spiritual warfare, you will see that I ALWAYS pray by the **authority of Jesus Christ** and the **Holy Spirit's power** over the devil and his demons. Believers do not have their own authority and power over them. Only through the death and resurrection of Jesus Christ and being born-again by the Holy Spirit can they defeat their spiritual enemy.

CAUTION: If followers of Jesus have opened their lives to evil, their supernatural hedge of protection (Job 1:10) may be broken, allowing demons to influence them. They should not enter this open spiritual warfare if this is the case. Instead, they must repent of sin and ask the Holy Spirit to fill them with His presence and power. Only after this, and only if the Holy Spirit leads them, should they conduct spiritual warfare.

WHAT DO YOU THINK?

Why must believers not enter into spiritual warfare if they have opened their lives to evil in the supernatural realm through occult and other demonic-inspired practices?

Spiritual Warfare in a Hotel Room
The battle is mainly in the mind and heart, EXCEPT when it's not! You will see one of these exceptions in this story. I've already described two of my experiences with demons in a location in a previous chapter. You may never experience these open warfare encounters with demons, but you must be prepared just in case.

The hotel room. In 1986 my company transferred me from Florida to Michigan. We drove our two cars with our two dogs (Casey & Zach) and stopped at a hotel for the first night of the trip. When I entered the lobby to check in, I knew there was a problem. There was tension and strife with the hotel staff in the lobby, not just the "I'm having a bad day" stuff. When we entered our hotel room, we could sense a presence there. Because of my prior experiences, I knew these were demons. I felt a coldness in the room as well as evil. Our two dogs were on the floor as we unpacked for the night. In unison, they both looked up into the air and moved their heads back and forth as they watched demons move through the room. We could see our dogs were scared. We briefly prayed for protection over the room and our dogs and left for dinner. I should have requested another room, but we were tired and hungry since it was late in the evening.

When we returned from dinner, Zach, our small Poodle, was hunched over and quivering in fear against a wall in the room. We then realized we had a serious spiritual battle to fight. Clearly, they wanted us to fear them so we would leave "their room." But we were not buying their lies! This room was ours for the night, and we were not going to leave. (Linda was new to spiritual warfare with demons and was initially uncertain about what was occurring. However, later we had other experiences that enabled her to understand this better.) Linda and I prayed intensely, asking Jesus and the Holy Spirit to help us bind these demons for the night. We quoted relevant scripture, such as *the Spirit who lives in you is greater than the spirit who lives in the world* (1 John 4:4 NLT). We spent probably an hour quoting Bible verses and praying over every foot of the room, including the closet, bathroom, and shower. We were not giving them any place to hide! We commanded them to leave, rebuked them in the name of Jesus Christ, and bound them from harassing us. We had loosed them from the room and began to feel their presence diminishing. Finally, the room was at peace. We, and our dogs, slept well the rest of the night.

WHAT DO YOU THINK?

Why do you think the demons may have returned the next day after we left?

Bible Verses about Spiritual Warfare Tactics

Biblical truth can be used to put demons in their proper place of submission to Jesus Christ. Truth and the Lordship of Jesus over everything are the foundation of all spiritual warfare. Believers use the authority of the name of Jesus and the indwelling power of the Holy Spirit to stand firm in the victory Jesus has over their enemy.

Summary of tactics. Following are the tactics from scripture we use in spiritual warfare with their meanings:

- Quote appropriate scripture – From memory or read from a Bible or smartphone

- Command – Declare, charge, transmit a message

- Rebuke – Censure, admonish; archaic – to turn back

- Bind – Tie up, restrict

- Loose – Untie, set free

Every tactic must be done in the name of Jesus Christ because His name is who He is as God.

Following are scriptures that identify some spiritual warfare tactics:

> Now when Jesus saw that a crowd was quickly gathering, he rebuked the unclean spirit, saying to it, "Mute and deaf spirit, I command you, come out of him and never enter him again." (Mark 9:25 NET)

> But when the archangel Michael, contending with the devil, was disputing about the body of Moses, he did not presume to pronounce a blasphemous judgment, but said, "The Lord rebuke you." (Jude 1:9 NET)

> Next I saw Joshua the high priest standing before the angel of the LORD, with Satan standing at his right hand to accuse him. The LORD said to Satan, "May the LORD rebuke you, Satan! May the LORD, who has chosen Jerusalem, rebuke you! Isn't this man like a burning stick snatched from the fire?" (Zachariah 3:1-2 NET)

She continued doing this for many days. But Paul was greatly annoyed, and turned and said to the spirit, "I command you in the name of Jesus Christ to come out of her!" And it came out at that very moment. (Acts 16:18 NET)

I *[Jesus]* tell you the truth, whatever you bind on earth will have been bound in heaven, and whatever you release *[loose]* on earth will have been released *[loosed]* in heaven. (Matthew 18:18 NET, author's emphasis)

But no one can enter a strong man's house and plunder his goods, unless he first binds the strong man. Then indeed he may plunder his house. (Mark 3:27 ESV)

PERSONAL APPLICATION

Describe an encounter you've had with demons in this kind of spiritual warfare. What did you do in your battle against them? Now that you've read these tactics, what could you have done differently?

The following are additional scriptures to use in spiritual warfare. These represent the believer's submission to Jesus as the Lord of their lives and demonstrate a grateful trust in God.

But thanks be to God, who gives us the victory through our Lord Jesus Christ! So then, dear brothers and sisters, be firm. Do not be moved! (1 Corinthians 15:57-58 NET)

Little children, you are from God and have overcome them, for he who is in you is greater than he who is in the world. (1 John 4:4 ESV)

Praise the LORD! Praise God in his sanctuary; praise him in his mighty heavens! Praise him for his mighty deeds; praise him according to his excellent greatness! (Psalms 150:1-2 ESV)

For I know that the LORD is great And that our Lord is above all gods. Whatever the LORD pleases, He does, In heaven and in earth, in the seas and in all deeps. (Psalms 135:5-6 NASB)

WHAT DO YOU THINK? (ADVANCED)

Why do demons hate believers to praise and worship Almighty God in their presence? Why do they leave when this occurs under the presence and power of the Holy Spirit?

Demons Must Submit to Jesus' Authority

There are stories in the Bible about demons taking possession of a person and causing them harm. Somehow the individuals opened their lives to allow this to occur. However, when the demons encountered Jesus, they were forced to leave the person when He commanded them to do so.

Following are several stories from the Bible about demons submitting to the authority of Jesus Christ (He is God!) and leaving people:

> Just then there was a man in their synagogue with an unclean spirit; and he cried out, saying, "What business do we have with each other, Jesus of Nazareth? Have You come to destroy us? I know who You are—the Holy One of God!" (Mark 1:23-26 NASB)

> As the boy was approaching, the demon threw him to the ground and shook him with convulsions. But Jesus rebuked the unclean spirit, healed the boy, and gave him back to his father. (Luke 9:42 NET)

> They were all amazed and began to say to one another, "What's happening here? For with authority and power he commands the unclean spirits, and they come out!" (Luke 4:36 NET)

This next verse states that Jesus gives His followers this same authority over demons:

> After Jesus called the twelve together, he gave them power and authority over all demons and to cure diseases. (Luke 9:1 NET)

Jesus' Lordship. When people are genuinely saved, they have asked Jesus to be their Savior and Lord. Jesus' Lordship means they sincerely want Him to take charge. They want His will more than their own for their lives (James 4:7).

CAUTION: People who are not followers of Jesus Christ don't have His authority over the presence and power of demons. If they try to use Jesus' name, the demons know the people don't have the indwelling Holy Spirit and Jesus' authority over them. They may respond and actually harm these unsuspecting people (Acts 19:13-16). So, if you are not a born-again follower of Jesus Christ actively living under His Lordship (1 Peter 3:15), do not engage the enemy in spiritual warfare.

WHAT DO YOU THINK?

What does it mean for believers to live under the Lordship of Jesus Christ?

Greater Is He Who Is Within You

Remember this verse, *You are from God, little children, and have conquered them, because the one who is in you is greater than the one who is in the world. . . . We are from God; the person who knows God listens to us, but whoever is not from God does not listen to us. By this we know the Spirit of truth and the spirit of deceit.* (1 John 4:4 NET)

The Holy Spirit must live within. In the following verses, Jesus warned that demons want a place to occupy and will do anything to keep it. He says that when a demon is cast out, it looks for another place to occupy. When it doesn't find one, it gets more demons and returns to its original location to reoccupy it. If the Holy Spirit is not living within that person due to their salvation in Christ, the demon can reclaim its place there. This last situation is far worse than the former.

When an unclean spirit goes out of a person, it passes through waterless places looking for rest but not finding any. Then it says, "I will return to the home I left." When it returns, it finds the house swept clean and put in order. Then it goes and brings seven other spirits more evil than itself, and they go in and live there, so the last state of that person is worse than the first. (Luke 11:24-26 NET)

The *house swept clean and put in order* indicates the person had reclaimed their life after the demon left. However, they did not ask Jesus to be their Savior and Lord, so the Holy Spirit did not come to live with them. Their *house* was, therefore, still spiritually empty, leaving room for the return of more demons.

Praise be to God for His indescribable gift of salvation in Jesus Christ! It's through this eternal relationship that His followers live a victorious life. There is joy and peace when they know Jesus protects them from evil.

> But the Lord is faithful, and He will strengthen and protect you from the evil one. (2 Thessalonians 3:3 NASB)

> Don't be afraid, for I am with you. Don't be discouraged, for I am your God. I will strengthen you and help you. I will hold you up with My victorious right hand. (Isaiah 41:10 NLT)

Believers owe everything to Jesus. This includes giving them His victory over the devil and his demons who are already defeated and condemned.

> In this way, He disarmed the spiritual rulers and authorities. He shamed them publicly by His victory over them on the cross. (Colossians 2:15 NLT)

> No, despite all these things, overwhelming victory is ours through Christ, who loved us. (Romans 8:37 NLT)

PERSONAL APPLICATION

As a born-again believer, you have the Holy Spirit living within you. When was there a time you felt His protection when you sensed evil around you? If the idea of a spiritual battle scares you, what must you do to overcome the fear?

Remember, there is a life of peace when God's perfect love lives in the followers of Jesus Christ (1 John 4:18)!

WHAT CHRISTIANITY IS REALLY LIKE

34

Christ's Church May Be Different Than You Think

The Christian church is not a physical building with the name "church." Christ's church is not an organization, association, or denomination. **The Christian church is simply all born-again followers of Jesus Christ wherever they are located.** These Christians have committed their hearts and lives to Jesus as their Savior and Lord.

> God has put all things under the authority of Christ and has made Him head over all things for the benefit of the church. And the church is His body; it is made full and complete by Christ, who fills all things everywhere with Himself. (Ephesians 1:22-23 NLT)

The "house of God." In the New Testament, the first Jewish Christians continued to attend their local Synagogue on Saturdays and worshiped at the Temple in Jerusalem. However, they knew now they were the "house of God" since the Father, Jesus, and Holy Spirit had come to live within them. As you see in the next verse, all born-again followers of Jesus are the temple of God on earth.

> Do you not know that you are God's temple and that God's Spirit dwells in you? (1 Corinthians 3:16 ESV)

> Jesus answered and said to him, "Truly, truly, I say to you, unless one is born again he cannot see the kingdom of God." (John 3:3 NASB)

WHAT DO YOU THINK?
Why are people who have gone to church all their lives not part of Christ's church unless they have committed themselves to Jesus Christ as their Savior and Lord?

Jesus Christ's Purpose for His Church

If you have attended church for a while, you may have heard people say the Christian church's purpose is to glorify God and worship Him. I would certainly agree. It's also a place for believers to be taught and trained (discipleship) to grow and mature as followers of Jesus. Churches committed to Jesus may have a mission statement that includes carrying out Jesus Christ's "Great Commission." In the following verses, you see that this Commission involves making disciples for Jesus, baptizing them as evidence of genuine faith, and teaching them to understand and live by the Bible, God's word.

> And Jesus came and said to them, "All authority in heaven and on earth has been given to me. Go therefore and make disciples of all nations, baptizing them in the name of the Father and of the Son and of the Holy Spirit, teaching them to observe all that I have commanded you. And behold, I am with you always, to the end of the age." (Matthew 28:18-20 ESV)

Since Jesus is the head of His church, He determines what each local church should be doing to build the Kingdom of God on earth. Therefore, local church pastors and leaders must seek His will for their church.

WHAT DO YOU THINK?
Suppose some churches focus on evangelism or healing people broken in heart or body. Why can they also be helping fulfill the Great Commission?

The Birth of Christ's Church and Christianity

You can read about the birth of Christianity in the New Testament book of Acts, Chapter Two. The Christian church was born out of a one-time spectacular event known as Pentecost. It was the Holy Spirit who gave it birth on that day.

When the day of Pentecost arrived, they were all together in one place. And suddenly there came from heaven a sound like a mighty rushing wind, and it filled the entire house where they were sitting. And divided tongues as of fire appeared to them and rested on each one of them. And they were all filled with the Holy Spirit and began to speak in other tongues as the Spirit gave them utterance. (Acts 2:1-4 ESV)

NOTE: After its birth, Christianity was initially referred to as "The Way" (Acts 9:2). Later, believers were first referred to as "Christians" by the people of Antioch (Acts 11:26). The word Christian means those belonging to Christ. It only occurs three times in the Bible. Other names used are believers, brothers and sisters, and followers of Christ.

Christ's church grew quickly. His church began with about a hundred and twenty followers of Jesus gathered in a room praying on the morning of Pentecost. Another three thousand believers were added that same day as the Apostle Peter spoke powerfully (by the Holy Spirit) about Jesus Christ to the crowd.

"Therefore let all the house of Israel know for certain that God has made Him both Lord and Christ—this Jesus whom you crucified." Now when they heard this, they were pierced to the heart, and said to Peter and the rest of the apostles, "Brethren, what shall we do?" Peter said to them, "Repent, and each of you be baptized in the name of Jesus Christ for the forgiveness of your sins; and you will receive the gift of the Holy Spirit. For the promise is for you and your children and for all who are far off, as many as the Lord our God will call to Himself." (Acts 2:36-39 NASB

WHAT DO YOU THINK?
Based on the above scripture, what happens to a person's heart that causes them to want to be saved by Christ?

Oneness of Christ's church. There is one God in three persons. There is also a unity, a oneness in Christ's church. The following verses reveal this unique oneness:

For there is one body and one Spirit, just as you have been called to one glorious hope for the future. There is one Lord, one faith, one baptism, and one God and Father, who is over all and in all and living through all. (Ephesians 4:4-6 NLT)

You can see that there is unity, a oneness, permeating every aspect of Christianity. This unity also involves each person of the Trinity of God. The following describes this unity of Christ's church:

- *One body* (consisting of all believers as the body of Jesus Christ)
- *One Spirit* (Holy Spirit who lives in all believers)
- *One glorious hope for the future* (spending eternity with God)
- *One Lord* (Jesus Christ is in charge of the lives of His followers)
- *One Faith* (salvation based on the Good News of Jesus' death, burial, and resurrection)
- *One baptism* (into the family of God by the Holy Spirit when born-again)
- *One God and Father* (Father God of all believers. No other world religion proclaims their god to be *Abba*, who loves unconditionally)

PRACTICE IT
Are you attending a church that practices this unity? Do they strive to glorify God together in all they do? If not, is the Lord asking you to find one that does? Perhaps you should find one now that does?

What a Healthy Christian Church Does

There are several ways I could describe a healthy Christian church. You could find one that promotes the spiritual disciplines identified in the chapter "Knowing God through Christian Practices." Another way is to identify one that practices what the first followers of Jesus Christ did when they met. You can see these practices in the following verses:

And they devoted themselves to the apostles' teaching and the fellowship, to the breaking of bread and the prayers. And awe came upon every soul, and many wonders and signs were being done through the apostles. And all who believed were together and had all things in common. And they were selling their possessions and belongings and distributing the proceeds to all, as any had need. And day by day, attending the temple together and breaking bread in their homes, they received their food with glad and generous hearts, praising God and having favor with all the people. And the Lord added to their number day by day those who were being saved. (Acts 2:42-47 ESV)

The above verses describe the fundamentals of a healthy Christian church. Notice the focus is on God throughout their practices.

- Teaching: preaching, teaching, and studying the word of God
- Fellowshipping: meeting together regularly and enjoying each other
- Observing the Lord's Supper, Communion (Luke 22:14-20; 1 Corinthians 11:23-26)
- Praying: praying together and individually
- Helping others: sharing possessions, including financially, with those in need
- Worshiping God: participating in a weekly church service by worshiping God in song and learning about Him from preaching and teaching
- Gathering in small groups: Meeting in homes to continue the above during the week

It's important to remember that these Christians were committed to consistently doing these practices together. That's what the phrase *devoted themselves to* means. It's the key to understanding the motivation and behavior of a healthy Christian church.

Treatment of others. A spiritually healthy group of believers will demonstrate the following characteristics toward one another in all they do, even when deeply offended.

So, as those who have been chosen of God, holy and beloved, put on a heart of compassion, kindness, humility, gentleness and patience; bearing with one another, and forgiving each other, whoever has a complaint against anyone; just as the Lord forgave you, so also should you. (Colossians 3:12-13 NASB)

WHAT DO YOU THINK?
Why does a spiritually healthy church focus on God?

IMPORTANT: Sometimes, Christians say they would like to go back and participate in the early church because it was so enthusiastic about following these practices. However, most of the letters in the New Testament were written by the apostles to correct errors in Christian beliefs or some unacceptable behavior of these early believers. So, no church is perfect. That's because it's composed of imperfect people. Therefore, please don't look for perfection in any local church.

Pastors and Leaders of a Healthy Church

Find a local church where pastors and leaders are spiritually and emotionally healthy. One where they have a humble heart in serving God and others. You can see from the following verses that they (referred to as an *elder*) are to share with the Apostle Peter genuine care and protection of God's people:

> So as your fellow elder and a witness of Christ's sufferings and as one who shares in the glory that will be revealed, I urge the elders among you: Give a shepherd's care to God's flock among you, exercising oversight not merely as a duty but willingly under God's direction, not for shameful profit but eagerly. And do not lord it over those entrusted to you, but be examples to the flock. Then when the Chief Shepherd appears, you will receive the crown of glory that never fades away. (1 Peter 5:1-4 NET)

In the New Testament, church pastors and leaders were also sometimes called *overseers*. They were appointed to govern, lead, and teach in Christian churches. The Apostle Paul describes their qualifications and character as follows:

> It is a trustworthy statement: if any man aspires to the office of overseer *[elder]*, it is a fine work he desires to do. An overseer *[elder]*, then, must be above reproach, the husband of one wife, temperate, prudent, respectable, hospitable, able to teach, not addicted to wine or pugnacious, but gentle, peaceable, free from the love of money. He must be one who manages his own household well, keeping his

children under control with all dignity (but if a man does not know how to manage his own household, how will he take care of the church of God?), and not a new convert, so that he will not become conceited and fall into the condemnation incurred by the devil. And he must have a good reputation with those outside the church, so that he will not fall into reproach and the snare of the devil. (1 Timothy 3:1-7 NASB, author's emphasis)

WHAT DO YOU THINK? (ADVANCED)

Why do you think Jesus Christ has such strict requirements for pastors and leaders in His church?

Pastors and leaders who serve with Christ's love for His people should be honored and respected for their dedication to Christ and the congregation.

Elders who do their work well should be respected and paid well, especially those who work hard at both preaching and teaching. (1 Timothy 5:17 NLT)

They must have a solid knowledge of the Bible and be able to teach it accurately.

He must have a strong belief in the trustworthy message he was taught; then he will be able to encourage others with wholesome teaching and show those who oppose it where they are wrong. (Titus 1:9 NLT)

WHAT DO YOU THINK? (ADVANCED)

What can happen to the people in a congregation when the pastors and leaders don't know the Bible well? Why do you think they may also not know the Father God, Jesus Christ, and the Holy Spirit well?

The following verses say pastors and church leaders who use their spiritual gifts wisely will help believers actively participate in the church's activities and ministries. As a result, everyone will increase their knowledge of God and mature in faith. In other words, they will grow spiritually.

And He gave some as apostles, and some as prophets, and some as evangelists, and some as pastors and teachers, for the equipping of the saints for the work of service, to the building up of the body of Christ; until we all attain to the unity of the faith, and of the knowledge of the Son of God, to a mature man, to the measure of the stature which belongs to the fullness of Christ. (Ephesians 4:11-13 NASB)

How to Find a Healthy Christian Church

You can find information about a particular church in your area in the following ways.

1. Read the statement of faith on the church's Internet website. They usually provide descriptions of their beliefs, which indicate what's important to them. Some questions to ask yourself about their beliefs:

    *   Are they focused on fulfilling the Great Commission?

    *   Are any of their beliefs contrary to the Bible?

    *   Are any of their beliefs contrary to those in this book's chapter "Christian Beliefs: Salvation?"

2. Ask people who attend the church about the following:

    *   Have they seen the pastors, leaders, and people consistently following their church's beliefs?

    *   What leadership style do they see in the pastors and leaders?

    *   Do they exhibit a deep devotion to serving Christ and people?

    *   Are the sermons and teachings consistently and accurately based on the Bible?

3. Ask them if the church regularly practices the fundamental activities in Acts 2:42-47 above.

4. Ask the opinions of other pastors and people in your community about the church. Does it have a reputation for devotion to Christ and serving Him? Of course, opinions are not necessarily facts. So, check out the facts on your own as well.

IMPORTANT: Ask the Lord Jesus to lead you to a church where you can find a spiritual family and home. There are likely many churches in your local area, so follow the leading of the Holy Spirit and choose wisely. Remember that no church is perfect because all churches are composed of people who are not perfect.

PRACTICE IT
If you are not in a Christian church that meets most of the above indicators of being spiritually healthy, perhaps now is the time to ask the Lord (through His Spirit) to lead you to one of His choice?

Jesus is Lord of all! Therefore, you will not be wrong by following the leading of His Spirit as you seek His will in all things.

35

Tale of Three Churches

Following are true stories about three different churches. The first church exemplifies what a spiritually alive and healthy church can experience. Conversely, the symptoms of a spiritually unhealthy church are visible in the second and third churches.

WHAT DO YOU THINK?
If honoring and living for the Father God, Jesus Christ, and the Holy Spirit is not the center of worship, what is the reason for a church's existence? Who or what do they strive to honor instead of God?

Church One: The Lord Built a Spiritually Alive Church

In 1990, the Lord led Linda and me to a small church in Michigan with about fifty people. Many in the congregation were in their 70s or older. The worship services were formal, with rituals, and little opportunity to experience God's presence. Also, many didn't seem motivated to study the Bible and grow spiritually.

The pastor had only been there a short time when we arrived, but the Lord had given him a desire for the church to change and grow spiritually. He wanted worship services where people could encounter God and experience His awesome presence. Linda and I connected with the pastor and his wife and began to meet with them. We started a home group ministry with only the pastor, his wife, and a few other newcomers. The Holy Spirit continued to bring other Christians to our little church. These also wanted to grow spiritually and experience the presence of God and His Spirit. Soon I started to teach an adult Sunday School class. Unfortunately, most of the older congregation thought Sunday School was only for children. Hence, it mainly included newcomers to the church.

WHAT DO YOU THINK?
What evidence was there that God (not man) was orchestrating this growth in the church?

Choir of Angels Sing with Us

The Lord made it clear that He wanted us to start an additional worship service "contemporary" in style. We knew contemporary meant the Lord's Spirit was to be our guide and empower the worship services with His presence. Over the following months, we prayed, planned, and developed a strategy to implement the Lord's will. The time had now come, so we advertised the new contemporary service through multiple media sources. The services included singing, prayer, preaching, and an altar call. **It was to be the Lord's service with the Holy Spirit in control.** It would fail if the Spirit didn't show up with His presence and power. This was to be about worshiping our God and Savior, not about us.

WOW! We were stunned! We had over fifty people in our first new service. This was about the same number of people in the entire church when we first attended. And we did experience the presence of God and the power of the Holy Spirit as we sang songs of praise and worship to our great God!

> Praise the LORD! How good to sing praises to our God! How delightful and how fitting! (Psalms 147:1 NLT)

About halfway through our singing, I heard something supernatural – a choir of angels was accompanying us. I stopped and just listened to them praise their God and our God. This was incredible – a multitude of angels was worshiping the Father with us!

PERSONAL APPLICATION
How would you have felt if you were there and heard a magnificent choir of Heaven's angels sing?

Later I thought about how the shepherds must have felt when they saw and heard a wonderful choir of angels sing praises to God.

Suddenly, the angel was joined by a vast host of others—the armies of heaven—praising God and saying, "Glory to God in highest heaven, and peace on earth to those with whom God is pleased." (Luke 2:13-14 NLT)

Some of us were talking about the service when it was over. When I mentioned I heard a choir of angels sing praises to God with us, several others, including two young girls, said they also heard them. The girls then pointed to an area in the upper corner of the sanctuary and said, "Look, some are still here!" I never saw these angels, but I certainly enjoyed hearing them praise God (Hebrews1:6)!

The altar call. Before the service, we had asked the Holy Spirit to bring people to the altar He wanted us to pray for. He did this and performed His work through several of us as we prayed for eight or ten people. He would often give a word of knowledge (a spiritual gift) about the hurts He wanted to heal. I laid my hands on and prayed for one woman. The Holy Spirit told me she had a broken relationship with a close family member, and He wanted to heal it. She broke down in tears and asked me how I knew this. I told her I didn't, but God did and wanted to heal her heart and that of the other person. She said she had a quarrel with her daughter ten years prior and had not spoken to her since. I told her the Holy Spirit impressed upon me that the Father would restore their relationship. She needed, however, to contact her daughter with love and forgiveness. She called me several days later to say she had done this, and they both cried and forgave each other. Her loving heavenly Father did what He said He would do when she obeyed Him.

PERSONAL APPLICATION

How would you have responded if you were there, and God healed you physically or emotionally? What would have been your response to God for this miraculous blessing?

Symptoms of a Spiritually Unhealthy Church

Have you ever attended a church, and something didn't seem right? Perhaps it was because the church was spiritually unhealthy.

Spiritually unhealthy churches may result from pastors and leaders who lack the love of Christ in their hearts. They may also not preach, teach, and lead by biblical principles. Instead, they tend to focus more on themselves than on God. Some may even lead people astray from God and a personal relationship with Him. These churches are sometimes referred to as "toxic churches."

Based on what a spiritually healthy church is like, how would you describe a spiritually unhealthy one?

Symptoms of a spiritually unhealthy church congregation. Following are some questions to ask about a congregation to determine if it's spiritually unhealthy:

- Does the congregation worship and glorify God for who He is and what He does?

- Is the worship service focused on what pleases God or what the people want to experience?

- Does the music help people worship the Savior and Father with a humble heart of love and adoration?

- Do people serve because they want Jesus to get the credit, or do they want the credit and glory for themselves?

Symptoms of spiritually unhealthy pastors and leaders. Following are some types of pastors and leaders whose churches you want to avoid. Unfortunately, they exist in many Christian denominations. They create spiritually unhealthy, toxic churches because they are:

1. Rule-based (legalistic): Following their rules is more important than living a life of grace, truth, and love. (Colossians 2:20-23)

2. Hypocrites: They don't practice what they preach and teach. (Matthew 23:1-5)

3. False teachers/preachers: They misuse and distort the Bible to achieve their own purposes. (2 Peter 2:2)

4. False prophets: They pridefully proclaim to hear from the Holy Spirit when they have not. They give the congregation false hope, wrong guidance, and lead them away from God. (Matthew 7:15)

5. Skim milk preachers: They don't teach and preach the substance of the Bible to enable people to be saved and mature as followers of Christ. (Hebrews 5:13)

6. Immoral: They prey on the weak to fulfill their own desires. (2 Peter 2:19)

WHAT DO YOU THINK? (ADVANCED)

Why can these spiritually unhealthy churches be destructive to the faith and spiritual life of those who want to follow Jesus Christ? Why should believers avoid them and find a spiritually healthy church?

Church Two: Some Leaders May Not Live the Christian Life You Expect

The following story illustrates the damage hypocritical leaders can do to people who want to know God and live a Christian life. The pastor in this church was a wonderful man of God, so this story is not about him. Instead, it is about some church leaders who refused to live their lives in obedience to God. (Perhaps because they were not born-again followers of Jesus?)

They didn't practice it. Adam attended children's Sunday School and worship services for many years growing up. In high school, he began to see that some of the leading men in their church were living blatantly like non-Christians. So, in his junior year, he told his mother that he would never go to church again because it was full of hypocrites. For the rest of his younger life, he avoided church and Christians until he later committed his life to Jesus. (Unfortunately, other people have told me this same story about why they stopped attending church.)

My comment. I have been a follower of Jesus Christ for over forty-five years and have attended churches in many denominations. I can tell you, without a doubt, that there are hypocrites in many churches today. However, don't be dismayed, and don't stop going to church. And don't go to church looking for hypocrites. Instead, go to a church the Lord wants you to be in and worship Almighty God and His Son, Jesus Christ. And enjoy spiritual life with other followers of Jesus Christ who worship God and strive to mature as Christians.

WHAT DO YOU THINK?

Why should our attention always be on God and not on the imperfect people around us, whether in or out of church?

Be involved. God says in the following verses that believers are to find opportunities to fellowship with other Christians and encourage them in their faith in Christ. They must be actively involved in a spiritually healthy church to do this (where there may also be some hypocrites).

Let us hold fast the confession of our hope without wavering, for He who promised is faithful; and let us consider how to stimulate one another to love and good deeds, not forsaking our own assembling together, as is the habit of some, but encouraging one another; and all the more as you see the day drawing near. (Hebrews 10:23-25 NASB)

Church Three: Some Leaders May Reject God's Plan

This next story is about pastors and church leaders who rejected God's plan to follow their own.

They chose human reasoning rather than God's revealed will. We moved to this state and participated in a large church there. The Lord began to send people from out of state to speak at several local churches. They all brought the same prophetic message: God wanted to build a global prayer and Christian training center in our area. Several specified it was to be located on a mountain top with a 360-degree view to pray for the nations. Many people from our church and other local churches were excited and started praying for this to happen according to God's plan and will.

Later as we persisted in prayer, our pastor told us about a multi-story house for sale behind our church property. He asked us to pray about buying it as a place to start the Prayer Center. Donations from our church members and surrounding churches poured in for this purchase. With more than sufficient funds, our church soon purchased the house. The top floor was designated our temporary Prayer Center until the Global Prayer Center launched. We consistently experienced the presence of God and the power of the Holy Spirit as we prayed there. God was calling us to prayer, and He was answering prayers. In some cases, He set Christians free from sins and unhealthy influences that limited their ability to serve Him. We felt that He was preparing His people for His promised Global Prayer Center.

PERSONAL APPLICATION

When have you experienced this kind of prayer with the powerful presence of God and the Holy Spirit? Explain how you felt in the presence of Almighty God.

After a few months, several important things occurred. First, someone donated land on a nearby mountain top for the Center. The land provided an unobstructed 360-degree view to pray for the nations, just as God had told us. We rejoiced in what we saw as a wonderful provision from God! Indeed, we thought the vision was going to happen! Then came the announcement that a non-Christian agency had been consulted about what to do with the house while waiting for funds to start construction on the

Global Prayer Center. The decision dictated the house was now off-limits for prayer and all other Christian activities. We were devastated. How could this be? Didn't God provide it as the initial Prayer Center? Wasn't He meeting us there consistently as we prayed? Unfortunately, the decision ended the Global Prayer Center in our area. Key pastors and leaders had rejected God's plan to pursue their own plan.

NOTE: This story is in the book for you to know people can exercise their self-will to resist or refuse God's provisions and plans.

Seek the Lord and His church. You must find a church with a group of believers that practice the fundamentals of a healthy Christian church. The Lord will guide you through the Holy Spirit to one where you can fellowship with maturing followers of Jesus, enjoy worshiping God, serve, and study the Bible together.

36

Christian Beliefs: Salvation

Earlier in the book, I said everyone believes in someone or something. By now, you know how strongly I believe in the God of the Bible. I want you to understand that Christianity is not just another religion. It differs from all other religions because it proclaims that the God who created the universe wants to have an eternal relationship with you. God's love for you and His desire for you to know Him is what makes Christianity unique.

On the Internet, you will find a variety of lists and descriptions of Christian beliefs. This is because people have different perspectives on almost everything. The following four chapters describe the beliefs I think are important to understanding Christianity.

Categorizing the Beliefs

Since salvation is at the core of the Christian religion, it's the first chapter on Christian beliefs. I have separated the beliefs into the following four chapters:

- Salvation
- Trinity
- Christ's Church
- Eternity

I provide verses after each belief for your additional study. I also include the following "What Do You Think?" question to further enhance your understanding.

WHAT DO YOU THINK?
Reword this belief's description in a few sentences to help you remember it.

Sin, Rebellion: Everyone Needs Salvation

Before I describe beliefs related to salvation, it's essential to define the underlying reason why everyone needs to be saved. It's the word "sin" that people don't like to hear. Another word for sin is rebellion. Either way, it's defying God and His will for people to have eternal life with Him through Jesus Christ.

If you have ever done archery, think of missing the target with your arrow. A common definition of sin is to miss the mark of God's perfection. In other words, people can't be good enough for the Father to declare them perfect. This is what the following verse means:

> As the Scriptures say, "No one is righteous—not even one." (Romans 3:10 NLT)

Everyone has committed the two types of sin identified in the Bible:

- Sins of omission are those actions people should be doing but are not. God says it is a sin to know what we ought to do and then not do it. (James 4:17 NLT)

- Sins of commission are those people are doing but should not do. A list of some of these can be found in Colossians 3:8, *But now is the time to get rid of anger, rage, malicious behavior, slander, and dirty language.* (NLT)

PERSONAL APPLICATION
Which type of sin is the most common to you? Why do you think this is true?

What is the "unpardonable sin?" Unfortunately, there is confusion among Christians about what the unpardonable sin is. However, Jesus made it clear in the following verses that it's blasphemy against the Holy Spirit:

> But when the Pharisees heard this they said, "He *[Jesus]* does not cast out demons except by the power of Beelzebul, the ruler of demons!" . . . "But if I cast out demons by the Spirit of God, then the kingdom of God has already overtaken you. . . . For this reason I tell you, people will be forgiven for every sin and blasphemy, but the blasphemy against the Spirit will not be forgiven. Whoever speaks a word against the Son of Man will be forgiven. But whoever speaks

against the Holy Spirit will not be forgiven, either in this age or in the age to come. (Matthew 12:24-32 NET, author's emphasis)

The only unforgivable sin is to say that the work of the Holy Spirit is done by a demon. And so this implies that He is a demon. This, of course, is a lie since the Holy Spirit is God. How hard a person's heart to God must be for them to deny the Holy Spirit's existence as God!

WHAT DO YOU THINK?

When people blaspheme the Holy Spirit like this, why does it indicate their hearts are hardened to God beyond forgiveness?

Jesus is Savior and Lord. However, there is another unforgivable sin, which is not accepting Jesus Christ as Savior and Lord. This is not blasphemy, but there is no forgiveness and no salvation without repentance and acceptance of Jesus. This unbelief is a sin of omission, whereas blasphemy of the Holy Spirit is a sin of commission.

For God did not send his Son into the world to condemn the world, but to save the world through him. Whoever believes in him is not condemned, but whoever does not believe stands condemned already because they have not believed in the name of God's one and only Son. (John 3:17-18 NIV)

WHAT DO YOU THINK?

Write a list of the Christian beliefs you would want people to understand about salvation. Compare your list to the beliefs in this chapter. Why would you expect there to be a difference?

Beliefs about Salvation

The following three beliefs are essential to understanding the significance of salvation.

Belief #1: Salvation (Rescued!)

To be saved is another way of saying people need to be rescued. Every person needs to be rescued from the eternal consequences of living a life without Jesus Christ as Savior and Lord. This is the essence of rebellion and sin. They may have committed other sins identified in the Bible, but only the rejection of Jesus separates people eternally from God.

The one who believes in the Son has eternal life. The one who rejects the Son will not see life, but God's wrath remains on him. (John 3:36 NET)

Belief Description:

A person's life without Jesus condemns them to an eternity without hope and without God (John 3:18; Revelation 20:11-15). Only the death of Jesus Christ as the payment for sins and His resurrection from the dead rescues (redeems) people from this eternal fate without Him. This salvation is by God's grace. It's a free gift from the Father that can't be earned. He offers it simply because He loves people and wants them to spend eternity with Him.

> For by grace you have been saved through faith; and that not of yourselves, it is the gift of God; not as a result of works, so that no one may boast. (Ephesians 2:8-9 NASB)

> This is good and acceptable in the sight of God our Savior, who desires all men to be saved and to come to the knowledge of the truth. For there is one God, and one mediator also between God and men, the man Christ Jesus, who gave Himself as a ransom for all, the testimony given at the proper time. (1 Timothy 2:3-6 NASB)

Some verses about this belief: Isaiah 53:1-12; Matthew 1:21, 27:11-54, 28:1-6; Luke 1:67-70; John 3:16-18, 5:24; Acts 2:21-24; Romans 3:21-26; 1 Corinthians 15:1-4; 2 Corinthians 5:17-19; Ephesians 1:7, 2:8-9; 1 Timothy 2:3-6.

WHAT DO YOU THINK?

Reword this belief's description in a few sentences to help you remember it.

The Good News saves. God says through the Apostle Paul that the Good News (Gospel) saves people. The following verses describe this Good News:

> Now I make known to you, brethren, the gospel which I preached to you, which also you received, in which also you stand, by which also you are saved, if you hold fast the word which I preached to you, unless you believed in vain. For I delivered to you as of first importance what I also received, that Christ died for our sins according to the Scriptures, and that He was buried, and that He was raised on the third day according to the Scriptures. (1 Corinthians 15:1-4 NASB)

The three elements of the Good News stated in the above verses follow:

- *Christ died for our sins, just as the Scriptures said.*
- *He was buried, and*
- *He was raised from the dead on the third day, just as the Scriptures said.*

Believing this and accepting Jesus as Savior and Lord is what saves people.

Virgin birth. If Jesus was not born by the Holy Spirit to a virgin, then He is not God, and there is no salvation through Him. However, the following verse says Jesus was born to the virgin Mary by the Holy Spirit and, therefore, is the Son of God.

God sent the angel Gabriel to Nazareth, a town in Galilee, to a virgin pledged to be married to a man named Joseph, a descendant of David. The virgin's name was Mary. . . . The angel answered, "The Holy Spirit will come on you, and the power of the Most High will overshadow you. So the holy one to be born will be called the Son of God." (Luke 1:26-35 NIV)

WHAT DO YOU THINK? (ADVANCED)

How would you describe the virgin birth of Jesus to someone who knew nothing about Christianity?

Belief #2: Death of Jesus Christ

There is no forgiveness of sin without the death of Jesus Christ, the Son of God. Even a hardened Roman soldier watching the crucifixion recognized this as he saw Jesus die.

And at the ninth hour Jesus cried with a loud voice, "Eloi, Eloi, lema sabachthani?" which means, "My God, my God, why have you forsaken me?" . . . And Jesus uttered a loud cry and breathed his last. And the curtain of the temple was torn in two, from top to bottom. And when the centurion, who stood facing him, saw that in this way he breathed his last, he said, "Truly this man was the Son of God!" (Mark 15:34-39 ESV)

Belief Description:

Through the death of Jesus Christ, people are forgiven of all past, present, and future sins. When the Father looks at His born-again child, He sees them as perfect, as if they never sinned. He has given them the perfect righteousness of Jesus Christ, the Son of God. This means they stand before the Father in a right relationship with Him. There is no longer any condemnation resulting in eternal separation from Him. They no longer need to fear death, as many non-believers do.

> Christ died once for all time as a sacrifice to take away the sins of many people. (Hebrews 9:28 NLT)

> *Christ's one act of righteousness brings a right relationship with God and new life for everyone.* (Romans 5:18 NLT, author's emphasis)

PERSONAL APPLICATION

How much do you think the God of the Bible loves you? Do you know of any other so-called god that loves you?

Some verses about this belief: Isaiah 53:4-11; Mark 15:33-39; John 19:38-42; Acts 10:39, 26:20; Romans 3:10, 3:24-28, 5:15-18; Galatians 3:1; 2 Timothy 1:10; Hebrews 2:14-15, 5:7, 9:28.

WHAT DO YOU THINK?

Reword this belief's description in a few sentences to help you remember it.

Belief #3: Resurrection of Jesus Christ

Christianity is a false hope without the resurrection of Jesus Christ (1 Corinthians 15:17-20). But it's not false hope because Jesus has risen from the dead, just as He said would happen!

> Then the angel spoke to the women. "Don't be afraid!" he said. "I know you are looking for Jesus, who was crucified. He isn't here! He is risen from the dead, just as He said would happen. Come, see where His body was lying." (Matthew 28:5-6 NLT)

Belief Description:

The tomb was empty, where Jesus Christ's dead body was laid. He was not there because He had risen from the dead by God's supernatural power. The resurrection of the Son of God uniquely separates Christianity from all other religions. (By the way, all His followers will also experience this resurrection.)

> I am the living One. I died, but look—I am alive forever and ever! And I hold the keys of death and the grave. (Revelation 1:18 NLT)

Jesus said to her, "I am the resurrection and the life. Whoever believes in me, though he die, yet shall he live." (John 11:25 ESV)

Some verses about this belief: Psalm 16:9-10; Mark 16:1-6; Matthew 27:62-66, 28:5-6; Acts 1:1-3, 2:24, 31, 3:15, 4:2, 10, 33. 5:30, 10:39-41, 13:30; Romans 1:1-4, 6:9-10; 1 Corinthians 15:3-8, 16-20, 50-53; 1 Thessalonians 4:14; Revelation 1:18.

WHAT DO YOU THINK?
Reword this belief's description in a few sentences to help you remember it.

The following verses say that no one other than the Son of God, Jesus Christ, can save people. And that no one can be good enough to save themselves.

And there is salvation in no one else, for there is no other name under heaven given among men by which we must be saved. (Acts 4:11-12 ESV).

Salvation is not a reward for the good things we have done, so none of us can boast about it. (Ephesians 2:9 NLT)

WHAT DO YOU THINK?
Why is salvation at the core of Christian beliefs? What does having a personal relationship with God have to do with salvation?

Christianity is not just a religious belief system. Because of the life, death, and resurrection of Jesus Christ, it's an eternal living relationship with God Himself.

37

Christian Beliefs: Trinity

I don't think the beliefs in this, and the next two chapters are necessary for salvation, but they are still important. They identify other foundational beliefs that differentiate Christianity from other religions. Of course, you know now that beliefs about the Trinity underlie the Christian faith.

Belief #4: Trinity

The word "Trinity" doesn't appear in the Bible. Biblical scholars created it to identify the unity, yet separateness, of the three persons of God.

Belief Description:

The Father, the Son, Jesus Christ, and the Holy Spirit are all equally God in every aspect of their being and nature. They are ONE God (one divine whole) existing as three separate persons. Their different names imply that they each have different functions in their relationships with each other and people. For example, God chose to be the Father God and for believers to be His children. Jesus chose to be the Savior and Lord of the Father's children. The Holy Spirit chose to be the Helper, Teacher, and Guide living within the Father's children.

> Jesus told His disciples, "Therefore, go and make disciples of all the nations, baptizing them in the name of the Father and the Son and the Holy Spirit." (Matthew 28:19 NLT)

Some verses about this belief: Genesis 1:26-27; Isaiah 61:1; Matthew 28:19; Luke 1:35; Acts 2:32-33; Romans 8:9-11; 3; Galatians 4:6; 1 Thessalonians 1:2-5; 2 Thessalonians 2:13-14; 1 Peter 1:2; 1 John 4:2-3, 13-14.

WHAT DO YOU THINK?

Reword this belief's description in a few sentences to help you remember it.

Monotheism and the Trinity of God. Monotheism is the belief that there is only one God. Polytheism is the belief there is more than one god. The Jewish religion of Judaism declares there is only one God. The religion of Christianity has its foundation in Judaism and declares there's only one God. As you see in the verse below, Jesus, the Son of God, states there is only one God:

> Jesus answered, "The foremost is, 'Hear, o Israel! The LORD our God is one LORD.'" (Mark 12:29 NASB)

So both Judaism and Christianity are monotheistic religions. Yet, many verses in the New Testament of the Bible clearly portray God as the Trinity (the Triune God). How this can be is a mystery to the limited human mind.

Some additional verses about the God of the Bible being one God are Deuteronomy 4:35, 6:4; Isaiah 45:20-24; Mark 12:29, 32; John 10:30; James 2:19.

WHAT DO YOU THINK? (ADVANCED)

How would you describe the difference between polytheism and monotheism?

Belief #5: God (Father God, Jehovah)

When we see the word *God* in the Bible, it typically identifies the first person of the Trinity. Sometimes, it also refers to the Trinity, emphasizing their oneness. In the Hebrew language of the Old Testament, God gives Himself one personal name, *Yahweh* (Exodus 3:13-14). Because the people of Israel thought of this as His sacred name, they referred to it as "YHWH," leaving out the vowels. In English Bibles, this is sometimes written as *I AM WHO I AM*, lord (with small capital letters), *Adonai*, or *Jehovah*. Many names and titles for God reveal aspects of His divine nature and represent who He is, such as *El Shaddai* (God Almighty) or *Jehovah-shalom* (God is our peace).

In both the Old and New Testaments, God is referred to as the Father of His children.

> The LORD is like a father to His children, tender and compassionate to those who fear Him. (Psalm 103:13 NLT)

And because we are His children, God has sent the Spirit of His Son into our hearts, prompting us to call out, "Abba, Father." (Galatians 4:6 NLT)

In the New Testament, the Aramaic name *Abba* means He is the Father God who loves His children intimately and personally. It's sometimes thought of as "daddy" or "papa" to denote His deep familial love for His children.

Belief Description:
God, the Father, is all-knowing, all-powerful, and ever-present. He resides on His throne in Heaven. He is sovereign, eternal, and never changes. He is a spirit by His nature. Yet throughout the Bible, He describes Himself in physical terms to help people relate to Him. He is loving and compassionate, just, and righteous by His nature. All good things are from Him. He has blessed His children with every spiritual blessing from Heaven through Jesus. Jesus told His disciples when they saw Him, they were seeing the Father (since He is the exact image of His Father). This oneness is part of the mystery of the Trinity.

The following verse indicates God exists everywhere, is all-knowing, and all-powerful:

He counts the number of the stars; he names all of them. (Psalms 147:4 NET)

Some verses about this belief: Exodus 3:14; Numbers 23:19; Proverbs 15:3; Psalms 139:7-12, 147:4; Isaiah 57:15; John 3:16, 4:24, 5:26, 14:19, 16:27; Romans 3:26, 8:15; 1 Corinthians 8:6; 2 Corinthians 1:3; Galatians 4:6; Ephesians 1:3.

WHAT DO YOU THINK?
Reword this belief's description in a few sentences to help you remember it.

Belief #6: Jesus Christ (Savior and Lord)
Jesus Christ is fully God, just as the Father and the Holy Spirit are also fully God. He is identified as the second person of the Trinity.

Belief Description:
The Father created everything through His Son, Jesus Christ. It's Jesus who spoke everything into existence. It's also Jesus who, by speaking, sustains everything the Father wants to continue to exist. The Father has given Jesus absolute authority over

all creation, including the devil and his demons. When Jesus Christ came to earth (first coming), He was fully human and fully God. He is, therefore, the Son of Man and the Son of God. The virgin Mary was His biological mother, and the Holy Spirit was His spiritual father. Jesus lived on earth, enduring all the temptations of being human, yet never sinned. The only way to be made acceptable to the Father is through His death and resurrection. He is God's ONLY plan to bring people into an eternal relationship with Himself.

> Jesus replied, "I am the way, and the truth, and the life. No one comes to the Father except through me." (John 14:6 NET)

Following are several Scriptures that describe Jesus as God:

> The Son radiates God's own glory and expresses the very character of God, and He sustains everything by the mighty power of His command. (Hebrews 1:3 NLT)

> Now He is far above any ruler or authority or power or leader or anything else—not only in this world but also in the world to come. God has put all things under the authority of Christ and has made Him head over all things for the benefit of the church. (Ephesians 1:21-22 NLT)

Some verses about this belief: Genesis 1:3-30; Isaiah chapter 53; Matthew 1:18-23, 8:29, 28:5-6; Luke 22:69-70; John 1:1, 14; Acts 4:12, 7:55-56; Ephesians 1:21-23; Hebrews 1:2-3, 4:15; Philippians 2:5-11; Colossians 1:15-23; Revelation 19:11-21.

WHAT DO YOU THINK?
Reword this belief's description in a few sentences to help you remember it.

Belief #7: Holy Spirit (Spirit of God and Christ)

The Spirit of God (the Spirit of Jesus) is also fully God in all aspects of His nature. He's the third person of the Trinity and was also involved in Creation. He supernaturally impregnated the virgin Mary to conceive Jesus Christ as the Son of God and the Son of Man. He was sent to start the Christian church at Pentecost when He came to live within the first believers.

Belief Description:

When people profess faith in Jesus Christ as their Savior and ask Him to be the Lord of their life, the Holy Spirit comes to live within them. Only then do they become a Christian. He causes believers to know in their spirit that they are the Father God's children. He is the Father's seal and guarantee that He will save them. He is their Helper, Teacher, and Guide in all of life. He communicates the will of the Father and Jesus to believers. He also helps them control their thinking, which results in greater peace and spiritual life. He empowers them to serve and live as the Father desires.

No Christian can live the Christian life in ways that please the Father without living by the Spirit. When Jesus was on earth, He did everything by His authority and the power of the Holy Spirit within Him. The Holy Spirit empowers and provides every born-again believer with spiritual gifts that enable them to serve according to His will. He helps them understand how to pray. He is the one who convicts people of their sins and draws them to salvation in Jesus Christ.

> I will ask the Father, and He will give you another Helper, that He may be with you forever; that is the Spirit of truth, whom the world cannot receive, because it does not see Him or know Him, but you know Him because He abides with you and will be in you. (John 14:16-17 NASB)

> Now all of us can come to the Father through the same Holy Spirit because of what Christ has done for us. (Ephesians 2:18 NLT)

Some verses about this belief: Genesis 1:2; Isaiah 61:1-3; Joel 2:28-32; Mark 1:10; Luke 1:35, 4:1, 11:13, 20; John 14:16-17, 26, 15:26, 16:7-14; Acts 1:8, 2:1-4, 13:2-4; Romans 8:5-11, 14-16, 26-27; 1 Corinthians 3:16; Galatians 5:25; Ephesians 1:13-14, 2:18; 1 John 4:13.

WHAT DO YOU THINK?

Reword this belief's description in a few sentences to help you remember it.

The Father, Jesus Christ, and the Holy Spirit desire every person to be saved and spend eternity with them. They want the followers of Jesus to know and experience their reality in daily life. God is not far off. He is near and lives within born-again followers of Jesus Christ.

PERSONAL APPLICATION
Which person of the Trinity do you feel closest to, and why?

The existence of the Trinity, the Triune God of three persons in one God, is unique to world religions. If the Trinity, three persons of God, did not exist, there would be no Christian religion.

38

Christian Beliefs: Christ's Church

God created people in His image for them to experience life as His children. Jesus Christ's church is comprised of all believers wherever they are located. The Holy Spirit wrote the Bible (through men of God) to reveal the true nature of God, His desire for an eternal relationship with people, and to provide guidance to a life that pleases the Father.

WHAT DO YOU THINK?
Why is knowledge of the Bible essential to understanding who people are and, therefore, what Christ's church is?

Belief #8: People
God created people to love and enjoy for all eternity. His love is not determined by who they are or what they can do. It is based solely on His divine nature of love.

> In this is love: not that we have loved God, but that he loved us and sent his Son to be the atoning sacrifice for our sins. (1 John 4:10 NET)

Belief Description:
God created people in His image. They have a spirit, soul, and body. From Hebrews 4:12, we see that a person's spirit and soul are distinct and have unique purposes. The spirit – When a person commits their heart and life to Jesus Christ, the Holy Spirit comes to live within them, and they are born-again. When this occurs, their spirit (which was dead to God before salvation) is made alive to God. It's through their spirit

that they can experience and communicate with God. The soul – We may think of it as composed of emotions, desires, thoughts, motivations, and conscience. The soul is how a person interacts with people and life in the natural world. The body – The physical body allows people to live within the physical world God created.

> God created mankind in his own image, in the image of God he created them; male and female he created them. (Genesis 1:27 NIV)

> Now may the God of peace himself make you completely holy and may your spirit and soul and body be kept entirely blameless at the coming of our Lord Jesus Christ. (1 Thessalonians 5:23 NET)

WHAT DO YOU THINK?
How would you describe the difference between the spirit and soul to someone who didn't know about them?

Some verses about this belief: Genesis 1:27; Psalms 8:3-6; Isaiah 6:5; Jeremiah 17:5; John 14:16-17; Romans 8:16; 1 Corinthians 2:9-13, 14:14-16; Ephesians 2:1-7; 1 Thessalonians 5:23; 2 Timothy 4:22; Hebrews 4:12; 1 John 4:10.

WHAT DO YOU THINK?
Reword this belief's description in a few sentences to help you remember it.

Belief #9: The Church

Some people may say, "What do you mean my church building is not the church?"

> Christ is also the head of the church, which is His body (Colossians 1:18 NLT).

WHAT DO YOU THINK?
Why is there a lack of understanding about Christ's church and who belongs to it? Why do people like to think of their facility is their church?

Belief Description:

The church is not a building, organization, or denomination. Jesus Christ's church is all born-again believers living everywhere on earth and in Heaven. Only people who have accepted Jesus Christ as their Savior and asked Him to be the Lord of their life are part of His church. These are the ones who can accurately claim to be Christian. The local church facility is where these Christians gather to worship God, learn, and serve.

> And He put all things in subjection under His feet, and gave Him as head over all things to the church, which is His body, the fullness of Him who fills all in all. (Ephesians 1:22-23 NASB)

> I am writing to God's church in Corinth, to you who have been called by God to be His own holy people. (1 Corinthians 1:2 NLT)

Some verses about this belief: Acts 13:1, 14:23, 16:4-5, 20:28; 1 Corinthians 1:2, 12:27; Ephesians 1:21-23, 2:19-22, 3:10, 4:4-6, 5:22-32; Colossians 1:18; 1 Peter 5:1-5.

WHAT DO YOU THINK?
Reword this belief's description in a few sentences to help you remember it.

Belief #10: The Bible

The Bible is not just another book about religion. It's so much more than black ink on paper. It's the living word of God because it is the living God's word. The Holy Spirit causes it to be alive in a person's mind and heart. No other book in the world can do this because all scripture, the entire Bible, is God-breathed (2 Timothy 3:16). The next verse says it's alive and active, powerful in what it can do in and through people:

> For the word of God is living and active, sharper than any two-edged sword, piercing to the division of soul and of spirit, of joints and of marrow, and discerning the thoughts and intentions of the heart. And no creature is hidden from his sight, but all are naked and exposed to the eyes of him to whom we must give account. (Hebrews 4:12-13 ESV)

WHAT DO YOU THINK?
What makes the Bible living and not just black ink on paper?

Belief Description:

There are many purposes and benefits to the Bible for everyone. However, its utmost importance is that it describes how to have a saving, personal relationship with the God of the Bible. It provides insights and wisdom about how to live a life that pleases the Father God. It has history, poems, stories, proverbs, prophecies, songs, and much more to benefit the heart, mind, and life of those who read, meditate on, and study it.

The Bible is God's written word provided for all people through the inspiration of the Holy Spirit. He's the person of God who put the thoughts and ideas into the minds of about forty men of God who wrote the sixty-six books of the Bible. The Bible was written over a period of 1,500 years and yet is cohesive and consistent. Since God inspired the Bible, there are no errors as originally written. Since it's God's word, it's truth. There are no lies or deceptions in the Bible. The Holy Spirit gives these written words spiritual life that can transform a person's heart and life. It can speak to the heart to provide encouragement and hope.

> For everything that was written in former times was written for our instruction, so that through endurance and through encouragement of the scriptures we may have hope. (Romans 15:4 NET)

Mysteries in the Bible. A mystery in the Bible is something for which God has partially concealed or hidden the entire meaning. For example, in 1 Corinthians 2:7, the Apostle Paul writes, " *No, the wisdom we speak of is the mystery of God—His plan that was previously hidden* (NLT). The nature of the Trinity of God is a mystery in the Bible. It isn't possible to understand with our limited human minds how the three separate persons of God can, at the same time, be one God. Therefore, our response to a biblical mystery requires faith in God to accept what He has chosen to reveal as sufficient for the time.

PRACTICE IT
How can you know that the Bible is true? How can the Holy Spirit help you believe His book is true? Why don't you take a few minutes to ask the Holy Spirit to help you know that you can trust Him and the Bible?

Some verses about this belief: Psalm 119:9-16; Isaiah 40:8; John 5:36-40, 16:13-15, 17:17; Romans 15:4; 2 Timothy 3:15-17; Hebrews 4:12; 1 Peter 1:25; 2 Peter 1:16-21.

WHAT DO YOU THINK?

Reword this belief's description in a few sentences to help you remember it.

People were created in God's image with a spirit, soul, and body. When they are born-again, they can worship, communicate, and enjoy the spiritual presence of the Father, Jesus Christ, and the Holy Spirit. Jesus Christ is the head of His church, and only people who committed their hearts and lives to Him are part of it. The Bible was written to help people know the God of the Bible for who He truly is. The uniqueness of the Christian religion can be seen by its people, Christ's church, and the Bible that describes it.

39

Christian Beliefs: Eternity

God created everything to exist for eternity. But Adam and Eve's rebellion against God resulted in creation being corrupted. There will be a new creation that will literally extend forever. This chapter focuses on beliefs about eternity that are foundational to the Christian religion.

Belief #11: Creation
The Old Testament book of Genesis includes God's story of creation. However, the truth of creation permeates the entire Bible. Therefore, when people decide not to believe in creation, they choose not to believe in the Bible and the God of the Bible.

Belief Description:

> The first verse in the Bible says God existed before He created anything:
> *In the beginning, God created the heavens and the earth* (Genesis 1:1 ESV).

God created everything out of nothing ("Ex Nihilo"). If you know chemistry, you are familiar with the Periodic Table. No element in the Table existed until God created it. By the way, scientists are still discovering new elements previously unknown to us but known to and created by God.

> By faith we understand that the entire universe was formed at God's command, that what we now see did not come from anything that can be seen. (Hebrews 11:3 NLT)

PERSONAL APPLICATION

What do you think about God when you consider that He created everything out of nothing?

God's creation displays His majesty and glory. Therefore, people must be aware that He exists.

> The heavens declare the glory of God; the skies proclaim the work of his hands. (Psalm 19:1 NLT)

Biblical creation answers several age-old questions of human existence, such as the following:

- How did people get here; where did we come from?
- Do people have a purpose? If so, what is it?

Some verses about this belief: Genesis 1:1-2:25; Job 26:7; Psalm 8:3, 19:1-4, 33:6-7, 90:2, 104:30, 145:9; Isaiah 45:18; John 1:1-4; Romans 1:20; Colossians 1:15-17; Hebrews 11:3; James 1:18.

WHAT DO YOU THINK?

Reword this belief's description in a few sentences to help you remember it.

The new heaven and new earth. God will ultimately destroy by fire this current creation because of the rampant rebellion of people against Him. He has delayed in doing so because He wants every person to repent and be saved.

> The Lord is not slow about His promise, as some count slowness, but is patient toward you, not wishing for any to perish but for all to come to repentance. But the day of the Lord will come like a thief, in which the heavens will pass away with a roar and the elements will be destroyed with intense heat, and the earth and its works will be burned up. Since all these things are to be destroyed in this way, what sort of people ought you to be in holy conduct and godliness, looking for and hastening the coming of the day of God, because of which the heavens will be destroyed by burning, and the elements will melt with intense heat! (2 Peter 3:9-12 NASB)

After this destruction, He will create an entirely new heaven and new earth. It will be a wonderful place of eternal existence for the followers of Jesus Christ. The Father and Jesus Christ will come down from Heaven to live with believers. There will never again be pain, suffering, or sin in this eternal home with God. There will be no crime or murder because everyone who has rejected Jesus Christ will not be there.

> Then I saw a new heaven and a new earth; for the first heaven and the first earth passed away, and there is no longer any sea. And I saw the holy city, new Jerusalem, coming down out of heaven from God, made ready as a bride adorned for her husband. And I heard a loud voice from the throne, saying, "Behold, the tabernacle of God is among men, and He will dwell among them, and they shall be His people, and God Himself will be among them, and He will wipe away every tear from their eyes; and there will no longer be any death; there will no longer be any mourning, or crying, or pain; the first things have passed away." And He who sits on the throne said, "Behold, I am making all things new." And He said, "Write, for these words are faithful and true." (Revelation 21:1-5 NASB)

PRACTICE IT

Imagine sitting with Jesus and the Father and talking with them face-to-face on the new earth. Why not talk to them now to thank them for this beautiful eternal home waiting for believers?

Belief #12: Eternity

God created human beings to exist forever. God has placed the reality of their eternal existence in every person's heart.

> He has planted eternity in the human heart, but even so, people cannot see the whole scope of God's work from beginning to end. (Ecclesiastes 3:11 NLT)

Eternity in the human heart means everyone has an innate longing for something more than human experience. It is an inner sense that they were made for something greater than themselves. But some refuse to acknowledge this. Perhaps it's easier for them to ignore God and the prospect of eternal life after death. Someone once said, "I just don't think about God!"

<table>
<tr><td>

WHAT DO YOU THINK?

Why do some people refuse to admit they will live forever? What do you think they may be afraid of?

</td></tr>
</table>

Belief Description:

Every person will spend eternity with or without God, depending on whether they accepted His free gift of salvation through Jesus Christ. After Judgment Day, the followers of Jesus Christ will go to the new earth for eternity (Revelation 21:1-3). People who have ignored this wonderful gift will be sent to the *lake of fire* forever. They will never experience the presence of God or His love and compassion. The *second death* in Revelation 20:14-15 refers to this eternal separation from God's presence.

> Then Death and Hades were thrown into the lake of fire. This is the second death, the lake of fire. And if anyone's name was not found written in the book of life, he was thrown into the lake of fire. (Revelation 20:14-15 ESV)

Some verses about this belief: Ecclesiastes 3:11; Isaiah 43:13, 57:15; John 3:16, 36; Romans 6:23; 1 John 2:25, 5:11-13; Revelation 20:14-15, 21:1-3.

<table>
<tr><td>

WHAT DO YOU THINK?

Reword this belief's description in a few sentences to help you remember it.

</td></tr>
</table>

Belief #13: Eternal Judgment

Jesus Christ will judge every human being who has ever lived. The Bible is clear that His judgments are just and true, for everyone reaps in eternity what they have sown in this life.

> Do not be deceived, God is not mocked; for whatever a man sows, this he will also reap. For the one who sows to his own flesh will from the flesh reap corruption, but the one who sows to the Spirit will from the Spirit reap eternal life. (Galatians 6:7-8 NASB)

Belief Description:

Judgment Day (Revelation 20:11-12) is not about where people will spend eternity. That was determined by whether they accepted Jesus Christ when their bodies died. Instead, it is about the nature of each person's eternal existence.

The following scriptures state that believers and non-believers will be judged on Judgment Day by how they lived their lives.

> Then I saw a large white throne and the one who was seated on it; the earth and the heaven fled from his presence, and no place was found for them. And I saw the dead, the great and the small, standing before the throne. Then books were opened, and another book was opened – the book of life. So the dead were judged by what was written in the books, according to their deeds. (Revelation 20:11-12 NET)

> Surely You repay all people according to what they have done. (Psalm 62:12 NLT)

> But I, the LORD, search all hearts and examine secret motives. I give all people their due rewards, according to what their actions deserve. (Jeremiah 17:10 NLT)

WHAT DO YOU THINK? (ADVANCED)

Why do you think these books contain the detailed life history of every believer and non-believer who has lived? Why would their personal information be used in their eternal judgment?

Book of Life. It seems this book contains the names of every believer who ever lived who will go to the new Jerusalem with God.

Believer's judgment. The following describes the judgment of believers based on how they lived their lives:

> For we must all stand before Christ to be judged. We will each receive whatever we deserve for the good or evil we have done in this earthly body. (2 Corinthians 5:10 NLT)

> Each man's work will become evident; for the day will show it because it is to be revealed with fire, and the fire itself will test the quality of each man's work. If any man's work which he has built on it remains, he will receive a reward. If any man's work is burned up, he will suffer loss; but he himself will be saved, yet so as through fire. (1 Corinthians 3:13-15 NASB)

> Watch out that you don't lose what we have worked so hard to achieve. Be diligent so that you receive your full reward. (2 John 1:8 NLT)

Non-believer's judgment. The following describes the judgment of non-believes based on how they lived their lives:

> But because you are stubborn and refuse to turn from your sin, you are storing up terrible punishment for yourself. For a day of anger is coming, when God's righteous judgment will be revealed. (Romans 2:4 NLT)

> He *[Jesus]* will come with His mighty angels, in flaming fire, bringing judgment on those who don't know God and on those who refuse to obey the Good News of our Lord Jesus. They will be punished with eternal destruction, forever separated from the Lord and from His glorious power. (2 Thessalonians 1:7-9 NLT, author's emphasis)

> But cowards, unbelievers, the corrupt, murderers, the immoral, those who practice witchcraft, idol worshipers, and all liars—their fate is in the fiery lake of burning sulfur. This is the second death. (Revelation 21:8 NLT)

Judgment for those who experienced God but still rejected Jesus. These are people who regularly attended church and experienced the realities of God. They may have served in church ministries and belonged to Christian organizations. However, they continually resisted their Savior and His salvation.

> "Dear friends, if we deliberately continue sinning after we have received knowledge of the truth, there is no longer any sacrifice that will cover these sins. There is only the terrible expectation of God's judgment and the raging fire that will consume His enemies . . . Just think how much worse the punishment will be for those who have trampled on the Son of God, and have treated the blood of the covenant, which made us holy, as if it were common and unholy, and have insulted and disdained the Holy Spirit who brings God's mercy to us . . . It is a terrible thing to fall into the hands of the living God." (Hebrews 10:26-31 NLT)

WHAT DO YOU THINK?
Why do you think the judgment of the above-described people will be so severe?

Judgment of the devil and his demons. The devil and his demons have no hope. They sealed their eternal destiny when they rebelled against God in Heaven (Revelation

12:7-9). Since their rebellion, they have known this destiny, and they fear it (Matthew 8:29).

> The devil who had deceived them was thrown into the lake of fire and sulfur where the beast and the false prophet were, and they will be tormented day and night forever and ever. (Revelation 20:10 ESV)

No reincarnation. By the way, there is no reincarnation, no second chances after physical death. People will face the judgment of God for their one life on earth.

> Just as people are destined to die once, and after that to face judgment. (Hebrews 9:27 (NLT)

> Finally, the poor man died and was carried by the angels to be with Abraham. The rich man also died and was buried, and his soul went to the place of the dead. There, in torment, he saw Abraham in the far distance with Lazarus at his side. (Luke 16:22-23 NLT)

WHAT DO YOU THINK?
Why does the idea of reincarnation give people false hope about their eternity?

Some verses about this belief: Psalms 62:12; Ecclesiastes 12:14; Jeremiah 17:10; Ezekiel 24:14; Daniel 7:22; Matthew 7:2, 21-23, 8:29, 12:36-37, 23:33-36; Luke 16:22-23; John 3:16-18, 36, 12:48, 16:11; Romans 2:1-8, 12; 1 Corinthians 3:11-15, 11:31-32; 2 Corinthians 5:10; Galatians 6:7-8; 2 Thessalonians 1:5-10; Hebrews 9:27, 10:26-31: James 3:1; 2 Peter 2:4; 2 John 1:8; Revelation 12:7-9, 19:19-20, 20:10-15, 21:8.

WHAT DO YOU THINK?
Reword this belief's description in a few sentences to help you remember it.

Eternal Life with God

All the religions of the world require faith and belief in their teachings. However, because the Bible is God's living word, it can be trusted as a guide to eternal life with the one true God, the Father, Jesus Christ, and the Holy Spirit.

> I give them eternal life, and they will never perish, and no one will snatch them out of my hand. My Father, who has given them to me, is

greater than all, and no one is able to snatch them out of the Father's hand. (John 10:28-29 ESV)

PRACTICE IT
I hope the reality of eternal judgment based on how you live your life encourages you to live for God. But is there something that hinders you from believing Jesus Christ will personally judge you? Does this thought offend or scare you? If so, will you repent now to receive His forgiveness?

The next chapter, "A Glimpse of Heaven," may help you believe what eternity will be like with the God of the Bible.

Eternity is forever! If you have not already done so, now is the time to accept Jesus Christ as your Savior and Lord. Please refer to the chapter "Prayer to Know God" for more information about this.

PART F

YOU HAVE NOTHING TO LOSE AND EVERYTHING TO GAIN

40

A Glimpse of Heaven

Is Heaven Real?

Some people ask questions like the following, "Is Heaven real?" or "How do I know Heaven actually exists?" What about purported visions of Heaven and Jesus? Can they be true? This chapter addresses these and other questions about the reality of Heaven.

God created Heaven. He created Heaven as a city with permanent foundations for His throne and residence.

> Abraham was confidently looking forward to a city with eternal foundations, a city designed and built by God. (Hebrews 11:10 NLT)

WHAT DO YOU THINK?
Have you thought about Heaven being a city? This implies many people live together under some form of government, culture, and social order. Why do you think this might describe what Heaven is like?

What is Heaven? It is the abode of the Father God, His Son, Jesus Christ, and the Holy Spirit (even though they exist everywhere). The Father and Jesus sit on their thrones in Heaven (Hebrews 8:1-2). Since God is supernatural, Heaven is supernatural as well.

> Your throne, O LORD *[Father God]*, has stood from time immemorial. You Yourself are from the everlasting past. (Psalms 93:2 NLT, author's emphasis)

But to the Son *[Jesus]* He *[Father God]* says, "Your throne, O God, endures forever and ever. You rule with a scepter of justice." (Hebrews 1:8 NLT, author's emphasis)

From the throne came flashes of lightning and the rumble of thunder. And in front of the throne were seven torches with burning flames. This is the sevenfold Spirit of God. (Revelation 4:5 NLT)

Heaven is where God presides over His multitude of mighty angels.

The highest angelic powers stand in awe of God. He is far more awesome than all who surround His throne. (Psalms 89:7 NLT)

I saw the Lord sitting upon a throne, high and lifted up; and the train of his robe filled the temple. Above him stood the seraphim. Each had six wings: with two he covered his face, and with two he covered his feet, and with two he flew. And one called to another and said: "Holy, holy, holy is the LORD of hosts; the whole earth is full of his glory!" And the foundations of the thresholds shook at the voice of him who called, and the house was filled with smoke. (Isaiah 6:1-4 ESV)

We see that God reigns from His throne in Heaven over His entire creation.

God reigns over the nations, God sits on His holy throne. (Psalms 47:8 ESV)

Yours, O LORD, is the greatness and the power and the glory and the victory and the majesty, for all that is in the heavens and in the earth is yours. Yours is the kingdom, O LORD, and you are exalted as head above all. Both riches and honor come from you, and you rule over all. In your hand are power and might, and in your hand it is to make great and to give strength to all. (1 Chronicles 29:11-12 ESV)

WHAT DO YOU THINK?

Imagine experiencing Jehovah God's *greatness*, *power*, *glory*, *victory*, and *majesty* as He sits on His throne in heaven. Why is it impossible to describe what this will truly be like (2 Corinthians 12:4)?

Following are other names for Heaven:

Paradise:

> And he said, "Jesus, remember me when you come into your kingdom."
> And he said to him, "Truly, I say to you, today you will be with me in
> Paradise." (Luke 23:42-43 ESV)

Mount Zion, city of the living God, and the Heavenly Jerusalem:

> But you have come to Mount Zion, the city of the living God, the
> heavenly Jerusalem (Hebrews 12:22 NET)

Where is Heaven? It's thought of as being located "above" the earth (Deuteronomy 5:8). However, we don't know its precise location. But Heaven's current location is temporary since there will be a new heaven and new earth (Revelation 21:1). In this future, God will bring Heaven down to the new earth as the new Jerusalem (Revelation 21:1-3). The new earth with this new Jerusalem will be the Father's, Jesus', and the Holy Spirit's eternal dwelling place with all the followers of Jesus.

Heaven Is Indescribable

The magnificent beauty and glory of Heaven are beyond human imagination and understanding.

> That is what the Scriptures mean when they say, "No eye has seen, no
> ear has heard, and no mind has imagined what God has prepared for
> those who love Him." (1 Corinthians 2:9 NLT)

> I *[Apostle Paul]* was caught up to paradise and heard things so astounding
> that they cannot be expressed in words, things no human is allowed to
> tell. (2 Corinthians 12:4 NLT, author's emphasis)

Visions of Heaven. A vision from God is a supernatural experience where the Holy Spirit enables a person to see beyond the natural into the supernatural realm. Visions of Heaven are, therefore, supernatural experiences. The Apostle Paul describes his supernatural vision of Heaven in 2 Corinthians 12:1-4. But in the following verse, he says he didn't know whether his physical body was supernaturally transported to Heaven or he had a vision of it in his mind:

> I was caught up to the third heaven fourteen years ago. Whether I
> was in my body or out of my body, I don't know—only God knows.
> (2 Corinthians 12:2 NLT)

WHAT DO YOU THINK?

Why does the Apostle Paul's vision of Heaven imply that people today could also see a vision of Heaven or Jesus?

In the following verses, we see that multiple people in the New Testament were given a vision of Heaven or heard Jesus speak from Heaven:

> But Stephen, full of the Holy Spirit, gazed steadily into heaven and saw the glory of God, and he saw Jesus standing in the place of honor at God's right hand. And he told them, "Look, I see the heavens opened and the Son of Man standing in the place of honor at God's right hand!" (Acts 7:55-56 NLT)

> After these things I looked, and there was a door standing open in heaven! And the first voice I had heard speaking to me like a trumpet said: "Come up here so that I can show you what must happen after these things." Immediately I was in the Spirit, and a throne was standing in heaven with someone seated on it! And the one seated on it was like jasper and carnelian in appearance, and a rainbow looking like it was made of emerald encircled the throne. (Revelation 4:1-3 NET)

> As he *[Saul before he was converted and became the Apostle Paul]* was going along, approaching Damascus, suddenly a light from heaven flashed around him. He fell to the ground and heard a voice saying to him, "Saul, Saul, why are you persecuting me?" So he said, "Who are you, Lord?" He replied, "I am Jesus whom you are persecuting!" (Acts 9:3-5 NET, author's emphasis)

WHAT DO YOU THINK?

Why do you think the Holy Spirit gives only a few people visions of Heaven or Jesus? Why doesn't He give everyone these visions?

Jesus Gives Mark a Vision of Heaven

I will call this couple Mark and Anne. Mark was a good friend who died in 2019 after a five-year battle with pulmonary fibrosis. He was a strong Christian man who loved his wife, Anne, and strove to live a godly life. I knew him through our church, adult

Sunday School class, and our Men's Bible Study Group. I remember his faith and desire to grow as a follower of Jesus Christ.

Mark's story begins. Two scriptures have particular meaning for me about Mark's constant battle with pain and suffering.

> For to me to live is Christ, and to die is gain. (Philippians 1:21 ESV)

> He will wipe away every tear from their eyes, and death shall be no more, neither shall there be mourning, nor crying, nor pain anymore, for the former things have passed away. (Revelation 21:4 ESV)

I know without a doubt Mark is in Heaven with his Savior and Lord, Jesus Christ, and his Heavenly Father. But, like many people, he had questions about what Heaven would be like. He was also concerned about leaving Anne, his family, and his friends.

Conversation between Mark and Anne. The following exchange between Mark and Anne occurred on the evening of October 13, 2019, as they watched TV. This happened two weeks before he went to his home in Heaven. The conversation went something like the following.

> Mark: "There is a bright, white light next to me."
> Anne: "Is it scary?"
> Mark: "No! It is just a presence."
> Anne: "Is it Jesus Christ?"
> Mark: "Maybe."

That night. The following short conversation occurred about three or four in the morning.

> Anne: "Mark, you have talked in your sleep all night. Why don't you stop talking and go to sleep?"
> Mark responded by saying: "I am not talking to you!"

That afternoon. I went over to visit Mark. Before I went into the bedroom, Anne told me about the above conversation.

> Paul: "How are you feeling today, Mark?"
> Mark: "I am not feeling well. I didn't get much sleep last night."
> Paul: "Why not?"
> Mark: "Jesus Christ was here and talking with me."
> (Mark had evidently been talking with Jesus for five or six hours that night.)
> Paul: "What did the Lord say to you?"

Mark: "He told me I would be going home to Heaven soon."
Paul: "Did the Lord show you Heaven?"
Mark: "Yes."
Paul: "What's Heaven like? What did you see there?"

Mark replied with words similar to the Apostle Paul's when the Lord showed him a vision of Heaven, saying it was inexpressible.

> I was caught up to paradise and heard things so astounding that they cannot be expressed in words, things no human is allowed to tell. (2 Corinthians 12:4 NLT)

End of Mark's vision. Mark was very tired, so I left at this point.

My imagination – Mark in Heaven

In my imagination, I see Jesus showing Mark around Heaven to let him know what a wonderful place his future home will be. I wonder if Jesus might have included the following descriptions of Heaven. This, of course, is all in my imagination because I know that Heaven is indescribable. I don't know what Jesus actually told and showed Mark. However, the following Bible verses are accurate and provide some understanding of what Heaven is like.

The Father's appearance and throne. "Mark, I am first going to take you to visit with my Father in His throne room." The following words describe the Father God's appearance and throne. I think Mark would have bowed down in contrite humbleness at the holiness and majesty of his God!

> At once I was in the Spirit, and behold, a throne stood in heaven, with one seated on the throne. And he who sat there had the appearance of jasper and carnelian, and around the throne was a rainbow that had the appearance of an emerald . . . . From the throne came flashes of lightning, and rumblings and peals of thunder, and before the throne were burning seven torches of fire, which are the seven spirits of God, and before the throne there was as it were a sea of glass, like crystal. And around the throne, on each side of the throne, are four living creatures, full of eyes in front and behind: the first living creature like a lion, the second living creature like an ox, the third living creature with the face of a man, and the fourth living creature like an eagle in flight. And the four living creatures, each of them with six wings, are full of

eyes all around and within, and day and night they never cease to say, "Holy, holy, holy, is the Lord God Almighty, who was and is and is to come!" (Revelation 4:2-8 ESV)

Innumerable angels. Mark would not have been able to count the number of angels he saw in Heaven.

> No, you have come to Mount Zion, to the city of the living God, the heavenly Jerusalem, and to countless thousands of angels in a joyful gathering. (Hebrews 12:22 NLT)

WHAT DO YOU THINK?

What would it be like to see these innumerable angels in Heaven worshiping and serving Jehovah God? What would you like to ask some of them when you arrive there?

Only followers of Christ are in Heaven. As Mark looked around and saw more people than he could count, he was reminded of the following scripture:

> After these things I looked, and here was an enormous crowd that no one could count, made up of persons from every nation, tribe, people, and language, standing before the throne and before the Lamb dressed in long white robes, and with palm branches in their hands. They were shouting out in a loud voice, "Salvation belongs to our God, who is seated on the throne, and to the Lamb!" (Revelation 7:9-10 NET)

Then Jesus said, "I want you to know, Mark, that not everyone will go to Heaven. Only those who accepted me as their Savior and Lord and are born-again by the Holy Spirit will be here."

> Jesus answered, "Truly, truly, I say to you, unless one is born of water and the Spirit he cannot enter into the kingdom of God." (John 3:5 NASB)

Jesus may have reminded Mark that the believer's home is in Heaven because they are a citizen of Heaven.

> But we are citizens of heaven, where the Lord Jesus Christ lives. And we are eagerly waiting for Him to return as our Savior. (Philippians 3:20 NLT)

He may have warned that if a person's passions are for acquiring earthly wealth, they will miss out on heavenly treasures.

> Don't store up treasures here on earth, where moths eat them and rust destroys them, and where thieves break in and steal. Store your treasures in heaven, where moths and rust cannot destroy, and thieves do not break in and steal. Wherever your treasure is, there the desires of your heart will also be. (Matthew 6:19-21 NLT)

WHAT DO YOU THINK? (ADVANCED)
The above verses are about the condition of the heart. You may recall the five types of hearts God attempts to reach with His word in the chapter "Everyone Needs to Be Rescued." But only one type treasures their knowledge of and relationship with Jesus above all else. Why do you think it's easy for some people to treasure their earthly wealth more than eternity with God?

Believer's body in Heaven. I think Mark saw believers walking around in Heaven. He noticed they had a visible form. It was not just their spirit floating in the air. Jesus may have said to Mark, "Let's go over to the house of the Apostle Paul. I want you to meet him."

> For we know that when this earthly tent we live in is taken down (that is, when we die and leave this earthly body), we will have a house in Heaven, an eternal body made for us by God Himself and not by human hands. We grow weary in our present bodies, and we long to put on our heavenly bodies like new clothing. For we will put on heavenly bodies; we will not be spirits without bodies. (2 Corinthians 5:1-3 NLT)

NOTE: The bodies of believers in Heaven are not the resurrected eternal bodies like that of Jesus. They will receive that later. Many Christians believe it will be at the second coming of Jesus Christ (Revelation 19:11-14).

Full knowledge of heavenly things. The believer's spirit and soul in Heaven will have abilities they can't have in their mortal body on earth. Mark realized he would know and understand the divine and supernatural later when he finally arrived at his home in Heaven.

Now we see things imperfectly, like puzzling reflections in a mirror, but then we will see everything with perfect clarity. All that I know now is partial and incomplete, but then I will know everything completely, just as God now knows me completely. (1 Corinthians 13:12)

No marriage. "Mark, your beautiful Christian wife, Anne, will not be your wife in Heaven." At first, Mark didn't like this idea. But he noticed his thoughts were constantly centered on his Father God and Jesus Christ, not Anne. And that his heart was constantly filled with praise and worship of God.

> For when the dead rise, they will neither marry nor be given in marriage. In this respect they will be like the angels in Heaven. (Matthew 22:30 NLT)

You will have a place to live. Next, Jesus told Mark, "I will take you to the home I have reserved for you." Jesus Christ has already prepared a place in Heaven for His followers.

> There are many dwelling places in my Father's house. Otherwise, I would have told you, because I am going away to make ready a place for you. And if I go and make ready a place for you, I will come again and take you to be with me, so that where I am you may be too. (John 14:2-3 NET)

PERSONAL APPLICATION

What do you think your place of residence in Heaven will be like?

You will receive an inheritance. "Mark, would you like to know about my inheritance I will share with you?" Of course, Mark was eager to know about this. When a follower of Jesus goes to Heaven, they will receive an inheritance from the Father.

> And if children, then heirs—heirs of God and fellow heirs with Christ (Romans 8:17 ESV)

> The Spirit is God's guarantee that He will give us the inheritance He promised and that He has purchased us to be His own people. He did this so we would praise and glorify Him. (Ephesians 1:14 NLT)

Mark realized he couldn't have imagined what his Father God had prepared for him in Heaven as a joint heir with His Son, Jesus Christ.

> But, as it is written, "What no eye has seen, nor ear heard, nor the heart of man imagined, what God has prepared for those who love him." (1 Corinthians 2:9 ESV)

No tears or pain. Mark noticed no one was sad or crying. When he asked Jesus about this, He replied, "There will never be any death, suffering, sorrow, or pain in Heaven."

> He will wipe every tear from their eyes, and there will be no more death or sorrow or crying or pain. All these things are gone forever. (Revelation 21:4 NLT)

PERSONAL APPLICATION
Imagine what it will be like in Heaven to have no pain or suffering, no crime or indecency. Would you feel safe and secure? If you had a severe health condition on earth, how grateful would you feel toward the Father for never again having that terrible pain and suffering in Heaven?

No killing of animals. Mark was getting hungry by now, so he asked Jesus where the nearest restaurant was located. He felt like a good steak. Jesus reminded him that even though people on earth kill animals for food, this will not be so in Heaven. Remember, there is no death in Heaven.

> The wolf and the lamb will feed together. The lion will eat hay like a cow. But the snakes will eat dust. In those days no one will be hurt or destroyed on My holy mountain. I, the LORD, have spoken! (Isaiah 65:25 NLT)

Our pets. Mark asked Jesus if his cat would be in Heaven when it died. I don't know what Jesus' response would be. This is a question many pet owners have. I wonder if pets might be in Heaven since animals will be there.

Serve God in Heaven. Mark asked Jesus what he would be doing in Heaven. Jesus replied, "Since there is no death or need for rest in Heaven, you will continually serve the Father. Does this sound boring to you, Mark? It will not be!"

Therefore they are before the throne of God, and serve him day and night in his temple; and he who sits on the throne will shelter them with his presence. (Revelation 7:15 ESV)

WHAT DO YOU THINK?

Perhaps there will be jobs in Heaven. Why do you think there may be manufacturing, farming, distribution centers, retail stores, and government jobs in Heaven?

Adam and Eve had jobs in Heaven. God created Adam and Eve as eternal humans who could not die. As such, they were to work and serve God in the Garden of Eden before their fall. The following verses say that God gave them work to do in the Garden of Eden:

The LORD God took the man and put him in the garden of Eden to work it and keep it. (Genesis 2:15 ESV)

If God intended Adam and Eve (and their offspring) to have work to do as eternal humans before their fall, then perhaps this indicates He has the same intention for believers in Heaven and the new earth.

Following are other verses that may indicate that believers could have jobs in Heaven and the new earth:

He said therefore, "A nobleman went into a far country to receive for himself a kingdom and then return. Calling ten of his servants, he gave them ten minas, and said to them, 'Engage in business until I come.' . . . When he returned, having received the kingdom, he ordered these servants to whom he had given the money to be called to him, that he might know what they had gained by doing business. The first came before him, saying, 'Lord, your mina has made ten minas more.' And he said to him, 'Well done, good servant! Because you have been faithful in a very little, you shall have authority over ten cities.'" (Luke 19:12-17 ESV)

If there is work, it won't be hard labor that resulted from Adam's fall when they were cast out of the Garden of Eden. Instead, I believe it will be enjoyable without hardship or pain.

And I heard a voice from heaven saying, "Write this down: Blessed are those who die in the Lord from now on. Yes, says the Spirit, they are blessed indeed, for they will rest from their hard work; for their good deeds follow them!" (Revelation 14:13 NLT)

The end of my imaginary story about Mark in Heaven. Only two weeks later, Mark went home to be with His Savior and Lord forever!

WHAT DO YOU THINK?
After reading these Bible verses about Heaven, why do you think it's a real place?

Want to read more about Heaven? *The Case for Heaven* by Lee Strobel provides research-based evidence to validate the existence of Heaven. He interviews various experts to answer such questions as what happens after we die, what our experiences will be like in Heaven, why our view of eternity matters, and much more.

Myths about Heaven

There are erroneous ideas about Heaven which are not found in the Bible. Therefore, searching the Bible to verify assertions about what Heaven is like is essential.

The following are myths about Heaven that are not in the Bible. They can draw people away from the truth and give false hope about eternity.

- Heaven doesn't exist (so neither does hell)
- Jesus Christ is not the only way to get to Heaven
- Everyone goes to Heaven when they die
- People will join all their friends and family in Heaven (NOTE: some will not be in Heaven)
- Wealth obtained in this world can be taken to Heaven
- People who die with the "most toys win"
- People become angels with wings in Heaven
- People will sit on a cloud and play the harp in Heaven
- People can return to earth to look after a loved one or to complete "unfinished business"
- People can send messages back to earth, whether by a medium or other means

- People can pray or give money to help someone gain Heaven
- People can repent in Hell and be sent to Heaven

Ask the Holy Spirit to show you the truth if you believe these myths. Then ask the Father God to forgive you for believing a lie about His wonderful reality of Heaven.

PRACTICE IT
Which of these myths about Heaven have you believed to be true? Why do you want them to be true? Why don't you accept the truth about Heaven now and ask the Father to forgive you of these deceptions?

Do you have questions about Heaven and eternity? Heaven can be just a concept in your mind. Something you have read or heard about but can't fully grasp as reality. You may have questions like the following:

- Is there really a God?
- Does He love me and care about me?
- Will my soul and spirit go to Heaven when my physical body dies?

Few people have supernatural experiences, as Mark did about Heaven. If you have questions about your eternity, I suggest you speak with your pastor or someone you trust who knows the God of the Bible.

How to make Heaven your home. A friend and wonderful man of God sent me a small card to share with people. His purpose is to help people know how to make Heaven their eternal home. This is what is printed on the card.

Side one:

JESUS LOVES YOU

Side two:

> For God loved the world so much that He gave His one and only Son so that everyone who believes in Him will not perish but have eternal life. (John 3:16 NLT)

> For everyone has sinned, we all fall short of God's glorious standard. (Romans 3:23 NLT)

If you confess with your mouth that Jesus is Lord and believe in your heart that God raised Him from the dead, you will be saved. (Romans 10:9 NLT)

Jesus told him, "I am the way, the truth, and the life. No one can come to the Father except through Me." (John 14:6 NLT)

PERSONAL APPLICATION

If you are a follower of Jesus, what are you most looking forward to in Heaven? How do you think you will feel when you arrive there? Which family and friends do you think you will see there? Which ones don't care about Jesus and won't be there? What can you say to help them understand and believe their need to be rescued from the eternal consequence of rejecting Jesus?

If you are not a follower of Jesus, please don't wait until it is too late! Now is the time, not tomorrow, because tomorrow may not come. In the chapter "Prayer to Know God," you can learn more about praying to receive Jesus Christ as your Savior and Lord.

41

Prayer to Know God

Sometimes you hear people ask, "Isn't being a good person enough to get me into Heaven?"

> Your eyes are too pure to look on evil; you cannot tolerate wrongdoing.
> (Habakkuk 1:13 NIV)

> You therefore must be perfect, as your heavenly Father is perfect.
> (Matthew 5:48 ESV)

No one is perfect enough to live in God's holy presence. Every person (no matter how nice they are) has said, thought, and done things that displease God. He calls these behaviors "sin." The Greek word translated sin is sometimes referred to as "missing the mark" of God's perfection.

> For everyone has sinned; we all fall short of God's glorious standard.
> (Romans 3:23 NLT)

WHAT DO YOU THINK?
God is perfect, and people must also be perfect to spend eternity with Him. Why did Jesus suffer and die on the cross for people if they could be good enough to earn salvation?

There Is No Hope without Jesus Christ

The following verses describe a person's spiritual condition without Jesus Christ.

> In those days you were living apart from Christ. You were excluded from citizenship among the people of Israel, and you did not know the covenant promises God had made to them. You lived in this world without God and without hope. (Ephesians 2:12 NLT)

> For the sinful nature is always hostile to God. It never did obey God's laws, and it never will. That's why those who are still under the control of their sinful nature can never please God. (Romans 8:7-8 NLT)

I heard a pastor say that you "must step across the line" to choose to leave your old, condemned life and accept God's new eternal life. It's the most important decision you will ever make.

> There is no judgment against anyone who believes in Him *[Jesus]*. But anyone who does not believe in Him has already been judged for not believing in God's one and only Son. (John 3:18 NLT, author's emphasis)

There are born-again followers of Jesus who cannot state a specific date or event in time when they made this decision. But they know in their heart that they have committed themselves to Him as their Savior and Lord.

WHAT DO YOU THINK?

Why is this a conscious decision and not something that might happen by chance if people go to church long enough?

There is Good News! It's God's provision to rescue you from the eternal consequences of living your life without Jesus. You can be saved from these consequences and gain an eternal relationship with the Father God through Jesus Christ.

The Good News (the Gospel)

The Good News about Jesus Christ will save you if you put your faith in Him.

> For I am not ashamed of this Good News about Christ. It is the power of God at work, saving everyone who believes—the Jew first and also

the Gentile. This Good News tells us how God makes us right in His sight. This is accomplished from start to finish by faith. As the Scriptures say, "It is through faith that a righteous person has life." (Romans 1:16-17 NLT)

You see the three essential components of this Good News of Jesus Christ in the following verses.

Now I want to make clear for you, brothers and sisters, the gospel that I preached to you, that you received and on which you stand, and by which you are being saved, if you hold firmly to the message I preached to you – unless you believed in vain. For I passed on to you as of first importance what I also received – that Christ died for our sins according to the scriptures, and that he was buried, and that he was raised on the third day according to the scriptures. (1 Corinthians 15:1-4 NET)

PRACTICE IT

The following prayer uses these three components of the Good News. Please pray now from your heart to enter into an eternal relationship with the Father, Jesus, and the Holy Spirit.

Your Prayer to Know God

Dear God, thank you for loving me and caring about me. Thank you for wanting me to be with you forever and for sending Jesus to be my Savior and Lord. I believe that Jesus died on the cross for me, that He was dead and buried, and was raised back to life by your supernatural power, according to the scriptures.

Please forgive me for all my sins against you and people. I commit to live my life under your authority and rule, Jesus, as the Lord of my life. Thank you, Jesus Christ, for rescuing me from the eternal consequences of living my life without you.

Thank you, Father, for sending your Holy Spirit to live within me now to guide, help, and teach me. I know that I now have eternal life with you, my God!

If you sincerely prayed the above from your heart, you are now a born-again Christian, a follower of Jesus Christ. The Holy Spirit is living within you. Welcome to the eternal family of God!

You now have the following relationship with each person of the Trinity of God. You are a:

- Child of your Father God (Galatians 3:26)

- Disciple and brother/sister of Jesus Christ (Mark 3:35)

- Temple in which the Holy Spirit lives (1 Corinthians 6:9)

PRACTICE IT
Now that your relationship with God has changed, what is the first thing you want to ask the Holy Spirit now to do to help you begin this new eternal journey?

You have a new nature now since the Holy Spirit lives in you. In the next chapter, you will learn what to do to become a mature follower of Jesus Christ. Your goal is to know God and become more like Jesus in your character and new nature.

42

Resources for New and Maturing Believers

Now that You Belong to Him

In the chapter, "The Christian Church May Be Different than You Think," you saw that believers in a healthy Christian church should practice the following (Acts 2:42-47):

- Studying the word of God
- Fellowshipping: meeting together regularly and enjoying being with each other
- Observing the Lord's Supper, Communion (Luke 22:14-20; 1 Corinthians 11:23-26)
- Praying together and individually
- Helping others: sharing their time, talents, and treasure, including financially, with those in need
- Worshiping God: participating in a weekly church service by worshiping God in song and learning about Him from preaching and teaching
- Gathering in small groups: Meeting in homes during the week to continue the above

WHAT DO YOU THINK?

As a born-again follower of Jesus Christ, why do you think believers must develop these same regular habits? Why will they not grow to become a spiritually mature Christian without this?

Diversity of Christian Materials

There are many choices of Christian materials and resources to help you mature as a follower of Jesus Christ. Most of the ones I mention here are free. Just contact the Christian ministry to request them.

Journals. Write daily about your experiences with God. This is called journaling. What's the cost – paper and a pen. Writing about God's involvement in your life can produce the following benefits:

- You learn to recognize His voice as He communicates, teaches, and guides you (this is often the Holy Spirit).

- Your faith in God and His reality in your life is strengthened.

- You will be able to tell others about God's love, care, and involvement in your life years later.

PERSONAL APPLICATION

Why would writing about God strengthen your faith in His reality in your life? Why does knowing His reality encourage you to discipline yourself to do the things needed to grow spiritually?

Music to worship God. I listen to Christian music at home every day. I sing with other believers Sunday during worship service. For me, worshiping God in music is about sensing His presence and fellowshipping with Him in my heart, mind, and spirit. As I sing, my mind and heart become quiet from the day's noise. I experience peace and not agitation. The worship music I like does not ramp me up and stimulate me. Instead, it quiets me and brings me into God's presence with reverence for who He is as *Abba* and *Almighty God*.

New Christian materials. Many Christian churches and organizations offer free materials to help new (and maturing) Christians grow in their faith and spiritual life with God. The Billy Graham Evangelical Association offers such excellent materials:

- Billy Graham Evangelical Association – *https://peacewithgod.net/i-prayed-the-prayer/*

Daily Devotional

I suggest you read a daily devotional. Linda and I have read devotionals from all the following sources. They are free. We have appreciated their insights into the life of a follower of Jesus.

Following are links to free devotionals with which we are familiar and enjoy:

- Our Daily Bread – *https://odb.org* (Especially good for new believers)

- Ray Stedman – *https://www.raystedman.org/daily-devotions*

- Charles Stanley – *https://www.intouch.org/read/magazine/daily-devotions*

- Chuck Swindoll – *https://www.insight.org/resources/daily-devotional/individual*

- Billy Graham – *https://billygraham.org/devotions*

- Crosswalk.com provides access to devotionals by many Christian authors – *https://www.crosswalk.com/devotionals*

There are many devotional books you can also purchase. One excellent book is Alistair Begg's *Truth for Life, 365 Daily Devotionals*, published by The Good Book company: *(https://www.thegoodbook.com)*. Alistair is a pastor with many years of preaching and teaching God's word. His spiritual insights and practical applications to the life of a believer are remarkable.

PERSONAL APPLICATION
Why would reading a daily devotional help you know God better?

Discipleship Resources

Discipleship is a small group process that involves someone leading and teaching others. Bible study guides are used to provide structure and focus for the content and process. Discipleship is primarily about developing spiritual maturity in new and growing believers. Another benefit is that believers learn to rely on each other to be accountable for their spiritual growth. There is a reasonable cost for most discipleship study materials, but the benefits are well worth it.

The following are two sources that will help new and maturing believers grow in their Christian faith:

Dr. Ralph F. Wilson's book, *JesusWalk Beginning the Journey,* subtitle *Discipleship and Spiritual Formation* is an excellent resource for new

Christians to learn and be guided by a mentor during the early years of spiritual growth. It provides *A Curriculum for Training and Mentoring New Believers in the Christian Doctrines, Core Values, and Spiritual Disciplines*. There is a small cost for the book. In addition, there are free online resources for the book, which include video and audio for the lessons: *http://www.JesusWalk.com/beginning*.

The Beginning, First Steps for New Disciples, Disciples Path for Students, 5-Session Bible Study, by Lifeway Press. This series is based on how Jesus modeled discipleship in the Gospels. It leads new believers on a pathway to spiritual maturity where they also can become disciple-makers.

Participate in a Local Church

Find a local Christian church where the preaching and teaching are based on the Bible. Look for one that is discipleship-oriented that provides small group opportunities to help you grow and mature as a follower of Jesus Christ. Be sure they teach how the indwelling Holy Spirit can help you live the Christian life. If you can't find one, ask Christians in your community about a church like this. Read the chapter "The Christian Church May Be Different than You Think" for information about what a good Christian church should be like.

Participate in a Small Group

It's essential to be with other maturing Christians for encouragement and fellowship. We need each other. Participate in a teaching-based small group, such as a home group or adult Sunday School class. This may also be a discipleship small group, as mentioned earlier.

IMPORTANT: You must become a student of the Bible. As you know by now, it's the living word of God (Hebrews 4:12). Through the work of the Holy Spirit, it will change you. Too many new Christians stagnate in their spiritual growth and never learn to live as followers of Jesus Christ. Find someone who knows God and the Bible to disciple you. You are not alone. Enjoy your life with God and other believers.

PERSONAL APPLICATION
Why would studying and discussing the Bible with a small group of believers help you feel more accountable to grow spiritually?

Continue reading and studying. Regularly reading and studying the Bible is essential for new and maturing Christians. If you are new to the Bible, I suggest starting with the four Gospels in the New Testament (Mathew, Mark, Luke, and John). They describe the life of Jesus Christ while He was on the earth and will help you get acquainted with Him. The New Living Translation (NLT) is good for new and maturing believers if you don't have a Bible.

Many excellent books can help you grow as a believer. Ask a pastor or a mature Christian friend about books they would recommend. You might also want to purchase one or more of the books in the "Further Study" section of this book. They are written by reputable Christians and will help you live a life that pleases God.

43

In the End, It's Up to You

As you read this final chapter, consider again how different Christianity is from all other world religions.

Three Things Last Forever

Biblical Faith, Hope, and Love are from God and are eternal. They are, therefore, the basis of a Christian's trust and life with Him.

> And now these three remain: faith, hope, and love. But the greatest of these is love. (1 Corinthians 13:13 NET)

WHAT DO YOU THINK?
Why are faith, hope, and love associated with eternal life with God? If everything else seems to disappear, why do these three remain in a believer's life?

What Is Faith?

The following verses describe biblical faith as having confidence and trust that God is who He says He is and that He will do what He says He will do. Therefore, faith in God is not "blind faith" but rather is based on the substance of God's living word. So, faith comes from the Holy Spirit.

> Faith is the confidence that what we hope for will actually happen; it gives us assurance about things we cannot see. Through their faith, the

people in days of old earned a good reputation. By faith we understand that the entire universe was formed at God's command, that what we now see did not come from anything that can be seen. (Hebrews 11:1-3 NLT)

WHAT DO YOU THINK?

Why is genuine faith in God not thoughtless blind faith?

Through the indwelling Holy Spirit, Jesus Christ comes to live within the hearts of believers when they place their faith in Him for salvation and eternal life. This faith is grounded in the unconditional love of God for His children.

> I pray that according to the wealth of his glory he will grant you to be strengthened with power through his Spirit in the inner person, that Christ will dwell in your hearts through faith. (Ephesians 3:16-17 NET)

Faith in God brings joy and confidence in knowing that you will spend eternity with Him. It comes from the heart as well as the mind.

> Because of our faith, Christ has brought us into this place of undeserved privilege where we now stand, and we confidently and joyfully look forward to sharing God's glory. (Romans 5:2 NLT)

You can't please God without having faith in Him. You will not live your life for God when you don't trust Him. I think trusting God is the same as having faith in Him.

> And it is impossible to please God without faith. Anyone who wants to come to Him must believe that God exists and that He rewards those who sincerely seek Him. (Hebrews 11:6 NLT)

True faith requires action. The following verses say that faith in God requires action, or it's not real:

> What good is it, my brothers and sisters, if someone claims to have faith but does not have works? Can this kind of faith save him? If a brother or sister is poorly clothed and lacks daily food, and one of you says to them, "Go in peace, keep warm and eat well," but you do not

give them what the body needs, what good is it? So also faith, if it does not have works, is dead being by itself. (James 2:14-17 NET)

PERSONAL APPLICATION

In what ways do you trust the God of the Bible in your life? Why does this trust demonstrate your faith and confidence in Him, or perhaps a lack of these?

Stories – faith in action. You have seen the reality of faith in action in the stories in this book. Reread them if needed to help strengthen your faith in God. There are more at the end of this book. Your faith will grow over time as you experience God and allow the Holy Spirit to apply His living word to transform your heart and life.

What Is Hope?

Hope is similar to faith because they both involve the assurance that God will do what He says. As a result, there is a sense of confidence and certainty in the heart and life of believers. They base their decisions and actions on the hope God has given them for eternal life with Him.

All hope in God comes from His Holy Spirit and can bring joy and peace as you trust Him.

> I pray that God, the source of hope, will fill you completely with joy and peace because you trust in Him. Then you will overflow with confident hope through the power of the Holy Spirit. (Romans 15:13 NLT)

Followers of Jesus can find hope in God when they read and study the Bible.

> For everything that was written in former times was written for our instruction, so that through endurance and through encouragement of the scriptures we may have hope. (Romans 15:4 NET)

The following verse says that life without faith in Jesus Christ is living without God and without hope:

> In those days you were living apart from Christ. You were excluded from citizenship among the people of Israel, and you did not know the covenant promises God had made to them. You lived in this world without God and without hope. (Ephesians 2:12 NLT)

PERSONAL APPLICATION

What was your hope in life before you read this book? Was it for fame, popularity, wealth, power, or prestige? Was it just to get by, to survive the next day? Or does your hope rest securely on the reality of God and His eternal love for you?

What Is Love?

God's nature, His essence, is love. It's not a trait or characteristic that can change because it's who He truly is (Malachi 3:6). This is also true of faith and hope. And they all come from the Holy Spirit.

> For love comes from God ... because God is love. (1 John 4:7-8 NLT)

Unlike conditional human love, God's love is unconditional. Nothing you experience in life can come between you and His love. If you still doubt His unconditional, sacrificial love for you, read the following words from the Bible:

> Who is the one who will condemn? Christ is the one who died (and more than that, he was raised), who is at the right hand of God, and who also is interceding for us. Who will separate us from the love of Christ? Will trouble, or distress, or persecution, or famine, or nakedness, or danger, or sword?... For I am convinced that neither death, nor life, nor angels, nor heavenly rulers, nor things that are present, nor things to come, nor powers, nor height, nor depth, nor anything else in creation will be able to separate us from the love of God in Christ Jesus our Lord. (Romans 8:34-39 NET)

God knows you and loves you just as you are. Nothing you can ever do or say will change how deeply He loves you.

> O LORD, You have examined my heart and know everything about me. (Psalms 139:1 NLT)

He wants you to understand and experience His wonderful, all-encompassing love.

> And may you have the power to understand, as all God's people should, how wide, how long, how high, and how deep His love is. (Ephesians 3:18 NLT)

PRACTICE IT

Are you experiencing the Father's unconditional love? If not, ask Him now to show you why. Then, why not ask Him for forgiveness to enjoy His eternal unconditional love?

Remember to keep love alive. "When love stops growing, it starts dying." Life can be full of difficulties, so believers must be intentional about not giving up on their love for the Father, Jesus, and the Holy Spirit. Loving God and others require a life-long commitment to persevere. But the rewards are eternal!

Since God loves His children, He wants them to demonstrate His love toward one another. This proves they belong to God.

> Let all that you do be done in love. (1 Corinthians 16:14 ESV)

> Dear friends, let us continue to love one another, for love comes from God. Anyone who loves is a child of God and knows God. But anyone who does not love does not know God, for God is love. (1 John 4:7-8 NLT)

Life Is Not Easy!

I don't have to tell you this. You know it's not. Like most people, you've encountered various difficulties in your life.

> We can rejoice, too, when we run into problems and trials, for we know that they help us develop endurance. And endurance develops strength of character, and character strengthens our confident hope of salvation. And this hope will not lead to disappointment. For we know how dearly God loves us, because He has given us the Holy Spirit to fill our hearts with His love. (Romans 5:3-5 NLT)

But if Jesus Christ is your Savior and Lord, you can experience His peace and love amid life's difficulties.

> I have told you all this so that you may have peace in Me. Here on earth you will have many trials and sorrows. But take heart, because I have overcome the world. (John 16:33 NLT)

PRACTICE IT

If you don't have the peace of Jesus Christ in your heart, ask Him now to show you why. Then do what He wants to receive it.

The God of all comfort. God refers to Himself as the spiritual Father of His children. Your earthly father may not have comforted you in your trials, difficulties, and suffering. However, your Heavenly Father offers you His divine comfort, which gives you His supernatural peace, encouragement, and strength to persevere.

The following verses say that another reason God comforts you is so you can comfort others who are going through similar difficulties:

> All praise to God, the Father of our Lord Jesus Christ. God is our merciful Father and the source of all comfort. He comforts us in all our troubles so that we can comfort others. When they are troubled, we will be able to give them the same comfort God has given us. (2 Corinthians 3-4 NLT)

Be Intentional about How You Live

Don't just float along in your daily activities, perhaps even wishing for something to change. Instead, live your life intentionally in ways to please the Father God. As a follower of Jesus, ask the Holy Spirit to help you. Strive to do everything as if you are working directly for Jesus Christ.

> So, my dear brothers and sisters, be strong and immovable. Always work enthusiastically for the Lord, for you know that nothing you do for the Lord is ever useless. (1 Corinthians 15:58 NLT)

> Work hard to show the results of your salvation, obeying God with deep reverence and fear. (Philippians 2:12 NLT)

Grow in your spiritual life with God. Through His Spirit, the Father gives His children spiritual insight that enables them to grow in their knowledge of Him. As a result, believers can experience the wonders of life with God beyond their imagination, as you see in the following verses:

> I pray that the God of our Lord Jesus Christ, the glorious Father, will give you spiritual wisdom and revelation in your growing knowledge of him – since the eyes of your heart have been enlightened – so that you can know what is the hope of his calling, what is the wealth of

his glorious inheritance in the saints, and what is the incomparable greatness of his power toward us who believe, as displayed in the exercise of his immense strength. (Ephesians 1:17-19 NET)

My prayer for you. As I conclude this book, the above verses are my prayer for you.

The Father, Jesus Christ, and the Holy Spirit want you to experience their reality in your life because they desire a living relationship with you. No other religion offers this. I hope this book helps you find faith in the God of the Bible. I also hope you learn to live by the Spirit and allow the love of Christ to fill your heart and life.

Everyone Believes in Someone or Something

This book begins and ends with a core theme: everyone believes in someone or something. If you are an atheist, anti-theist, or evolutionist, you believe in something. Does your faith give you peace and confidence that what you believe is true and lasting?

PERSONAL APPLICATION
In what or in whom do you believe? Where have you placed your faith? Is it a faith with no foundation in truth and reality? Or is it a living faith based on the truth and reality of the God of the Bible?

You Have Nothing to Lose and Everything to Gain

You have nothing of earthly value to lose and everything of eternal value to gain when you ask Jesus Christ into your heart and life as Savior and Lord. The chapter "Prayer to Know God" provides a prayer for you to enter eternal life with God. He loves you so faithfully and dearly. I encourage you to take the time now to step into your eternal life with Him if you've not already done so.

FINAL PRACTICE IT
Will you choose to spend eternity with God now and enjoy His presence on earth as you learn to live with Him? If you are a follower of Jesus, what can you do differently to experience His presence and reality in your life more fully?

Call on me in prayer and I will answer you. I will show you great and mysterious things which you still do not know about. (Jeremiah 33:3 NET)

More Stories to Strengthen Your Trust in God

Following are several long stories to further your understanding of how God can supernaturally intervene in a person's life. They are intended to strengthen your trust in the God of the Bible. The subject matter varies, but all demonstrate His loving care, presence, and power. Take the time to study them. First, identify the spiritual principles from the Bible involved in each story. Then, consider how these biblical truths can impact your own life. You will discover that God can be found in situations where you may not readily recognize Him. He is everywhere and always present in the life of His children.

My First Health Breakdown

I committed my life to Jesus Christ in the summer of 1976. In the fall of 1976, my health broke down. This resulted from working 12 to 18 hours a day, seven days a week, for over three months for a company account in the upper Midwest. The subsequent three months of intensive Systems Engineering training added to the physical and mental stress. When I returned to my regular account in San Francisco, I was commuting an hour or more one way. The stress increased, and all this became more than my body could handle.

In the Spring of 1977, I reluctantly resigned from my company. I could no longer continue to work. I was sick, exhausted, and foggy-headed every day. In retrospect, I believe I damaged my body due to constant, excessive stress. I was told that my immune system was seriously compromised. The same doctors that were treating my mother began to treat me. Like my mother, I was diagnosed with "environmental sensitivities." I had become allergic, or sensitive, to much of the world in which I lived.

I will never forget this dinner. I lost fifty pounds over the next year due to severe food allergies and sensitivities. At the worst point, I remember one dinner in particular.

It consisted of three organic white figs, about eight raw organic cashews, and a small pile of organic sprouts. I felt helpless, yet I still knew Jesus had not abandoned me to a life like this. I sensed the Holy Spirit was telling me that the Father had a plan for my life that required better health.

PERSONAL APPLICATION

When has the Holy Spirit given you a sense of peace that difficult things would improve?

In 1980, I was rehired by my company. Thank God! I desperately needed a job and income. I had been too sick to work for nearly four years. I had sold everything of value. I was essentially homeless, broke, and without new skills for any job. My prior manager was gracious and gave me various work activities to help acclimate me to the work environment. This was another instance of God at work in my life through another critical person. All the organic foods, nutritional supplements, homeopathic medicines, and herbs had enabled me to start work again. However, I was still not well. I remember telling someone I would come home from work so sick I didn't know whether I wanted to throw up or pass out. I prayed continually for the Lord to finish healing me.

First Miraculous Healing

In the late Spring of 1983, I was attending a large Pentecostal church in Marin County, California. The pastor had an incredible evangelistic ministry in India. These events would bring thousands of Indian people to salvation and an eternal relationship with Jesus Christ. Before leaving on this trip, he asked the congregation to set aside their personal prayers for the two weeks he was away. Instead, he asked us to pray for God's will and work to be accomplished in India. And now was the last day of this event. As our Men's Group was standing in a circle praying, I began to feel a gentle warmth flow throughout my body. It was so subtle I wondered what it was.

As the following verse indicates, Jesus heals supernaturally:

> Through faith in the name of Jesus, this man was healed—and you know how crippled he was before. Faith in Jesus' name has healed him before your very eyes. (Acts 3:16 NLT)

The next morning when I woke up, I knew the Lord had finished healing me. Praise God! I felt well for the first time in years.

PERSONAL APPLICATION

When has Jesus Christ supernaturally healed you? Or perhaps He healed you through medical science, surgery, or natural health products? Either way, how did you know it was Him?

"I Love You as Much as I Love Everyone"

Linda and I attended Peter Lord's church in Titusville, Florida, in 1985/86. The heart of Peter's ministry was to connect people with God. He wanted people to know God, know His love for them, and learn to communicate in an experiential life with Him. One way he did this was to offer workshops where people had the opportunity to experience God speaking to them. The church had purchased an older motel nearby. People would go alone to an individual motel room to talk with God. The first question was to ask the Father God if He loved them. They would then wait silently for Him to respond. Later, they would return and report to the group what the Father said to them.

In the workshop Linda and I attended, Peter told the story about a man who had gone to church for years but refused to believe God loved him. He finally agreed to participate in the workshop. He returned from asking the first question, sobbing. When he asked God how much He loved him, the Father said something like the following, "I love you as much as I love everyone!" To know God loved him as much as He did all His children was beyond this man's imagination. Knowledge of this changed his life. He became an ardent follower of Jesus Christ, participating in church ministry and visibly enjoying the love of God in his heart and life for all to see.

Peter Lord answers many of the common questions about learning to communicate with God in his book *Hearing God*. It is a practical "how-to" book about experiencing God. If you are learning to communicate with God, this would be an excellent resource to guide you on this inspiring journey.

PERSONAL APPLICATION

How would you respond if you heard the Father God's voice in your mind tell you He loved you?

Sumo Wrestling and God's Protection

This story occurred in 1970, and it is an example of the Holy Spirit's protection. It's about how the Holy Spirit spoke through another person to save me from what would likely have been a seriously injured or broken back. I was twenty-three at the time. An injury like that would have dramatically altered the rest of my life. It's important to know God did this before I committed my life to Jesus Christ.

Tammy (my first wife) and I lived in a small fishing village near the base where I was stationed in Japan. Since I was the quarterback for our Navy base football team, I would occasionally bring a football home. When he was there, I would be greeted enthusiastically by an old man who sat on a stool across from our house. I found out later he was the village elder. One particular afternoon in the fall of 1970, he was especially animated as he pointed to the football I was carrying. Tammy taught English to a well-to-do Japanese lady, who arrived just as I went into the house. We could see Miyoko (I don't remember her name) talking with the elder. She came into the house excited. She said, "Paulsan," you have been given a great honor. The village elder asked you to participate in their annual sumo wrestling tournament. I told her I had been to a professional sumo wrestling tournament, and there was no way I would get into the ring with these mammoth athletes! Miyoko said I would disgrace the elder if I refused. So I asked her to tell him I would talk with my commanding officer to see if he would approve it, believing he wouldn't. However, he agreed and said a team of five could participate. But he warned that we had better be outstanding gentlemen!

WHAT DO YOU THINK?

Why do you think the Father may have used this village elder for me to experience His protection before I committed my life to Christ?

Tournament night. We were met the night of the tournament by a young Japanese man who spoke some English. He told us how to put on the belt ("mahashi") sumo wrestlers wear during training and a tournament. Our mahashi was made of stiff, new canvas, yes, canvas, not the silk the pros wear. As we were standing around waiting for our time in the ring, a stout, drunk Japanese man came up behind "Buddha," our 350-plus-pound center on the football team. He sneered at us, reached around Buddha, grabbed his mahashi from the front, and leaned back. Then, he lifted Buddha off the ground and carried him around. His intent, of course, was to instill fear in us. Shortly after this, we were told that we would be wrestling against the winners of the tournament weight classes. By halftime, we had lost every single match. However, we realized they were using our momentum against us. As we would try to turn them in one direction (say, to the left), they would just keep us moving in that direction and then toss us to the ground or out of the ring.

The Holy Spirit used a person to save me from a serious back injury. We finally began to win some matches. I won three in a row and had just thrown a Japanese wrestler out of the ring. I stood in the circle watching to make sure he was OK when I heard someone from our team shout, "Paul, look out behind you!" As I turned, I saw the drunken Japanese man rushing at me with his head down pointed toward the middle of my back. With adrenaline pumping, my mind raced to protect myself. I took two steps back toward him as he rushed at me, grabbed him by the back of his mahashi, then took two steps forward and flung him as hard as I could out of the ring. He landed headfirst into a tree, which cut his head and knocked him unconscious. I didn't realize the tree was there and was not trying to hurt him. As he lay there bleeding and unconscious, I looked up at our Navy and Air Force senior officers with their wives in the spectator stands. They were not pleased. Soon, the village elder and the tournament judge came to me in the ring. They bowed in a humble posture, asking me to forgive the drunken man's attempt to injure me. Our interpreter told me this and said they would ban the man from participating in their fall festival. The next day, people in the village treated me like a celebrity. For me, I was grateful to be walking around.

Perhaps the following scripture may help you understand God's protection:

> But you, LORD, are a shield that protects me; you are my glory and the one who restores me. (Psalms 3:3 NET)

PERSONAL APPLICATION
In what ways is this story meaningful to you?

The Mouse and Peeping Tom

The following story is not about the devil or demons but illustrates that things are not always what they seem.

When we were living in Japan, rumors were spreading among the six or seven military families residing in the village that a peeping Tom had been seen lurking around some of their homes. The wives were becoming more worried as a recent rumor indicated he had entered one of the homes.

On this particular night, I had worked a late shift and was extremely tired when I went to bed about midnight. I started to doze off when Tammy and I heard a noise in our bedroom. As I was waking up, my first thought was that the peeping Tom was in our home. I sprung out of bed with the idea I might be fighting for our lives. My mind was racing as I reached for the fluorescent light switch. As I did so, a hand slapped my chest. I was now in that "fight" mode of the adrenalin fight or flight. I reached for the light switch a second time, and the hand slapped my chest again. He was toying with me.

PERSONAL APPLICATION

How have you reacted in a fight or flight situation? Why do you think life experiences affected how you responded?

Now the fight was really on! I had a plan. So, I reached for the light switch a third time and grabbed his forearm as he slapped my chest. I had him now in my grasp. This was real! I heard Tammy scramble for the closet and close the sliding door. With all my strength, I flung the person across the bedroom. Just as the fluorescent light went on, I found myself lying on the bedroom floor, holding my left forearm. Both Tammy and I laughed at what just occurred. My left arm had gone to sleep as I lay in bed with it under my head. When I reached for the light switch with my right hand, my numb left arm flopped against my chest. I had been fighting with myself.

Just then, we heard the noise in our bedroom that started this. I looked around and saw a mouse by our dresser. I caught it gently with a t-shirt and let it go outside. What a relief! The battle was over. And our home was free of the noisy mouse. We found out later the peeping Tom had stopped lurking around before this incident.

I laugh about this story now and have shared it with friends over the years. However, as the following verses indicate, it is essential to realize that things are not always as they seem:

> And no wonder, for even Satan disguises himself as an angel of light. Therefore it is not surprising his servants also disguise themselves as servants of righteousness, whose end will correspond to their actions. (2 Corinthians 11:14-15 NET)

PERSONAL APPLICATION

When did your spiritual enemy attempt to deceive you by disguising himself? How did you recognize it was him?

Second Miraculous Healing

Linda and I were growing in our faith and life with God when we moved into our new home in Holly, Michigan, in 1990. We wanted to do a lot of work to "make it our own." The problem for me is that I tend to overdo things. I work hard at whatever I do.

Linda and I began with landscaping. On one occasion, I used a wheelbarrow for many trips to haul a mound of large rocks to our backyard. In addition to planting grass and many bushes, I built a large wooden deck. I poured a small concrete pad by the back garage door. I built a fence to keep our dogs safely in the backyard and constructed a storage shed.

I was working fifty-plus hours a week at my new job. In addition, I was working ten or more hours a week for ministries at our church. This was all too much for me. AGAIN, my health broke down. I began to experience extreme daily fatigue, problems concentrating, headaches, sensitivity to odors, and extreme muscle and joint pain. A minor activity overwhelmed me. My sleep was restless and left me still feeling exhausted the next morning. This continued for several years.

My primary care doctor was at a loss. He had never seen symptoms like these. He tried several treatments that failed to help me. He referred me to a specialist who diagnosed me with "Chronic Fatigue Syndrome" (CFS). There was not much known about it, including causes and treatments. There was no sign of Lyme Disease or Epstein-Barr virus that might explain the CFS. He tried everything he knew, but again nothing was helping.

PERSONAL APPLICATION
When have you experienced a seriously debilitating chronic illness where no medical treatment would provide restoration? How was your attitude toward God affected?

God can heal miraculously. God does not always heal, but sometimes He does in truly miraculous ways, as you will see next.

Full Gospel Business Men's Fellowship meeting. In 1992 my friend, Jack, took me to a local Full Gospel Business Men's Fellowship meeting. They would routinely pray for people with various needs and health problems. After the meeting, I talked with several of the men. They said the "old man" had the spiritual gifts of healing and would pray for me. I told him about my health problems as several other men gathered around me for prayer. Then I heard another man shout from across the room that the Lord just told him, "It's in his blood." The old man prayed a powerful prayer, but I didn't experience anything, not even the warm feeling I had with my first miraculous healing. I was discouraged. I had high hopes for another miracle.

When I got home, I went right to bed. I was exhausted. Shortly though, I began to feel an increasing warmth all over. There was a sensation of a rolling wave that started at the top of my head and gently moved down to the bottom of my feet. This continued as a cycle of movements. As the sensation increased, I noticed my body was feeling hotter. I called Linda into the bedroom and asked her to put her hand on my arm. She withdrew it quickly, saying my arm was very hot. This cycle continued for five or six hours until I finally got up about midnight to eat. I needed more energy for this. I went back to bed, and it continued throughout the night. The following morning, I was completely healed! I praised Jesus Christ and thanked Him for His undeserved loving-kindness!

> He is the one you should praise; he is your God, the one who has done these great and awesome things for you that you have seen. (Deuteronomy 10:21 NET)

Epstein-Barr virus. In Orlando, around 2003, a Hematology Oncologist told me she saw "markers" for the Epstein-Barr virus in my blood. This virus can result in Chronic Fatigue Syndrome. So it seems my health breakdown in Michigan in 1992 was likely due to exhaustive overwork and this debilitating virus. Remember, when I was healed, the Holy Spirit told a man at the Full Gospel Business Men's Fellowship meeting that the problem was "in his blood"? A virus, of course, can circulate in a person's blood. By the way, I didn't have cancer.

PERSONAL APPLICATION
When has the Holy Spirit shown you later what He had done previously for your benefit?

The end of stories. This concludes the stories of God's supernatural interventions. I hope they encourage you to believe in the reality of the Father God, His Son, Jesus Christ, and the Holy Spirit. I hope your faith and trust in them increases as you consider that they can do anything, anytime, anywhere.

Isn't it amazing! This God of the Bible is the ONE true God who created everything out of nothing and loves you deeply and eternally!

Along with the Old Testament's King David, let's praise our great and wonderful God for who He is and what He does.

> I will exalt You, my God and King, and praise Your name forever and ever. I will praise You every day; yes, I will praise You forever. Great is the LORD! He is most worthy of praise! No one can measure His greatness. Let each generation tell its children of Your mighty acts; let them proclaim Your power. I will meditate on Your majestic, glorious

splendor and Your wonderful miracles. Your awe-inspiring deeds will be on every tongue; I will proclaim Your greatness. Everyone will share the story of Your wonderful goodness; they will sing with joy about Your righteousness. (Psalms 145:1-7 NLT)

The Essentials: Who Is This God?

The following is a concise description of the God of the Bible derived from this book. It provides an abbreviated focus on the essentials of who He is as the Triune God. There is no one else in the world like Him!

Does the God of the Bible Exist?

Apparently, not to ninety-four percent of adult Americans. George Barna's 2020 *American Worldview Inventory* concludes that ninety-four percent of adult Americans have created their own idea of who they want God to be. That means only six percent believe in and live for God as He describes Himself in the Bible. Many studies indicate unbelief in the God of the Bible exists worldwide.

There Is Only One God

In the following verses, God says He alone is God. No other God in any form exists. He says that many people have created their own ideas of who He is, but they don't know Him as He truly is, the God of the Bible.

> What fools they are who carry around their wooden idols and pray to gods that cannot save! Consult together, argue your case. Get together and decide what to say. Who made these things known so long ago? What idol ever told you they would happen? Was it not I, the LORD? For there is no other God but Me, a righteous God and Savior. There is none but Me. Let all the world look to Me for salvation! For I am God; there is no other. (Isaiah 45:20-22 NLT)

God's Nature and Greatness

God is sovereign. This means He reigns and is supreme over everything. Nothing is outside His absolute authority. He is perfect in every respect. He is holy and separate from His creation. He is eternal and can't die. He can't be harmed or injured. He is the Creator of everything. He is just and righteous in all His ways. He is loving and compassionate toward people. In the following verse you see that He is mighty and majestic:

> O LORD, you are great, mighty, majestic, magnificent, glorious, and sovereign over all the sky and earth! You, LORD, have dominion and exalt yourself as the ruler of all. (1 Chronicles 29:11 NET)

God Exists as the Trinity (ONE God in Three Persons)

His greatness can be seen in the triune nature of His existence, ONE God (Mark 12:29) in three persons. This is the "Trinity," which are Jehovah (God the Father), His Son, Jesus Christ, and the Holy Spirit (Matthew 28:19). They are each equally God in every aspect of their being and nature.

God (Jehovah, Father God)

Christians identify Jehovah, the Father God as the first person of the Trinity. When we see the word *God* in the Old and New Testaments of the Bible, it's typically referring to Him. Sometimes, it also refers to the Trinity, emphasizing their oneness. In the Hebrew language of the Old Testament, God gives Himself one personal name, *Yahweh* (Exodus 3:13-14). Because the people of Israel thought of this as His sacred name, they referred to it as "YHWH," leaving out the vowels. In English Bibles, this is sometimes written as *I AM WHO I AM*, *lord* (with small capital letters), *Adonai*, or *Jehovah*.

Following are brief descriptions of God's personal name and other words for Him:

- *LORD* (*Yahweh* in Hebrew) – *Yahweh* is God's personal name. His name means God is self-existent. *Jehovah* is a translation in English Bibles for *Yahweh*.

- *God* (*Elohim* in Hebrew) – God is the strong one with great authority. Some people think of *Elohim* as the Creator God.

- *El Shaddai* (*God Almighty* in Hebrew) – God is the all-sufficient God, powerful to meet all His children's needs.

- *Abba* (*Father* in Greek) – Jehovah is the Father, daddy to His beloved children.

Jesus Christ (Son of God)

Christians identify Jesus Christ as the second person of the Trinity. He is entirely God and fully divine in His nature. He is found throughout the Old and New Testaments of the Bible and has many names and titles to help us understand who He is and what He does. *Jesus* is His personal name that He received when He was born to the Virgin Mary (Matthew 1:21). *Christ* is one of His New Testament titles, as *Messiah* is an Old Testament title.

No Christianity If Jesus Christ Is Not God

If Jesus Christ is not God, there is no New Testament Christianity. The entire Christian religion is based on this one simple fact – Jesus is God (John 20:28).

Son of God and Son of Man

Jesus Christ is called the Son of God and Son of Man in the New Testament (John 1:48-51). Each title represents who He is.

Son of God - No biological father. Jesus did not have a biological father. Instead, He had a spiritual father, the Holy Spirit (Luke 1:35). It was through Him that Jesus received His spiritual nature as the Son of God at conception. As the Son of God, He is fully divine, fully God, and equal to His Father, Jehovah, and the Holy Spirit.

Son of Man - Biological mother. Jesus' biological mother was a young virgin woman named Mary. It was through her that He received His human nature as the Son of Man at conception. Because she became pregnant by the Holy Spirit, we refer to this as the "virgin birth" of Jesus. As the Son of Man, He was fully human and did not rely on His supernatural divinity on earth (Philippians 2:5-7). He had a human body that became tired, hungry, and thirsty. Only in His human form as the Son of Man could Jesus' body suffer and die physically. His spirit/soul could never die because He is the eternal God.

Savior and Lord

Jesus is Savior. In order to save people from the eternal consequences of sin, He became the sacrifice for their sins. Because He sacrificed His physical human life, He became the *Savior* for all people. No one else can save people from the eternal consequences of their self-centered life (Acts 4:12).

Jesus is Lord. Jesus is referred to as *Lord* in the New Testament of the Bible (Philippians 2:9-11). For Him to be Lord means that believers have given Him control of their lives. He is in charge, not them. Therefore, maturing Christians continually seek to know and do His will in all things. There is no salvation for people if He is not the Lord of their life (Romans 10:9).

Holy Spirit (Spirit of God)

The Holy Spirit is identified as the third person of the Trinity. He is not some cosmic, impersonal force. Instead, He is a real person of God in the form of a spirit who loves and cares (Romans 15:30). He is the Spirit of Truth, Spirit of God, and Spirit of Jesus.

The One Called Alongside
He is the person of God who enables the followers of Jesus Christ to know God and live for Him. He was sent by the Father to teach, guide, and help believers (John 14:26). Jesus used the Greek word *Paraclete* to indicate the importance of the Holy Spirit to believers. In various Bible versions, this word is translated as *Helper* (NASB, ESV), *Comforter* (KJV), and *Advocate* (NET, NLT, NIV). It means one called alongside to help. It depicts how essentially close the Holy Spirit is to believers as He works within and through them. The Holy Spirit should be the believer's closest companion and co-worker in God's Kingdom. Because of this closeness, Jesus said that the Holy Spirit would never leave His followers.

He's God's Supernatural Power on Earth
The Holy Spirit was Jesus' supernatural power on earth. Everything Jesus did while on earth requiring divine power was done by the Holy Spirit working in and through Him (Matthew 12:28). This same Holy Spirit and His power are within every born-again follower of Jesus. The Holy Spirit is the Father's power at work within believers to enable them to accomplish His will and purposes (Ephesians 3:20).

GLOSSARY

The following glossary provides a quick reference to the meaning of some terms in this book. I use common definitions heard among the Christian community rather than theological terminology.

Abba: God Almighty is the Father God who refers to Himself in the New Testament of the Bible as *Abba*. This Aramaic word depicts Him in the personal sense as daddy or papa. It implies obedience and respect for Him as God. Even Jesus called Him *Abba* (Mark 14:36). This familial word indicates the Father's love for His children.

Angels: God created angels before He created the universe and earth. Several types of angels are described in the Bible. They are supernatural beings who exist to serve God. There are occasions when He sends them to help people. The devil and his demons were once angels but became corrupted when they rebelled against God in Heaven. People do not become angels or guardian angels for loved ones when they die.

Anointing with the Holy Spirit: The following scripture indicates that the Holy Spirit anoints Jesus' followers: *Nevertheless you have an anointing from the Holy One* (1 John 2:20 NET). We see from scripture that there are three ways in which the Holy Spirit anoints believers. 1. Special short-term ministry or situational anointings - Believers experience an increase of the Spirit's presence and power for particular purposes. 2. Permanent anointing of Spirit - 1 John 2:27 says the anointing of the Spirit *resides in you*, which implies permanence. 3. Spirit's anointing teaches truth - His anointing teaches and leads believers into truth. This guidance and teaching help believers avoid errors in the Christian faith that can mislead them.

Armor of God: Followers of Jesus Christ have a real spiritual enemy, the devil and his demons. Their tactics are filled with lies and deception. Their two goals are to prevent people from being saved and draw Christians away from their faith and life with Jesus. God has given every believer spiritual armor to protect them from this enemy. Each piece has a specific purpose, yet each is based on biblical truth. They are the belt of truth, the breastplate of righteousness, feet shod with the gospel of peace, shield of faith, helmet of salvation, and the sword of the Spirit. Prayer is also an essential part of spiritual warfare.

Baby Christians: Baby Christians have not matured as followers of Jesus Christ. There are two types identified in the Bible. Type One: New Christians who recently committed their lives to Jesus Christ. They are starting their journey as followers of His. Type Two: Perpetual baby Christians are people who were born-again sometime in the past. However, they have stopped, or perhaps never started, disciplining themselves to mature as followers of Jesus.

Baptism with the Holy Spirit: Baptism with the Holy Spirit represents the idea of being immersed in something. In this case, the new believer is immersed in the Holy Spirit's presence, power, and life. Jesus said people must be born-again by the Spirit to be saved and enter the Kingdom of God. When this occurs, it's the baptism with the Holy Spirit. It's the *promise of the Father* (Acts 1:4-5) and *gift of God* (John 4:10). The Father also promised this in the Old Testament book of Joel (Joel 2:28-29). Some born-again believers baptized with the Holy Spirit at spiritual birth have received what they refer to as a "second blessing of the Spirit." By this, they mean there was an incident when the Holy Spirit came upon them in a powerful way that changed their life by giving them more spiritual insight and power from the Holy Spirit.

Believer/Christian/Follower of Jesus Christ: I use these as synonyms throughout this book since they mean the same thing. They refer to people who, as one pastor said, "have stepped across the line" and accepted Jesus Christ as their Savior and Lord. However, some born-again believers may not remember the exact date or event of their salvation experience.

Born-Again: Jesus said that everyone must be born-again to enter the Kingdom of God (John 3:3). This occurs immediately when the Holy Spirit comes to live within people when they commit their hearts and lives to Jesus Christ as Savior and Lord. When they do this, they are saved. Conversely, people who are not born-again by the Holy Spirit are not saved and are not a Christian.

Christian Church: The Christian church is not a physical building with the name "church." It is not an organization, association, or denomination. The Christian church is simply all born-again followers of Jesus Christ wherever they are located.

Christian Practices/Spiritual Disciplines: Training to know God better develops spiritual habits that become a way of life. Christianity is not just about knowing religious doctrine. Importantly, it's about a spiritual life that the Holy Spirit is transforming through the practice of spiritual disciplines. Regularly practicing these enables believers to mature continually. In addition, these Christian practices enhance fellowship with the Father God, Jesus Christ, and the Holy Spirit.

Communicate (Talk) with God: Many people erroneously believe they should only communicate with God through an occasional formal prayer. The Bible doesn't support this idea. People can pray formally to the Father and spontaneously talk to Him, Jesus, and the Holy Spirit whenever they want. Communication with God, as with people, requires active listening. People don't need a priest, pastor, or anyone else to talk to God for them. Each person of God (see "Trinity") wants people to talk with Him. But be aware that some people say it's possible to talk to God or the dead through mediums or other occult practices. People who do this may find themselves communicating with demons instead.

Condemnation: Biblical condemnation results in eternal separation from the presence of God and His love. It's God's judgment of people who ignore the free gift of salvation through Jesus Christ. Their lack of belief condemns them according to John 3:18, *The one who believes in him is not condemned. The one who does not believe has been condemned already, because he has not believed in the name of the one and only Son of God* (NET). However, according to Romans 8:1, God says there is no condemnation for those who have accepted Jesus Christ as their Savior and Lord.

Conscience: The existence of conscience is part of human nature. God has given every person a conscience to discern right from wrong. However, people can be taught to believe something is right when it is actually wrong. Since people are not perfect, and neither are their cultures, a person's innate sense of right and wrong can be modified to be contrary to God. If in doubt, always look it up in your guidebook of truth, the Bible. The saying, "Let your conscience be your guide," is misleading. Instead, ask the Holy Spirit to be your guide.

Creation: The Bible describes God's creation in the first two chapters of the Old Testament book of Genesis. The first verse in the Bible says that God existed before He created anything, *In the beginning, God created the heavens and the earth* (Genesis 1:1 ESV). He is the all-powerful God who created everything out of nothing ("Ex Nihilo"). Since the people He made have a physical existence, He created the earth as a suitable physical environment within which they can live.

Death: The physical bodies of all people (and all life) eventually stop functioning and die. However, death is not the end of existence for people. Rather, their spirit/soul immediately leaves this earthly realm and goes to Heaven or Hell. Their destination depends on whether they accept Jesus as their Savior and Lord.

Devil and His Demons: They were once angels of God who rebelled and were cast out of Heaven. Now they strive to bring hate, destruction, and evil into the world and the lives of people. They are sometimes referred to as evil spirits or the spiritual enemy of believers. Their eternal fate is the lake of fire, where they will never again be able to harass God's people.

Disciple/Discipleship: In the New Testament Gospel of Matthew, Jesus told His followers to go into the world and make disciples for Him (Matthew 28:18-20). This is referred to as the "Great Commission." A disciple then, is a student and follower of Jesus Christ. Disciples exhibit lives that are being transformed by the Holy Spirit as they live for Jesus Christ. Discipleship is the process by which a Christian helps and teaches believers to know God and live and serve in ways that are pleasing to Him. Discipleship, therefore, is about spiritual growth whereby believers change to become more like Jesus Christ. There is no spiritual maturity without this transformational change in the hearts and minds of believers.

Eternal Relationship with God: No one has a personal relationship with God without being born-again. This occurs when people are rescued (saved) from the consequences of their sins through faith in Jesus. That's when they are born-again and receive an eternal relationship with each person of the Trinity – the Father God, Jesus Christ, and the Holy Spirit. This means they can have fellowship with God. They can experience His presence in their heart and life through their relationship with Him.

Evil: Can people be or do evil on their own? Perhaps, but the devil and his demons are a source of evil in this world because their nature is evil (John 8:44, Ephesians 6:12). They can influence people to do evil (2 Corinthians 5:10). Being and doing evil is not the same thing as being sinful. Sinfulness is about living by the self-centered old nature. Evil is about a person giving their heart over to demons, so it becomes corrupted and treacherous (John 8:44; Acts 5:3).

Evolution: This is referred to as the scientific theory of evolution by natural selection. It implies one species of plant or animal can change and evolve over great lengths of time to become a different species based on the prior one. This has been an unproven theory for many decades and can't ever be proven to be a scientific fact. Why?

Because God created everything. Some plants and animals have "adapted" to their environment, changing some specific inherited traits or characteristics over time. However, their entire species did not transform into a different and new species.

Faith: Biblical faith is confidence and trust that God is who He says He is and will do what He says (Hebrews 11:1-3). Faith requires action, or it's false (James 2:26). Faith grows over time deep within the soul as people experience God and allow Him to apply His living word to transform their hearts and lives.

Filling with the Holy Spirit: The Greek word for *filled* means to be full, filled to the top with no more room. Believers are to be so full of the Holy Spirit's presence, influences, and power that there is no room in their hearts and minds for their old self-centered life. Since believers still have their old nature, they will always have the internal battle to be filled with the Spirit.

Free Will: All human beings have the right and ability to make their own decisions. This is referred to as free will. God can do anything He wants. This is referred to as God's sovereign will. When people use their free will to disobey God, this is self-will.

Ghost: Some people believe that when a person's body dies, their spirit/soul can linger on earth for a while, sometimes to complete unfinished business or become a guardian angel. These are sometimes referred to as ghosts. However, this idea is inaccurate and contrary to the Bible's teachings. When people physically die, their spirit/soul goes directly to Heaven or Hell. There is no intermediate state where a person's spirit/soul lingers on earth. Therefore, supernatural experiences thought to be ghosts are either demons or fraud.

God (Father God, Jehovah): When we see the word *God* in the Bible, it typically identifies the first person of the Trinity. Sometimes, it also refers to the Trinity, emphasizing their oneness. In the Hebrew language of the Old Testament, God gives Himself one personal name, *Yahweh* (Exodus 3:13-14). Because the people of Israel thought of this as His sacred name, they referred to it as "YHWH," leaving out the vowels. In English Bibles, this is sometimes written as *I AM WHO I AM*, *lord* (with small capital letters), *Adonai*, or *Jehovah*. Many names and titles for God reveal aspects of His divine nature and represent who He is, such as *El Shaddai* (God Almighty) or *Jehovah-shalom* (God is our peace). (see "Abba")

God's Unconditional (Sacrificial) Love: God's love for people is unconditional and comes from His unchanging nature. His love is not dependent on how good or bad a person is – it's not conditional on the person's behavior. No one is good enough, so no one can earn God's love. Instead, He freely gives it. God's love is sacrificial, which He demonstrated by sending His Son, Jesus Christ, to die a horrible death on the cross for everyone's sins (1 John 4:10). Jesus' resurrection from the dead is proof of this love.

God's Will: God reveals His will to people because He wants them to know it and do it. As believers follow His will, they experience Him in ways they may not have thought possible. This is because the Holy Spirit is their Helper, Guide, and Teacher. He will help them navigate life and make decisions according to the Father's will. In Matthew 6:10, Jesus says to pray for God's will to be done: *Our Father in heaven, may Your name be kept holy. May Your Kingdom come soon. May Your will be done on earth, as it is in heaven* (NLT).

Good News/Gospel: The Good News is that Jesus Christ died for the sins of every person according to the scriptures, was buried, and was raised to life on the third day according to the scriptures. People are born-again and become Christians only when they respond to this Good News by accepting Jesus into their hearts and lives as Savior and Lord.

Grace: This is God's unmerited favor toward people. It can't be earned. It's given freely by God because of His unconditional love. Grace is a gift of God's divine help when human ability and effort are insufficient.

Heal (Healing): God can supernaturally heal a person of physical, mental, and emotional illnesses. He can also give insight to people and healthcare professionals that can help restore a person's health naturally. Being rescued from eternal condemnation by accepting Jesus is spiritual healing.

Heaven: When the physical body of a follower of Jesus Christ dies, their spirit/soul goes immediately to Heaven. The Father God, Jesus Christ, myriads of angels, and other believers welcome them with loving and joyful arms. Heaven is the eternal abode of God (Father God, His Son, Jesus Christ, and the Holy Spirit), even though they exist everywhere. Since God is supernatural, it's supernatural as well. It's the place where God presides over the entire creation and His multitude of mighty angels. Heaven above comes down to become the new Jerusalem at the end of time, where all believers will exist eternally, enjoying God's presence on the new earth (Revelation 21:1-3).

Hell: When the physical body of those who reject Jesus Christ dies, their spirit/soul goes immediately to Hell. After the Great White Throne Judgment, they will be sent to exist eternally in the lake of fire, where they will never experience God's presence, love, and peace (Revelation 20:11-15).

Holy (Holiness): The word holy in the Bible means to be set apart from the world for God and His use. Believers must be holy because God is holy (1 Peter 1:13-16). There are two aspects of holiness – status and process. First, believers are set apart for God when they are born-again. This is the status or state of being holy. Second, believers develop godliness (holiness) in their character and nature by being transformed from the self-centered old nature into the Christ-centered new nature. This ongoing process is also called sanctification.

Holy Spirit (Spirit of God and Christ): The Holy Spirit is identified as the third person of the Trinity. He has many names throughout the Bible, including the Spirit of God and Spirit of Christ. These indicate He is divine, fully God in nature, and part of the Trinity. The Holy Spirit opens people's hearts and minds to understand the Gospel that Jesus died for their sins, was buried, and resurrected to provide eternal life with God. When they profess their faith in Jesus Christ as Savior and ask Him to be the Lord of their life, the Holy Spirit comes to live within them. Only then are they born-again and become a Christian.

Hope: Hope, like faith, is an assurance that God will do what He says He will. There is a sense of confidence and certainty in biblical hope (Hebrews 11:1-3). Hope and faith are based on truth, not wishful thinking. Therefore, all hope in God comes from His Holy Spirit and can bring joy and peace as believers trust Him. Life without faith in Jesus Christ is a life without God and without hope (Ephesians 2:12).

Jesus Christ (Savior and Lord): He is identified as the second person of the Trinity. *Jesus* is His personal name (Matthew 1:21). *Christ* is a title that means the one chosen by God to save His people. Similarly, He is the *Savior*. He is fully God and fully divine in His nature. He is found throughout the entire Bible and has many names and titles that help us understand who He is and what He does. If Jesus Christ is not God, there is no Christianity. The entire Christian religion is based on the simple fact that Jesus is God. He is the only person who can rescue and save people from the consequences of their self-centered life. Jesus is referred to as *Lord*. There is no salvation for people if He is not the Lord of their life. For Him to be Lord means they have given Him control of their life. He's in charge, not them. This is what it means to live under His Lordship.

Jesus Christ's First and Second Coming: Jesus Christ came down from Heaven for salvation at His first Coming to be born in a manger in Bethlehem. He died, rose back to life, and ascended into Heaven from where He came. He will return for judgment at His Second Coming according to the Father God's plan (Acts 1:6-7).

Judgment: All followers of Jesus Christ will be judged by how they lived their life on earth. Since they are already rescued, this judgment is not about salvation but about whether they will receive eternal rewards for honoring Jesus with their lives. People who were unwilling to abandon their self-centered lives and did not accept Jesus as their Savior and Lord are not saved. They will be judged by how they lived without Christ. This judgment is about what their eternity will be like in the lake of fire without God.

Kingdom of God: When people receive Jesus as their Savior and Lord, they are immediately transferred from the kingdom of the devil into the Kingdom of God (Colossians 1:13). Believers, then, are part of the Kingdom of God under the authority and Lordship Of Jesus Christ. Since Jesus is the head of His church, He determines what each local church should do to build God's Kingdom on earth.

Lake of Fire: This is the eternal fate for the devil, his demons, and all people who ignore Jesus Christ as their Savior and Lord (Revelation 20:11-15). They will never experience the presence, love, and forgiveness of God. This is why sharing the Good News with people about being rescued from this fate is imperative.

Meditation: Biblical meditation means pondering or conversing with oneself. Meditating on a verse helps you remember and understand its meaning. As a result, you can apply it more accurately to your life. Meditating on scripture is another essential method for knowing God. Christian meditation does not involve emptying the mind. On the contrary, it consists in filling the mind with the word of God. It focuses on God and not oneself or a meaningless chant (Matthew 6:7). Christians can't learn about and know God with an empty mind. Instead, their mind must be full of scripture about who He is and what He does.

Messiah: Jehovah God promises in the Old Testament that He would send the Messiah to Israel (Micah 5:2). Jesus Christ is called the Messiah in Matthew 1:16. However, the Jewish people were expecting the Messiah to be a military and political leader who would free them from the tyranny of Roman government. But this was not the Father's purpose in sending Jesus. Instead, He came to save both Jewish and non-Jewish people from the eternal consequences of their sins.

Miracle: God overrides the natural world He created when He performs a supernatural feat. These miracles can't be explained by human reasoning.

Mystery: There are some verses and topics in the Bible that are simply a mystery. A mystery in the Bible is something for which God has partially concealed the complete meaning or even hidden the entire meaning. In 1 Corinthians 2:7, the

Apostle Paul writes, "*No, the wisdom we speak of is the mystery of God—His plan that was previously hidden*" (NLT).

Myth: These are erroneous ideas about reality. As such, they are untrue and should be disregarded by Christians. They may lead to confusion and misdirect people away from God's truth. For example, there are many myths about Heaven.

Natural World: People live in a natural world created by God for them to live within. The very existence of the natural world dictates there was an intelligent Designer of it. The theory of evolution cannot explain the complexities of the natural world, let alone the supernatural world.

New Heaven and New Earth. God will ultimately terminate this current creation by fire because of the rampant rebellion of people against Him. He has delayed doing so because He wants every person to repent and be saved. After its destruction, He will create an entirely new heaven and new earth. This will be a wonderful place of eternal existence for the followers of Jesus Christ. The Father and Jesus Christ will come down from Heaven to live among them in this new creation. There will never again be pain, suffering, or sin in this eternal home with God. There will be no crime or murder because everyone without Jesus Christ will not be there.

New Nature (Believers): When people commit their hearts and lives to Jesus Christ, they become a member of God's eternal family. They are born-again by the Holy Spirit. At that moment, He gives them a new nature that can mature over time to be like the nature of Jesus Christ. However, a lack of spiritual purpose, desire, and discipline to grow spiritually can prevent this growth. As a result, the old nature will continue to dominate them.

New Testament (Bible): The New Testament is the story of God and His relationship through Jesus Christ with all people. The Holy Spirit inspired its twenty-seven books through followers of Jesus Christ. The four gospels (Matthew, Mark, Luke, John) describe the life and person of Jesus Christ as God. Other books describe the start of the Christian church and how Christians should live to please God. Finally, there are prophecies about future events, especially in the last book of the Bible, Revelation.

Non-Believer/Non-Christian: Every person born into this world is born a non-believer in Jesus Christ. No one has "always been a Christian." Every non-Christian is condemned to an eternal fate that is without God and without hope. Therefore, every person must make a life-changing choice to receive Jesus Christ to become a born-again Christian and live eternally with God.

Old Nature (All People): When a person is physically born, they have a self-centered, old nature. A person's old nature never goes away. Only being born-again by the Holy Spirit can give a person a new nature centered on Jesus Christ. The old nature can then be gradually transformed into Christ's new nature during their lifetime on earth.

Old Testament (Bible): The Old Testament is the story of God and His relationship with His chosen people, Israel. The Holy Spirit inspired its thirty-nine books. All of them were written before the first coming of Jesus Christ. They are often categorized as follows: Pentateuch (first five books), historical books, poetical/wisdom books, and books of the major and minor prophets. There are 613 commands or laws in the Old Testament. At His first coming, Jesus Christ fulfilled over 300 Old Testament prophecies about His coming to earth.

Personal Testimony: The Holy Spirit will give believers opportunities to tell people about how they are different after God saved and changed them. This is referred to as a personal testimony. It contrasts the old and new natures and includes the following three parts:

- What I was like before I was rescued (old nature)
- How I was rescued
- What I am like now with the Holy Spirit living in me (new nature)

Prophecy: One definition is that a prophecy is an inspired utterance by a person given by the Holy Spirit. The Father God can speak to His people through prophecy. There are several types of prophecy in the Bible. Since this is not a study on prophecy, I will briefly describe only two types. The first are predictions that certain future events will occur, such as the first coming of Jesus Christ in the Old Testament. The second are proclamations of God's word. These are stating or speaking forth what God has made known. The Holy Spirit originates all prophecies in the Old and New Testaments (2 Peter 1:20-21). Prophecies from the Holy Spirit will always come true. Believers are to test prophecies to see if they are from God (1 John 4:1). One way to do this is to compare it to the Bible to see if it aligns with biblical truth and God's character. There are many warnings in the Old and New Testaments that false prophets would come and try to deceive people with false prophecies (Jeremiah 14:14; Matthew 7:15). False prophets and their fake prophecies should be ignored. The Holy Spirit gives some New Testament believers the spiritual gift of prophecy for the following purposes: *But one who prophesies strengthens others, encourages them, and comforts them* (1 Corinthians 14:3 NLT).

Redemption/Redeemed/Redeemer: No one can be perfect enough to earn the right to be saved and spend eternity with the Father because He is absolutely perfect. Jesus Christ is God and is also perfect. As the Redeemer, He paid the price with His death and rose from the dead to save all who would accept Him. Redemption means the Father sees the redeemed as having the perfection of Jesus.

Repentance: This means to stop doing what God says is wrong and start doing what He says is right. It's turning away from one thing and turning to God instead. There is no salvation without repentance of sin in Jesus' name.

Rescued/Saved: People have a terrible eternal fate if they have not accepted Jesus Christ as their Savior and Lord. This fate includes eternal separation from God, His love, and His presence. Therefore, every person must be rescued from this fate by accepting Jesus as their Savior and Lord.

Resurrection: The resurrection of the dead physical (human) body of Jesus Christ was a supernatural feat accomplished by God. It proves the reality of Jesus' claims that He is God, Savior, and Lord. All followers of Jesus will have their physical bodies resurrected at His second coming. The physical bodies of all who ignored Jesus Christ as their Savior and Lord will be resurrected on Judgment Day.

Righteousness: Righteousness protects the spiritual and emotional heart of the believer. It has two meanings in scripture similar to holiness – status and process. First, born-again believers are made right with God (status) when they accept the death and resurrection of Jesus Christ to rescue them from the consequences of their sins. Second, believers become more righteous and godly (holy) in their character and nature as they are transformed over time (process) to be more like Jesus Christ.

Saint: This is another name for a follower of Jesus Christ (Ephesians 1:1-3). It is derived from a similar Greek word translated as *holy*. These terms mean one who is set apart from the world and dedicated to God for His purposes. To be a saint has nothing to do with a person being more religious or self-sacrificing.

Second Death: There is a terrible eternal fate for those who ignored Jesus Christ as their Savior and Lord. This fate is condemnation, which results in eternal separation from God. This separation is referred to as the *second death* (The first death is that of the physical body.) Christians sometimes refer to it as "spiritual death" since these people will never experience the presence and love of God.

Self-will: All human beings have the right and ability to make their own decisions. This is referred to as free will. Self-will results from exercising free will in opposition to God's will.

Science: This is the study of the natural world created by God. Whether they know it or not, scientists seeking the truth without bias are learning about God because He is the intelligent Designer behind creation.

Sin: No one is perfect. No one can be good enough to earn salvation. Everyone does what displeases God. However, only one sin separates people from eternal life with God – the sin of not accepting Jesus Christ as their Savior and Lord. There are two types of sins identified in the Bible that everyone has committed:

- Sins of omission are actions people should do but are not doing: *Remember, it is a sin to know what to do and not do it.* (James 4:17 NLT)

- Sins of commission are actions people are doing but should not do. Following is one brief list of this type of sin: *But now is the time to get rid of anger, rage, malicious behavior, slander, and dirty language.* (Colossians 3:8 NLT)

Son of God: Jesus did not have a biological father. Instead, He had a spiritual father, the Holy Spirit. Jesus was the Son of God at His conception. As the Son of God, He is fully divine, fully God, and equal to His Father, Jehovah, and the Holy Spirit.

Son of Man: Jesus' biological mother was a young virgin woman named Mary. Through her, He received His human nature as the Son of Man as His conception. Because she became pregnant by the Holy Spirit, we refer to this as the "virgin birth" of Jesus. As the Son of Man, He is fully human. He had a human body that became tired, hungry, and thirsty. Jesus suffered and experienced temptations in His human form but did no wrong. Only in His human form as the Son of Man could Jesus' body suffer and die physically. His spirit/soul could never die because He is the eternal God. Jesus didn't use His divine, supernatural abilities and majesty as God when He lived as fully God and fully human in this world. Instead, he chose to forego these and rely on the Holy Spirit. Every supernatural miracle He did was by the Holy Spirit (Matthew 12:28). This enabled Him to demonstrate that His followers must also rely on the presence and power of the Holy Spirit.

Sovereignty of God: God is in complete control of everything, everywhere, all the time. Nothing exists outside of His absolute authority. He allows people to exercise their free will within the limits of His sovereign will.

Spirit, Soul, and Body: God created people in His image. They have a spirit, soul, and body. From Hebrews 4:12, we see that a person's spirit and soul are distinct and have unique purposes. The spirit – When a person commits their heart and life to Jesus Christ, the Holy Spirit comes to live within them, and they are born-again. When this occurs, their spirit (which was dead to God before salvation) is made alive to God. It's through their spirit that they can experience and communicate with God. The soul – We may think of it as composed of emotions, desires, thoughts, motivations, and conscience. The soul is how a person interacts with people and life in the natural world. The body – The physical body allows people to live within the physical world God created.

Spiritual: From a biblical perspective, only a born-again follower of Jesus is a "spiritual person." The Holy Spirit coming to live within a believer gives them spiritual life because their spirit is made alive to God. Therefore, spiritual growth and experiences occur because of His indwelling presence within believers.

Spiritual Fruit: A believer who is growing spiritually will increasingly exhibit the characteristics of the Holy Spirit. These are referred to as the fruit of the Spirit or spiritual fruit. The following verses identify this fruit: *But the Holy Spirit produces this kind of fruit in our lives: love, joy, peace, patience, kindness, goodness, faithfulness, gentleness, and self-control.* (Galatians 5:22-23 NLT)

Spiritual Growth: The Holy Spirit transforms the believer's old nature into the new nature of Jesus Christ within them. This spiritual growth occurs over time through the Holy Spirit as they regularly practice the spiritual disciplines. If believers are not changing through the Holy Spirit, they are not growing spiritually.

Spiritual Maturity: This is the consequence of spiritual growth. It's the visible manifestation of what has changed in the Christian's mind and heart.

Spiritual Warfare: Believers must wear the full armor of God to live a victorious life over their spiritual enemy. God's word in the Bible is living and active. It's a sword believers use to fight against their spiritual enemy (the devil and his demons). So, this spiritual war is not against people but is supernatural against demons. Most of this battle is in the believer's mind as a demon tries to distract, confuse, and render them helpless in God's Kingdom. Sometimes, it's open warfare when believers encounter demons who claim a certain location as their own. Spiritual warfare is needed to force them to leave it.

Spiritual Warfare Tactics: Biblical truth can be used to put demons in their proper place of submission to Jesus Christ. Truth and the Lordship of Jesus over everything are the foundation of all spiritual warfare. Believers use the authority of the name of Jesus and the indwelling power of the Holy Spirit to stand firm in the victory Jesus has over their enemy. Every tactic must be done in the name of Jesus Christ because His name is who He is as God. Following are tactics from scripture (with their biblical meanings):

- Quote appropriate scripture – From memory or read from a Bible or smartphone
- Command – Declare, charge, transmit a message
- Rebuke – Censure, admonish; archaic – to turn back
- Bind – Tie up, restrict
- Loose – Untie, set free

Supernatural World: There is something beyond the realm of this physical, natural world. It's the supernatural world. This realm is different from God's natural creation. It's the unseen world around us. God created it as well as the natural world. God and His angels are supernatural, and everything they do is supernatural. The devil and his demons are supernatural also, and everything they do is supernatural.

Transformed: The Holy Spirit wants to continually change born-again believers from their self-centered old nature into their Christ-centered new nature. This transformation occurs in small increments over their lifetime. These changes become evident as they gradually exhibit the fruit of the Spirit: love, joy, peace, patience, kindness, goodness, faithfulness, gentleness, and self-control.

Trinity: The word Trinity doesn't appear in the Bible. Biblical scholars created it to help people understand the unity, yet separate reality, of the three persons of God. They are God the Father, His Son, Jesus Christ, and the Holy Spirit. They are each equally God in every aspect of their being and nature. Some cultures and religions believe there are many gods. This is "polytheism." Judaism and Christianity believe there is one God. This is "monotheism." Christians believe in the Trinity, that there is one God in three persons.

Truth: It's an absolute that doesn't change with the culture or social norms. No lies, deceptions, or half-truths are involved with the biblical truth. Everything in the Bible is true because it's *God-breathed* (2 Timothy 3:16). Christians must base their decisions in life on God's truth. This means they must regularly read, study, and meditate on scripture.

Vision: A vision from God is a supernatural experience whereby the Holy Spirit enables a person to see beyond the natural into the supernatural realm. Visions of Heaven and Jesus are, therefore, supernatural experiences. The Apostle Paul describes his supernatural vision of Heaven in 2 Corinthians 12:1-4. But he also says he didn't know whether his physical body was supernaturally transported to Heaven, or he simply had a vision in his mind.

World: The word *world* in the context of many scriptures (such as John 16:7-11) doesn't mean the physical planet Earth. Instead, it refers to a society of people without God that has its own morals, standards, and values. These are created by people and are not typically aligned with the character of God and His word in the Bible.

FURTHER STUDY

The following is a suggested reading list. It's in chronological order as each one appears in the book. The reading list provides a variety of perspectives about God and Christianity that may be helpful in your life with God.

If you only want to purchase a few of these, I recommend the following books:

a. Alistair Begg, *Truth for Life, 365 Daily Devotionals* (India: The Good Book Company, 2021).

b. Francis Chan with Danae Yankoski, *Forgotten God*, subtitle *Reversing Our Tragic Neglect of the Holy Spirit* (Colorado Springs: David C. Cook, 2009).

c. Evidence that Demands a Verdict is an excellent book to help you develop a deeper understanding of Jesus Christ, Christianity, and the Bible.

Hosts Sam Rohrer and Dr. Gary Dull interviewed George Barna, "America's NEW 94% Religion: The Reality and Implications of an Unbiblical Worldview," *Stand in the Gap Today, American Pastors Network* (April 16, 2021).

(The title of George Barna's survey results is "America's Dominant Worldview." Sam Rohrer changed the title for his Stand in the Gap program to "America's New 94% Religion." Although the data provided in this book is from the Stand in the Gap program, it originated from the survey results report.)

Richard E. Simmons III, *Reflections on the Existence of God* (Birmingham: Union Hill Publishing, 2019).

Titus Kennedy, *Excavating the Evidence for Jesus: The Archaeology and History of Christ and the Gospels* (Eugene: Harvest House Publishers, 2022).

Josh McDowell and Sean McDowell, *Evidence that Demands a Verdict*, subtitle *Life-Changing Truth for a Skeptical World*, (Nashville, Thomas Nelson, 2017).

Josh McDowell and Sean McDowell, *More Than a Carpenter*, 3d ed. (Josh McDowell Ministry, 1977, 2005, 2009).

Francis Chan with Danae Yankoski, *Forgotten God*, subtitle *Reversing Our Tragic Neglect of the Holy Spirit* (Colorado Springs: David C. Cook, 2009).

Leonardo Blair, "Most adult US Christians don't believe Holy Spirit is real: study," *The Christian Post* (September 10, 2021).

Robert Boyd Munger, *My Heart – Christ's Home*, 2d ed. (Downers Grove: InterVarsity Press, 1954, 1986).

Jennifer Polland, "The 10 Most Read Books In The World," *https://www.businessinsider.com.au/the-top-10-most-read-books-in-the-world-infographic-2012-12#* (accessed October 27, 2021).

Richard J. Foster, *Celebration of Discipline*, subtitle *The Path to Spiritual Growth*, 3d ed. (New York: HarperCollins, 1978, 1988, 1998).

Adele Ahlberg Calhoun, *Spiritual Disciplines Handbook*, subtitle *Practices That Transform Us* (Downers Grove: InterVarsity Press, 2005, 2015).

John Hopkins Medical Center, *https://www.hopkinsmedicine.org/health/conditions-and-diseases/anatomy-of-the-brain* (accessed November 10, 2022).

Eric Metaxas, *Is Atheism Dead?* (Washington D.C: Salem Books, 2021).

Chip Ingram, *The Invisible War*, subtitle *What Every Believer Needs to Know about SATAN, DEMONS & SPIRITUAL WARFARE* (Grand Rapids: Baker Books, 2006, 2015).

Lee Strobel, *The Case for Heaven* (Grand Rapids: Zondervan, 2021).

Alistair Begg, *Truth for Life, 365 Daily Devotionals* (India: The Good Book Company, 2021).

Dr. Ralph F. Wilson, *JesusWalk Beginning the Journey*, subtitle *Discipleship and Spiritual Formation* (Loomis: JesusWalk, 2009).

Multiple Contributors, *The Beginning, First Steps for New Disciples*, Disciples Path for Students, 5-Session Bible Study (Nashville: Lifeway Press, 2014).

Peter Lord, *Hearing God*, 2d ed. (Bloomington: Chosen Books, 1988, 2011).

INDEX

CPSIA information can be obtained
at www.ICGtesting.com
Printed in the USA
JSHW061149180723
44955JS00001B/6